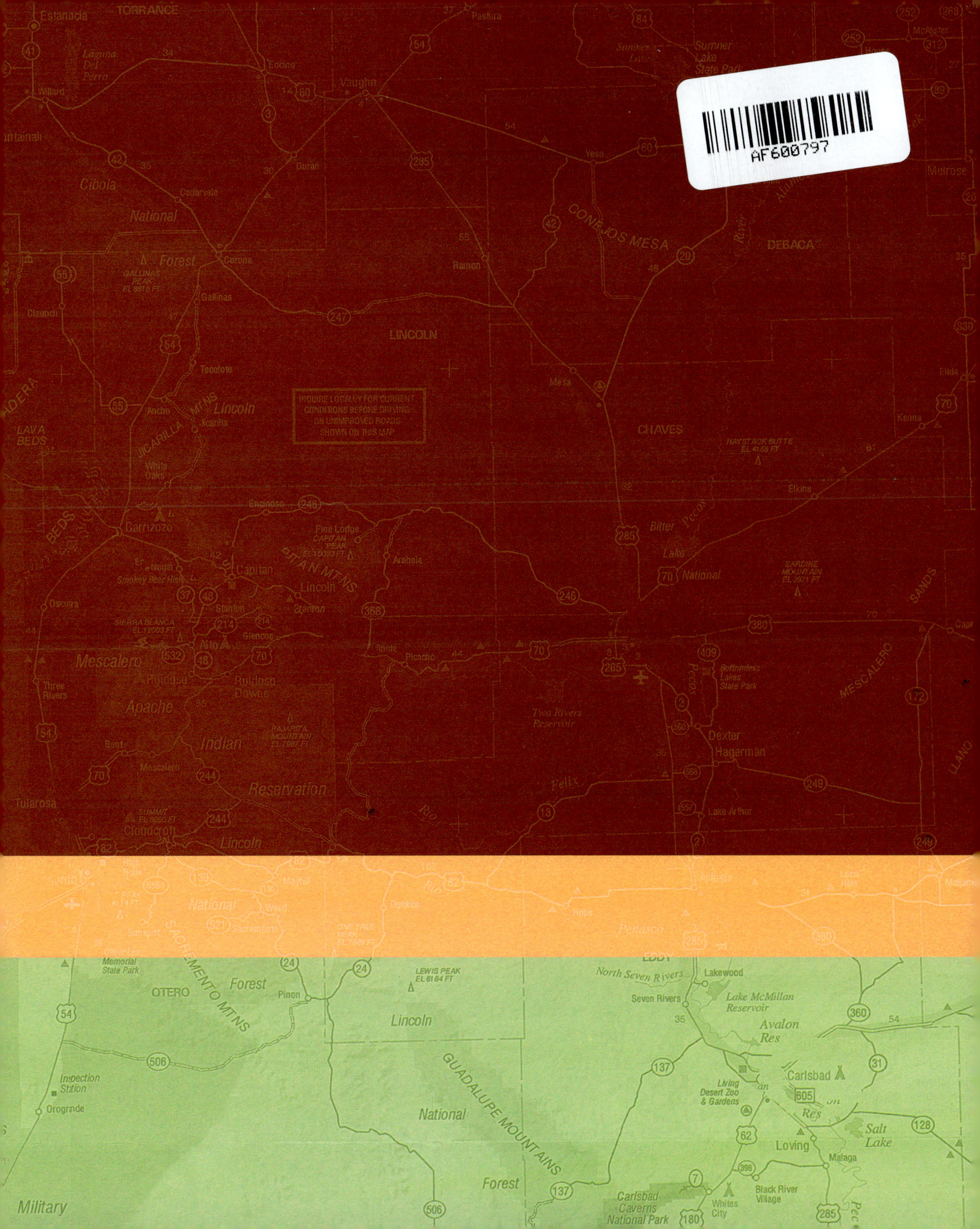
Estancia
TORRANCE
Willard
Encino
Vaughn
Pastura
Sumner Lake State Park
Cibola
National
Forest
Cedarvale
Duran
Yeso
CONEJOS MESA
DEBACA
Melrose
Corona
Ramon
Gallinas
Claunch
LINCOLN
Tecolote
Ancho
Jicarilla
JICARILLA MTNS
Lincoln
INQUIRE LOCALLY FOR CURRENT CONDITIONS BEFORE DRIVING ON UNIMPROVED ROADS SHOWN ON THIS MAP
LAVA BEDS
White Oaks
Mesa
CHAVES
Kenna
Elkins
Encinoso
Carrizozo
Pine Lodge
Arabela
Bitter
Lake
National
Capitan
Nogal
Smokey Bear Hist.
Lincoln
Oscuro
Stanton
SIERRA BLANCA
Alto
Glencoe
Mescalero
Ruidoso
Ruidoso Downs
Picacho
Three Rivers
Apache
Indian
Reservation
Bent
Mescalero
Two Rivers Reservoir
Bottomless Lakes State Park
Dexter
Hagerman
MESCALERO
Tularosa
Cloudcroft
Lincoln
Lake Arthur
Artesia
Mayhill
National
Sacramento
Dunken
Hope
EDDY
Memorial State Park
OTERO
Forest
SACRAMENTO MTNS
Pinon
LEWIS PEAK EL 6184 FT
Lincoln
North Seven Rivers
Lakewood
Seven Rivers
Lake McMillan Reservoir
Avalon Res
Inspection Station
Orogrande
GUADALUPE MOUNTAINS
National
Forest
Carlsbad
Living Desert Zoo & Gardens
Salt Lake
Loving
Malaga
Black River Village
Carlsbad Caverns National Park
Whites City
Military

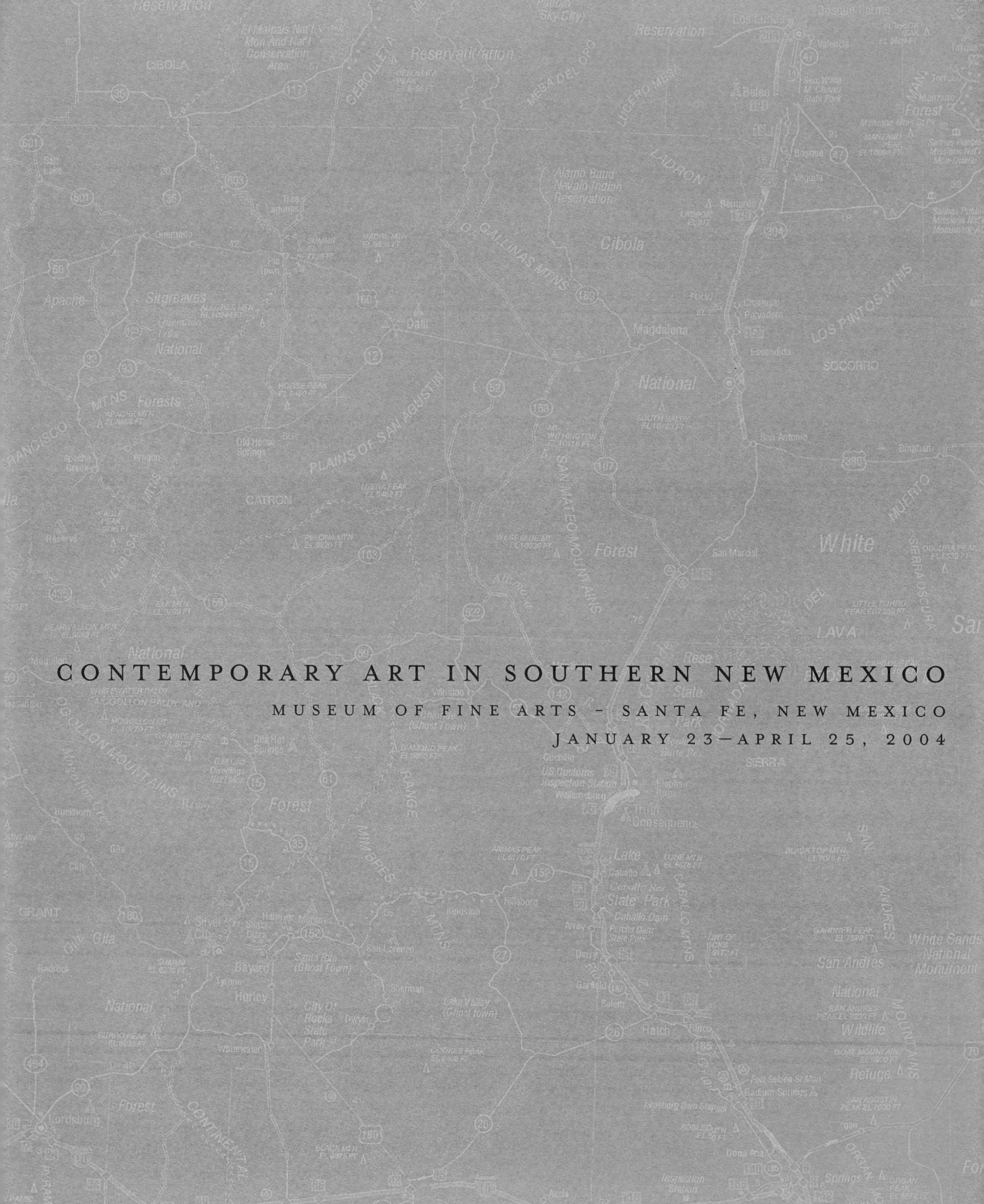

CONTEMPORARY ART IN SOUTHERN NEW MEXICO

MUSEUM OF FINE ARTS - SANTA FE, NEW MEXICO

JANUARY 23—APRIL 25, 2004

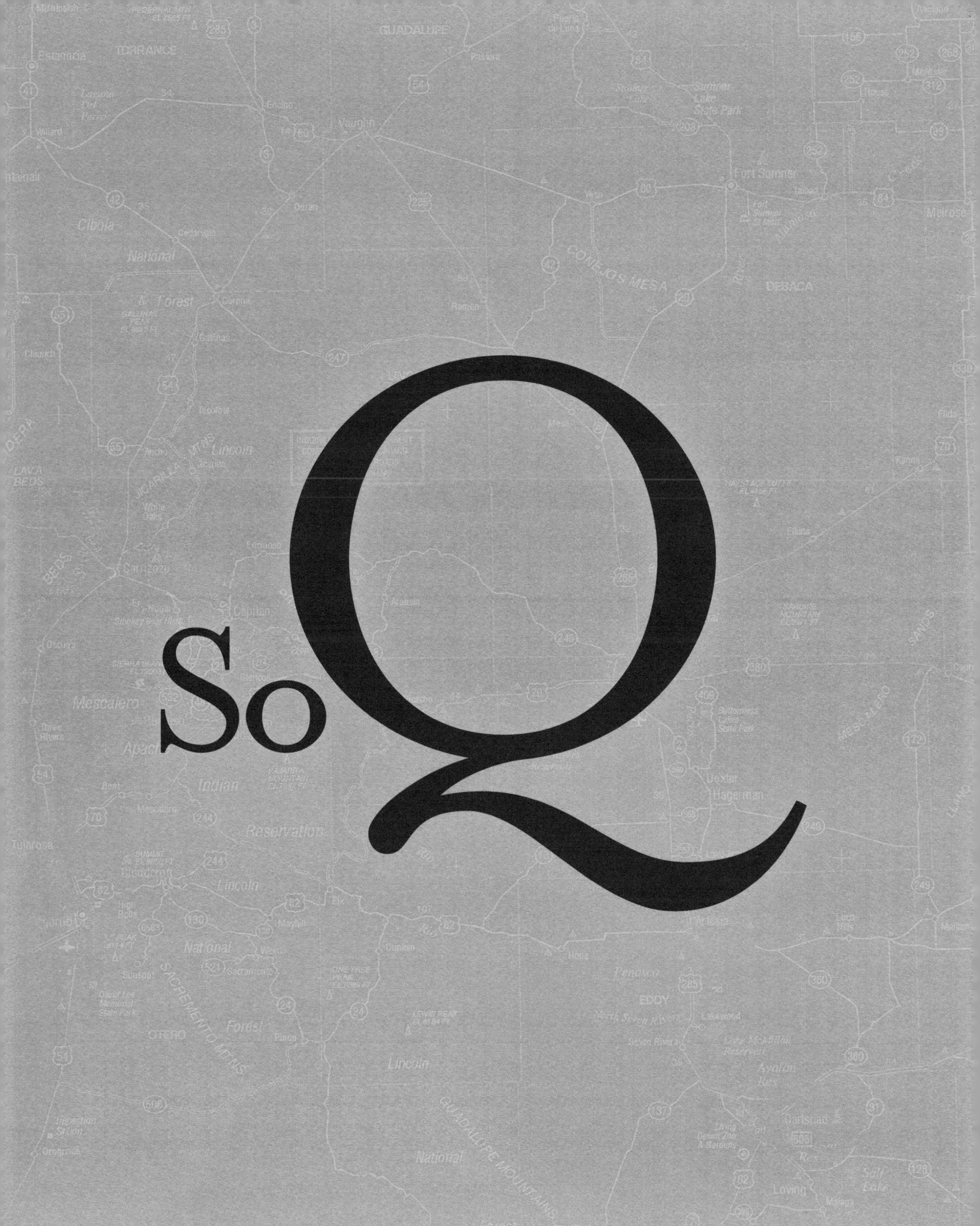
SoQ

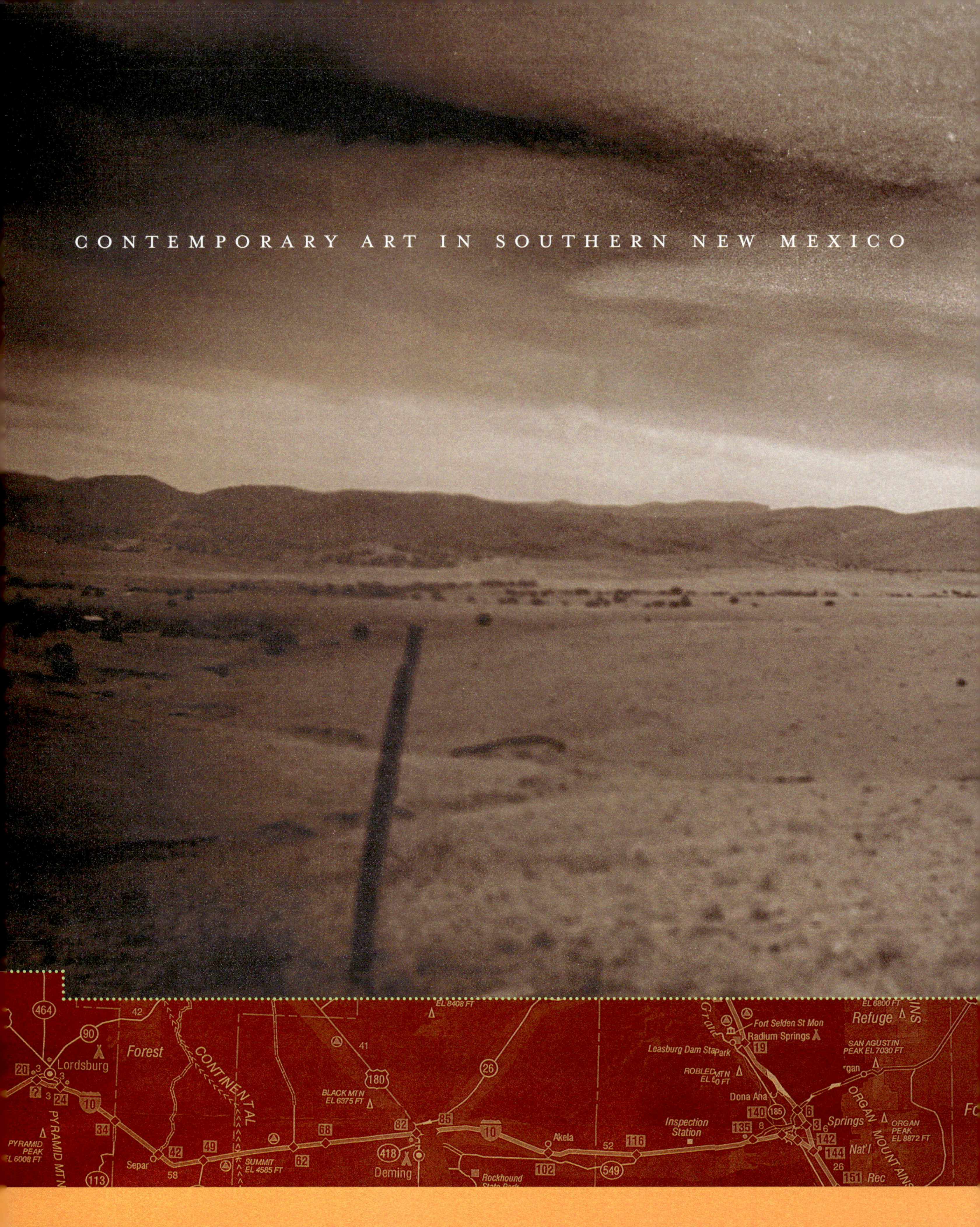

CONTEMPORARY ART IN SOUTHERN NEW MEXICO
Lordsburg
Forest
CONTINENTAL
PYRAMID MTN
BLACK MTN EL 6375 FT
EL 8408 FT
Separ
SUMMIT EL 4585 FT
Deming
Akela
Rockhound
Inspection Station
Fort Selden St Mon
Radium Springs
Leasburg Dam State Park
Dona Ana
Springs
ORGAN MOUNTAINS
ORGAN PEAK EL 8872 FT
SAN AGUSTIN PEAK EL 7030 FT
Refuge
EL 6800 FT
Nat'l
Rec

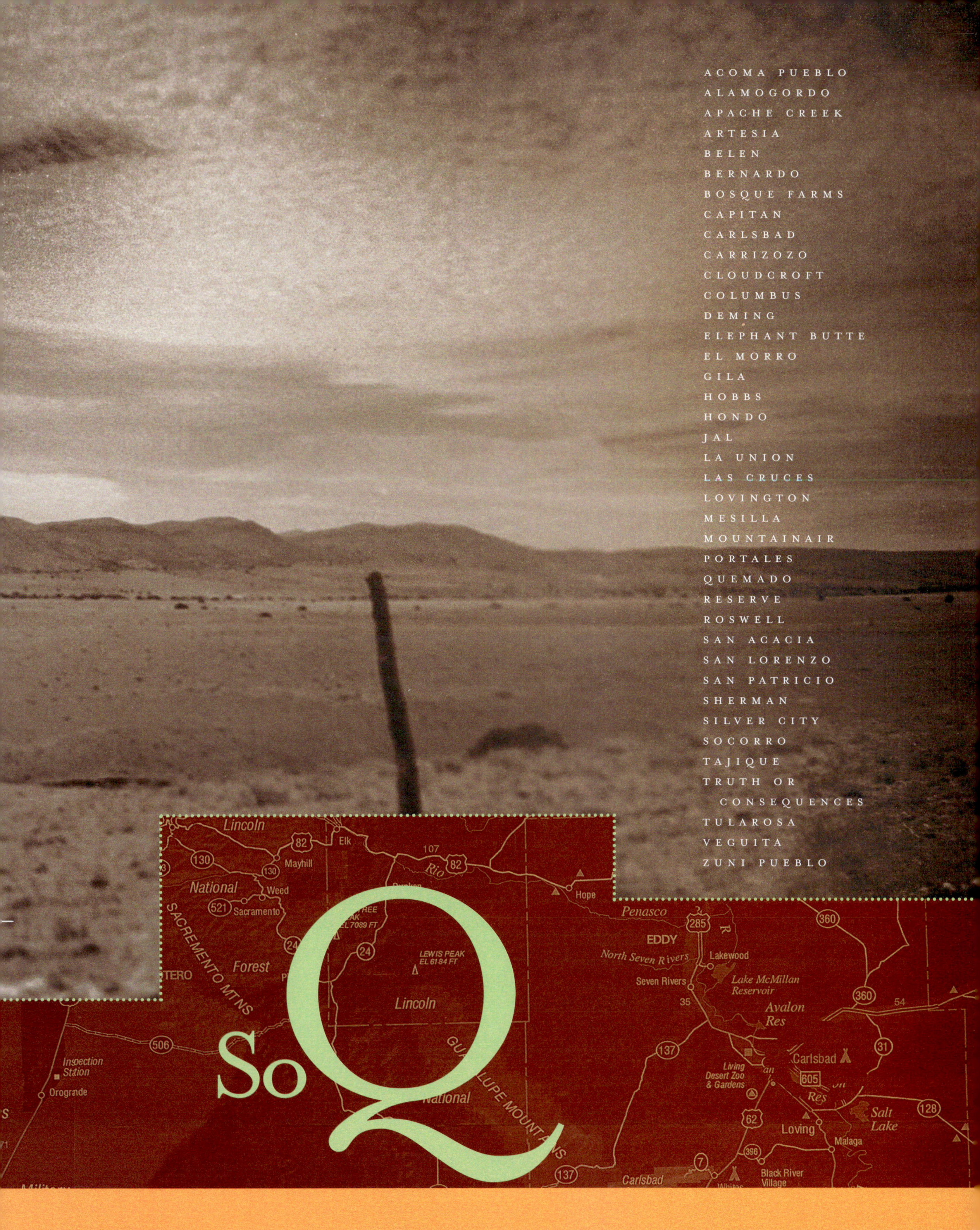
ACOMA PUEBLO
ALAMOGORDO
APACHE CREEK
ARTESIA
BELEN
BERNARDO
BOSQUE FARMS
CAPITAN
CARLSBAD
CARRIZOZO
CLOUDCROFT
COLUMBUS
DEMING
ELEPHANT BUTTE
EL MORRO
GILA
HOBBS
HONDO
JAL
LA UNION
LAS CRUCES
LOVINGTON
MESILLA
MOUNTAINAIR
PORTALES
QUEMADO
RESERVE
ROSWELL
SAN ACACIA
SAN LORENZO
SAN PATRICIO
SHERMAN
SILVER CITY
SOCORRO
TAJIQUE
TRUTH OR CONSEQUENCES
TULAROSA
VEGUITA
ZUNI PUEBLO
SoQ
Lincoln
Elk
Mayhill
National
Weed
Sacramento
SACRAMENTO MTNS
Forest
Hope
Penasco
EDDY
North Seven Rivers
Lakewood
Seven Rivers
Lake McMillan Reservoir
Avalon Res
LEWIS PEAK EL 6184 FT
Lincoln
Inspection Station
Orogrande
National
Living Desert Zoo & Gardens
Carlsbad
Loving
Salt Lake
Malaga
Black River Village
Carlsbad

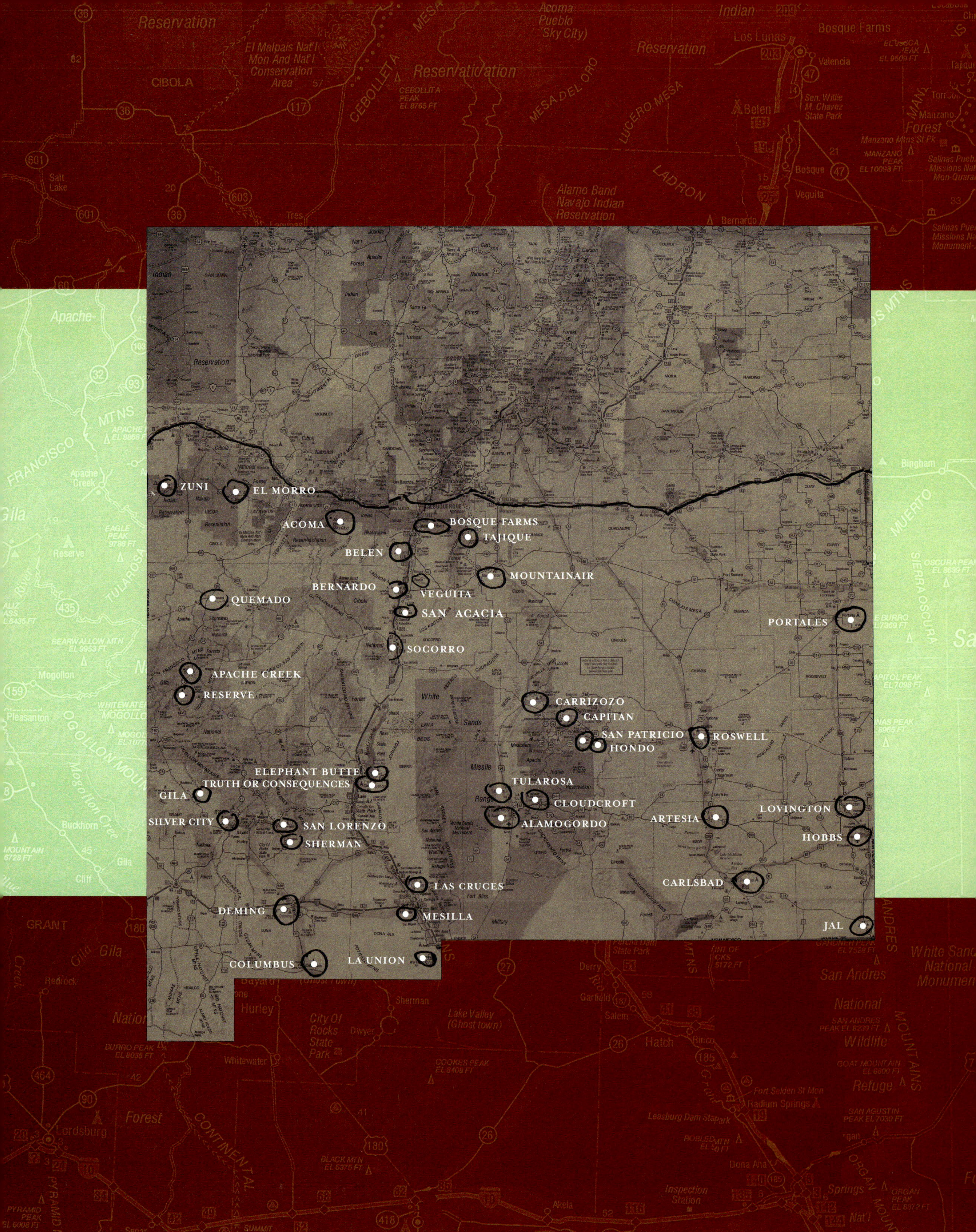

ZUNI
EL MORRO
ACOMA
BOSQUE FARMS
TAJIQUE
BELEN
MOUNTAINAIR
BERNARDO
VEGUITA
SAN ACACIA
QUEMADO
PORTALES
SOCORRO
APACHE CREEK
RESERVE
CARRIZOZO
CAPITAN
SAN PATRICIO
HONDO
ROSWELL
ELEPHANT BUTTE
TRUTH OR CONSEQUENCES
GILA
TULAROSA
CLOUDCROFT
SILVER CITY
SAN LORENZO
ALAMOGORDO
ARTESIA
LOVINGTON
SHERMAN
HOBBS
LAS CRUCES
CARLSBAD
DEMING
MESILLA
JAL
COLUMBUS
LA UNION

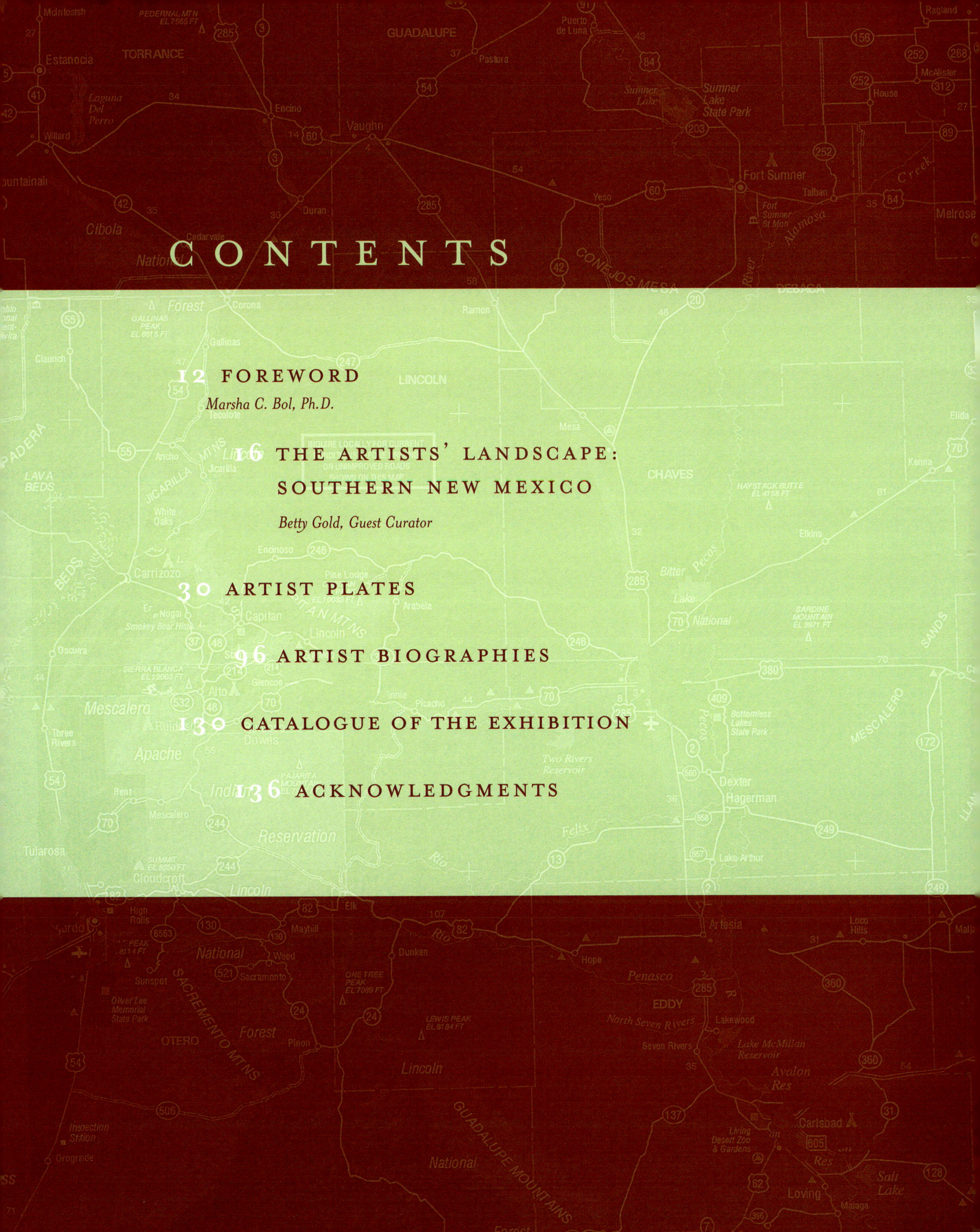

CONTENTS

FOREWORD

THE NEW MEXICO MUSEUM OF FINE ARTS is pleased and honored to present *SoQ: Contemporary Art in Southern New Mexico,* comprising the work of sixty-four artists working in thirty-nine cities, towns and hamlets of southern New Mexico.

When New Mexico State Representative J. Paul Taylor came to me with the idea for this exhibition in 2001, little did either of us realize what a monumental and historical undertaking this would turn out to be. Representative Taylor simply asked that the Museum of Fine Arts, as the state art museum of New Mexico, consider looking toward the southern portion of the state for an exhibition. This seemed a reasonable request—that is until I opened a map of New Mexico and reminded myself that fully two-thirds of the territory of New Mexico lie south of Interstate 40. I began to understand why never before, to my knowledge, had any museum or other arts institution undertaken such a project.

I look back now and realize that when I invited Betty Gold to become guest curator of this exhibition, the success of the project was assured. Gold is eminently qualified to direct such a project, having acquired and installed more than 8,000 works of art for five million square feet of building space worldwide during her tenure as manager of the corporate art department for the Atlantic Richfield Company and with many years of museum curatorial experience.

In addition to her qualifications, Gold brought an enthusiasm and commitment to this project that far exceeded any expectation that I might have hoped for. She took as her challenge the identification of meritorious artwork by personally visiting artists in as many cities, towns and villages, and driving as many country roads, south of Albuquerque as she could possibly travel. Everywhere Betty went she took her map of New Mexico, showing the working artists whom she visited all the red circles identifying the locales of the growing number of artists whose works were to be included in the exhibition. On Tuesday, February 4, 2003, Betty emailed me saying: "Howdy. I'm back from a trip to Belen, Veguita, Las Cruces, T or C and Socorro. It was really worthwhile to make it to the faculty show in Las Cruces. In Socorro, I went to an exhibition at New Mexico Tech and found a good artist from San Acacia [more red circles on the map!]. By the way, Bruce Lowney lives down by Zuni [another red circle]... Best...Betty."

In all, Betty made nine trips, traveling more than 5,000 miles, repeatedly bringing to my attention the wealth of work and talent happening throughout southern New Mexico. Gold's work as exhibition curator was made truly pleasurable by the many welcoming artists throughout southern New Mexico who have embraced this project.

The New Mexico Museum of Fine Arts turned eighty-five years old last year. When the museum was founded in 1917, the intention was to create a forum for showing the artwork of New Mexico artists. Artists signed up on a list to wait their turn to exhibit work in one of the museum's gallery alcoves. Of course, the number of artists in the state was far fewer than it would be eighty-five years later. No one knew in 1917 that New Mexico would become one of the leading arts centers in the country, no longer allowing the museum to continue as an open forum for all the state's artists.

Throughout its history, the Museum of Fine Arts has remained committed to collecting and exhibiting the artwork of the state and the region. Juried biennials of art created in New Mexico or the Southwest, presented in alternating exhibitions, took the place of the 1917 sign-up sheet as the museum sought to continue representing the artists over a wide geographic region. *SoQ* is the first exhibition, however, in the museum's history to focus solely on the artistic activity in the southern part of the state. I hope that you will be engaged and just a little surprised by the wealth of artistic offerings that this exhibition brings together for the first time.

The entire project began with the inspiration of Representative Taylor, who introduced a bill into the 2003 New Mexico State Legislature that appropriated funding for *SoQ*. We appreciate the Legislature's recognition of the importance of this project. We also appreciate the financial support of the Friends of Contemporary Art (FOCA). Gold, as guest curator, charted the course of the exhibition's development with her informed eye and broad experience. As the curatorial assistant, Martha Landry expertly coordinated as liaison between the curator and the Museum of New Mexico.

I especially want to thank the artists who have given generously of their talents and their time. I hope that they share in our pride in this historical undertaking.

Marsha C. Bol, Ph.D., *Director*

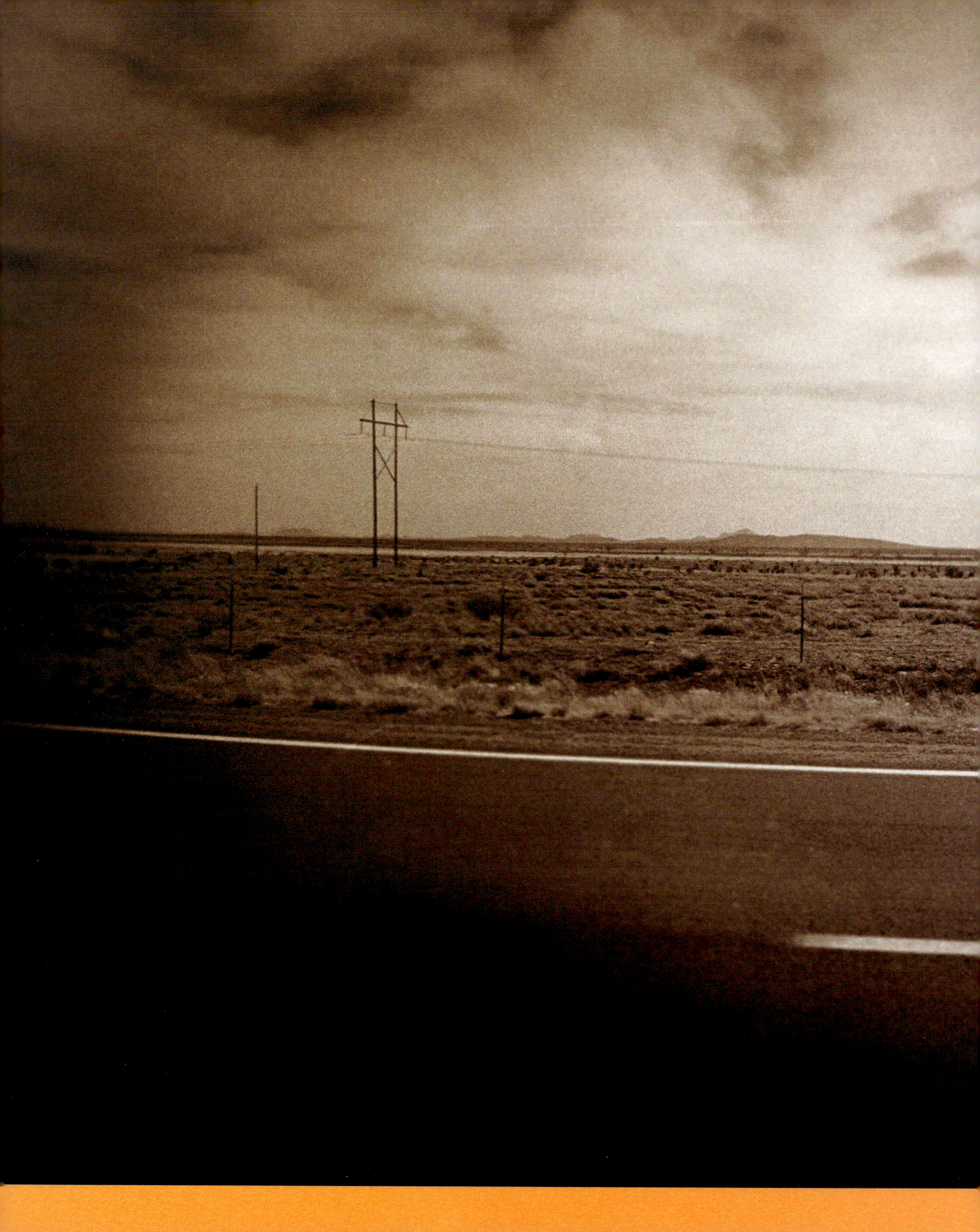

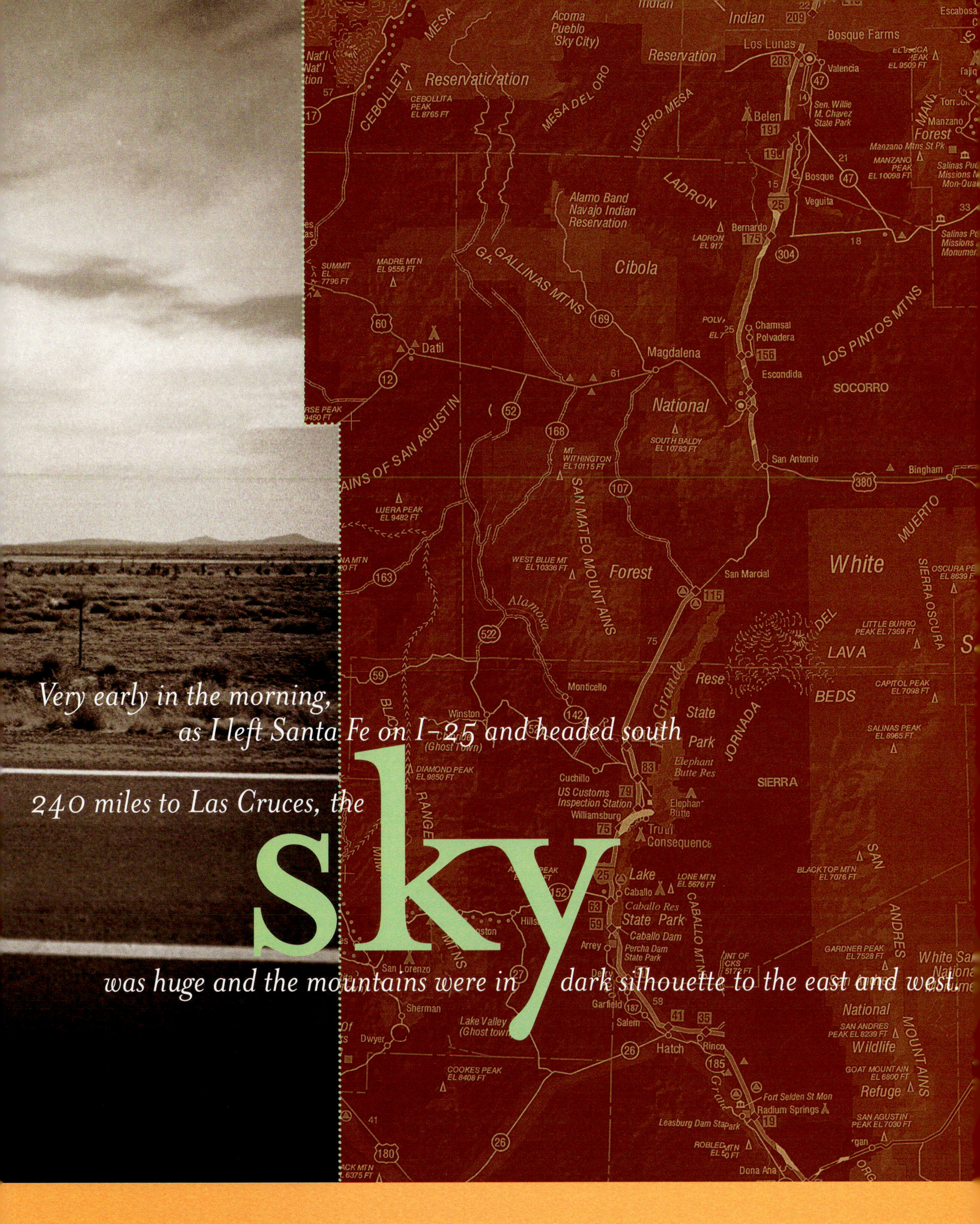

Very early in the morning,
as I left Santa Fe on I-25 and headed south

240 miles to Las Cruces, the

sky

was huge and the mountains were in dark silhouette to the east and west.

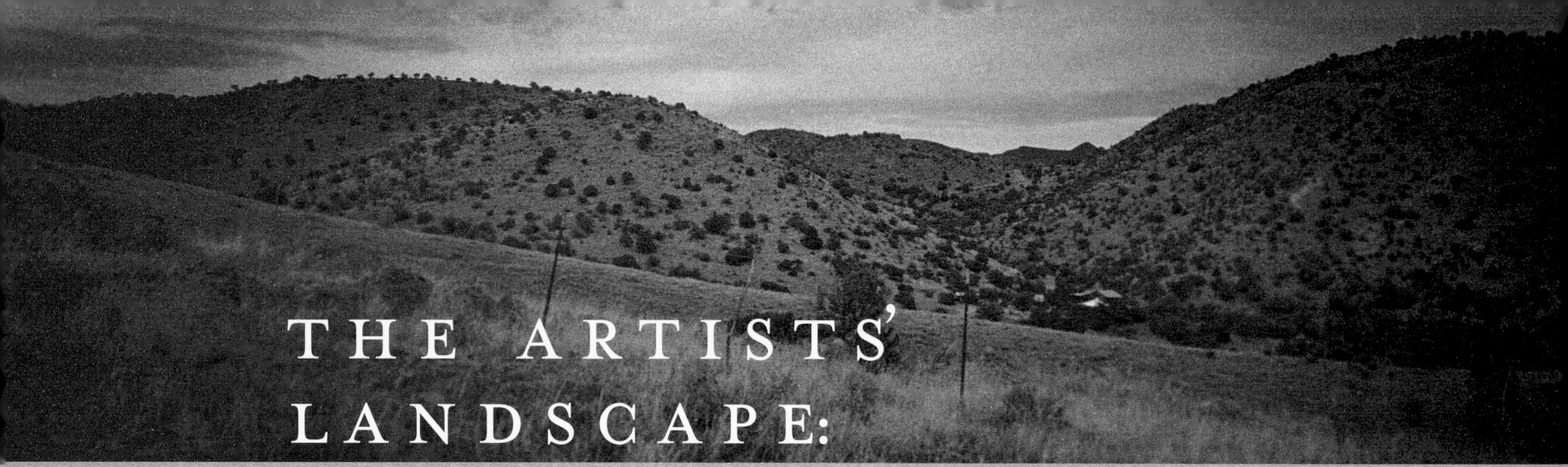

THE ARTISTS' LANDSCAPE: SOUTHERN NEW MEXICO

THE SIXTY MILES BETWEEN SANTA FE AND ALBUQUERQUE appear bereft of anyone living as far as the eye can see. But hidden fewer than ten miles from the highway, just out of sight, one passes various Native American pueblos: Cochiti Pueblo, where clay figures of storytellers and animals and fine drums from sheepskin and cottonwood are made; Santo Domingo Pueblo, where the Native people make exquisite shell jewelry and clay pots; and then San Felipe Pueblo, where more crafts are made. On my first trip to southern New Mexico to research this exhibition, I was already familiar with the arts hidden from view on these pueblos. I had hoped this unseen art might be a harbinger of the adventure that awaited me, of finding accomplished artists in the huge expanse of southern New Mexico. My first task was to identify what constituted "southern New Mexico," which for the purpose of this exhibition I defined as south of I-40, the highway that forms an east-west axis across the state, and dipping below Albuquerque, a city thought of as central New Mexico. As a result, the title of this exhibition is *SoQ,* an abbreviation for "South of Albuquerque." As far as is known, *SoQ* is the first exhibition to survey contemporary work from the entire southern New Mexico artistic landscape.

When I began my research for this exhibition, I assumed I would be traveling only to cities known to have active artist communities: Las Cruces, where there is a large art department at New Mexico State University and a university museum; Silver City, which is known as a town filled with galleries and is home to Western New Mexico University; and Roswell, which is home to the Anderson Museum of Contemporary Art and where there is a program for visiting artists to stay for six months to a year as artists-in-residence. But while searching the Internet one day, I found a site about Jal, New Mexico, that changed my perception about the scope of this exhibition. Jal is a town of fewer than 2,000 people in the extreme southeastern corner of the state. It was named after a cattle brand that was brought into the area in the 1880s. Jal is a ranching community and had also been an oil and gas town until the mid-1980s. To mark the occasion of the high school's reunion in 2000, local artist Brian Norwood decided to build a sculpture honoring the ranching heritage of the community. What Norwood envisioned was an outdoor sculpture of steel cut-outs of

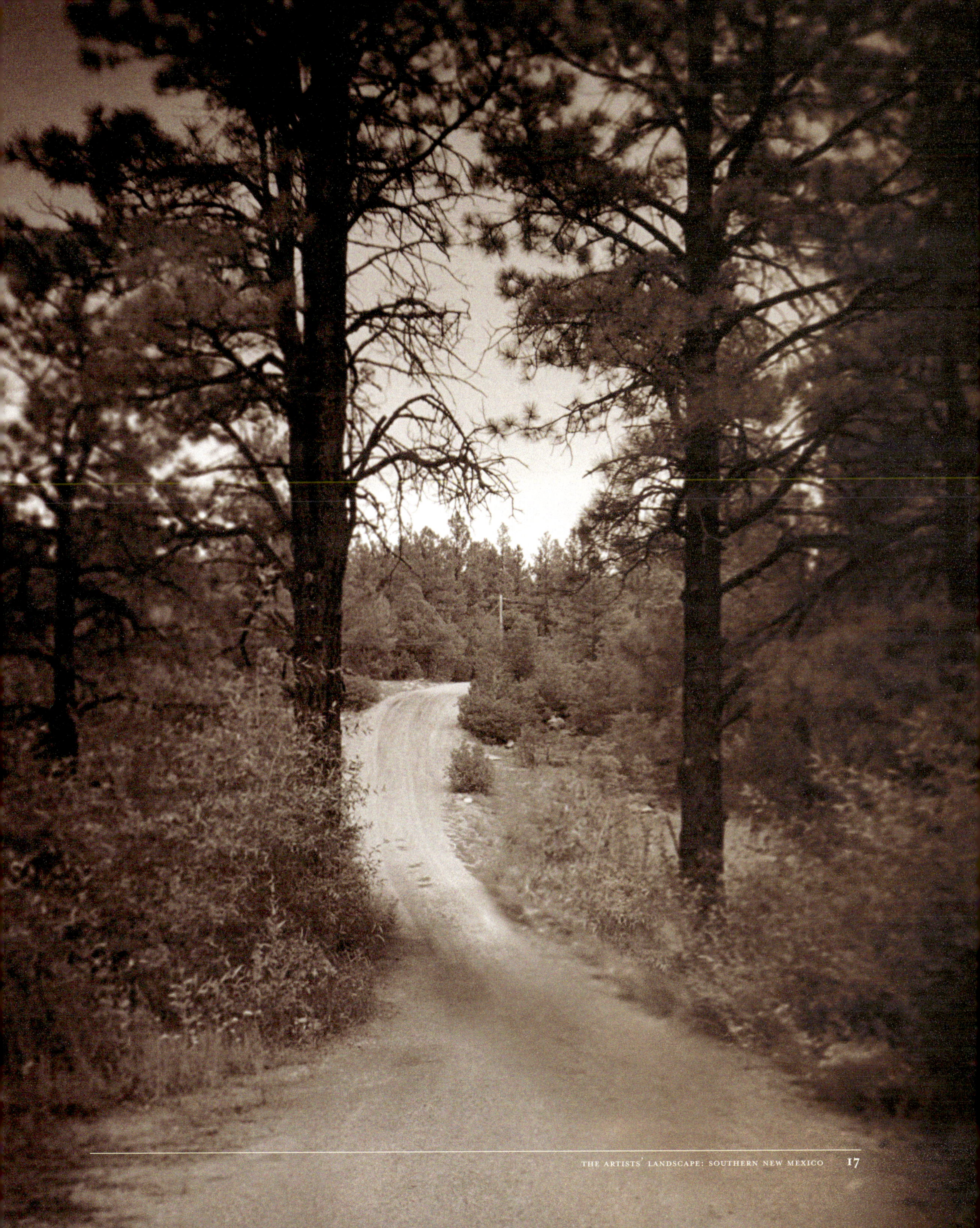

cowboys and cattle that was to be 400 feet long with the figures ranging in size from seven to twenty feet tall. It was to cost $15,000, a large sum for a town this size. With the help of the Jal Chamber of Commerce's volunteer staff the money was raised and the sculpture built in time for the reunion (which was not for a specific graduation class, but rather for anyone who ever attended the high school at any time).

Brian Norwood's vision to make a sculpture of such heroic dimensions in a town so isolated and small couldn't help but bring to mind the can-do spirit of the old West. To this curator, the creative drive, scale and scope of this project far outweighed the ordinary nature of the subject matter itself. I knew I wanted to honor this work and I felt confident that with enough research and luck, I would find work to demonstrate that there was a range of accomplished artists throughout the vast region of southern New Mexico. Inspired by Jal, the scope of *SoQ* changed; rather than highlighting only established artists from three cities, it ultimately exhibits the work of sixty-four artists from thirty-nine cities, towns and villages. The first of nine research trips was about to begin.

A half-hour or so south of Albuquerque there is a dramatic change of landscape. The green piñon trees of the north are gone and the land and hills are brown, but the open spaces and sky still proclaim "New Mexico." Not yet knowing all the art that awaited in villages a few miles east and west of I-25 south of Albuquerque, I drove the straight shot to Las Cruces, the first of four trips to this lovely city of 85,000 set beside the Organ Mountains, which rise like sharp, ragged cliffs in the background. There I met with Joshua Rose, the head of the art department at New Mexico State University, and with Jackie Mitchell Edwards, whose colorful painting *Prickly Pear #1* is in this exhibition. Edwards had been a corporate lawyer in New York, but she felt the pull of the Southwest. With her physician husband she moved to Las Cruces to pursue her dream of being a painter and opened JME Studios, now the leading contemporary art gallery in Las Cruces.

Next I headed north to Silver City, a town of 12,000 set in the Pinos Altos Mountains that was founded in 1870 after the discovery of silver. The history of this area goes back hundreds of years, with the Mimbres Indians living in the area in 1000 A.D. In much later times Silver City hosted Geronimo, Billy the Kid and Butch Cassidy. The impetus for this visit was Silver City's fall art and craft fair, which was advertised as a weekend festival with 100 artists and twenty-five galleries. The fair yielded the names of a few galleries and artists to check out on a future trip. Silver City's galleries are clustered on two streets so that a visitor can accomplish a lot in a short time.

Even at the early stages of my research, *SoQ* was beginning to take shape in my mind. No decision had been made, however, about the possibility of including artists no longer living. On my next trip to southern New Mexico I drove with Marsha Bol, director of the Museum of Fine Arts, to Las Cruces to meet with State Representative J. Paul Taylor.

Representative Taylor has long had an interest in the arts and is a collector extraordinaire of textiles, objects and contemporary art. A sixteenth-generation New Mexican, he lives in a magnificent adobe house on the plaza in Mesilla, a charming historical area adjacent to Las Cruces. The Taylors have generously promised their home to the Museum of New Mexico. Marsha and I had an unforgettable day visiting the Taylors' house and going to antique stores, artists' studios and the Branigan Cultural Center with Representative Taylor. After seeing so many contemporary artists, a decision was made to include a review of some of the early artists of southern New Mexico in the Women's Board Room gallery of the museum, concurrent with *SoQ*.

After taking Marsha to the airport, I headed back up I-25, stopping at Truth or Consequences (T or C), where, located next to the Ralph Edwards Trailer Park (named after the host of the "Truth or Consequences" radio program, after which the town is named), I visited painter Joe Waldrum's 9,000-square-foot Rio Bravo Fine Art gallery. Shock and awe—a 9,000-square-foot gallery in T or C! Here I saw Delmas Howe's dramatic paintings and found the work of landscape painter Dave Barnett, who lives just north of T or C in Elephant Butte, and the splashy, energetic paintings of Danielle Auprix, who moved to T or C from Canada.

My third trip was to Roswell to attend the thirty-fifth anniversary of the Anderson artist-in-residence program. Painter Donald Anderson, who founded and nurtured the important contemporary art scene in Roswell, is represented in *SoQ* by *Black Canyon*, a large, strong landscape painting that presents a resolved maturity to his work. Stephen Fleming, whose three biomorphic clay forms are included in this exhibition, is the director of the Anderson Museum of Contemporary Art. Together, Fleming and I went to see Stuart Arends, who lives outside Roswell in a contemporary house overlooking a lake—a perfect setting for his small but powerful hard-edged paintings. Then we drove forty miles beyond Roswell to Hondo to visit Luis Jimenez. His studio is filled with fiberglass sculptures, telling the story of his many years of fabricating muscular and mythic figures of the Southwest. In nearby San Patricio the accomplished landscape painter Michael Hurd, son of painters Peter Hurd and Henriette Wyeth, the artistic royalty of southern New Mexico, lives on the family hacienda. He is represented in *SoQ* with a wonderful garden scene, *Loveseat*.

I learned about a faculty show at New Mexico State University in Las Cruces and I headed down there later that week. It was an opportunity to see the work of more than a dozen artists in a single space. Based on that trip, I decided to arrange studio visits with several of the artists at a later date. On my way back to Santa Fe, I visited Socorro, an agricultural town of 9,000 people. Set in the Rio Grande Valley, its main crops are chiles and melons. It was developed as a town with the advent of the railroad in 1880 and is home to New Mexico Institute of Mining and Technology, where artist Loretta Lowman and I went to see an exhibition of her sculpture and photographs.

> The corridor between Socorro and Albuquerque boasts a number of talented artists. East of the highway, halfway between the two cities, is the charming ranching village of Veguita, where husband and wife Brian O'Connor and Iva Morris live. The imagery is not alike in their paintings, but both artists have a mystical quality to their work: O'Connor's is political in meaning while Morris' paintings show a satirical wit.

Sixty miles west of Albuquerque is Acoma Pueblo. Inhabited since 1150 A.D., it is still the home of 2,000 people and is known for the pottery of artists such as Sandra Victorino. A short distance from Acoma, along Highway 53, I drove through the spectacularly beautiful Cibola National Forest to El Morro, where painter Bruce Lowney has lived on 160 wooded acres for almost three decades. The isolation of Lowney's home and studio is typical of the artists in this exhibition and is the one

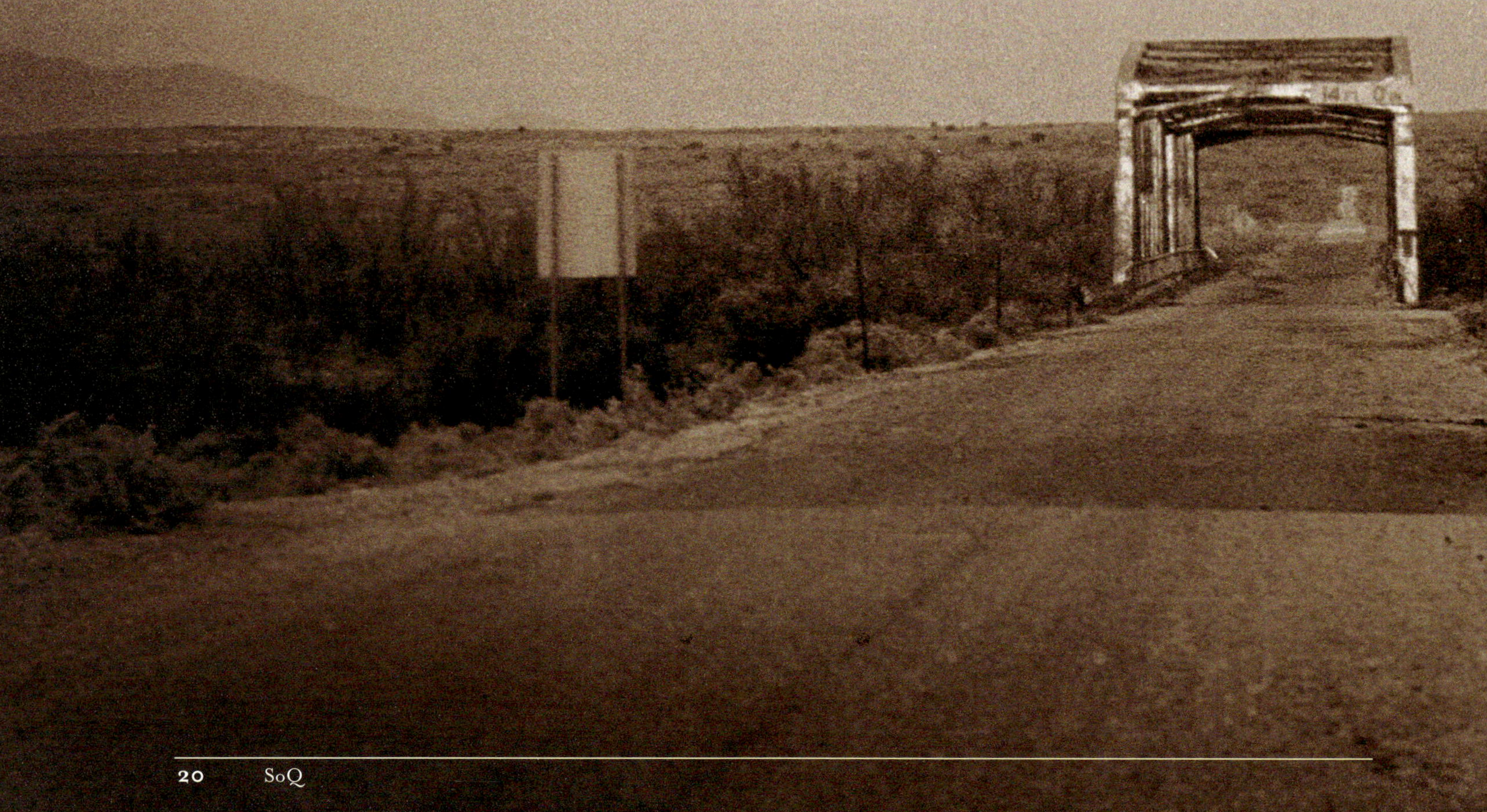

theme that distinguishes artists in southern New Mexico from artists in Albuquerque, Santa Fe and Taos. The isolated living conditions, always the artists' choice, free them from the pressures of gallery shows and the stimulation and influences of other artists and allow them the freedom to follow their own paths. This isolation also made finding the artists for *SoQ* almost a one-by-one event, spanning fifteen months and more than 5,000 miles.

> Highway 53 continues west through the tiny Navajo village of Ramah and then on to Zuni Pueblo, where potter Priscilla Peynetsa resides. Zuni is a charming village with several shops and a church with beautiful murals of life-size Zuni kachinas. Zuni is known not only for its potters but also for its inlaid jewelry and carved fetishes.

On my sixth trip I covered 1,000 miles in five days in order to visit as many artists as possible. I learned that what some artists describe as a "road" is in reality tire tracks on an expanse of desert dirt. The directions to many studios were wonderfully colorful: "Go to the end of the dirt road, turn left and follow the river, turn right at the old church past the boarded-up trading post,"often followed by the question, "Do you have four-wheel drive and a mobile phone?" The first destination on this trip was Bosque Farms, which is twenty miles south of Albuquerque. A lush farming and ranching community, Bosque Farms is home to Chip Simons. After selecting photographs from

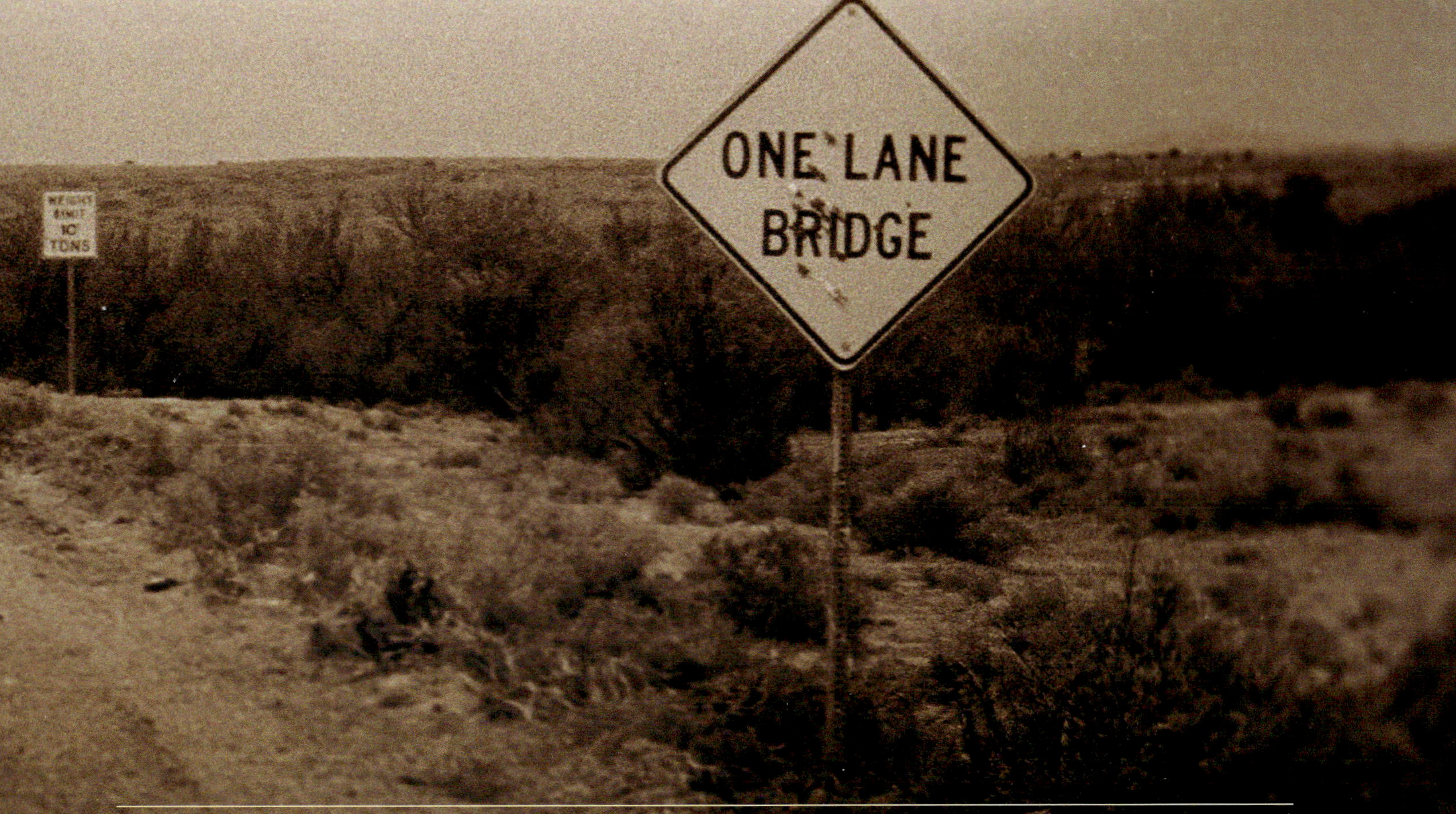

Simons, I traveled south forty miles to Bernardo, a village of about 100 people, where I got seriously lost trying to find Laura Wacha, on what felt to me like a desert moonscape. After reaching her by cell phone and asking her to meet me at the RV park (apparently the only landmark in Bernardo), I followed Wacha five dusty miles to her colorful mobile home to select a painting. I then managed to find my way back to I-25, stopping along the way to call some artists and postpone that afternoon's appointments until the next day—the result of the hours lost on the memorable moonscape.

Heading back down I-25, I turned west on Route 26 at Hatch, called the chile capital of the world. Every shop and home seemed to have a ristra of chiles hanging from the roof. I was on my way to Deming, where artist Gordon Dipple lives—then on to Silver City, where I started early the next day on a twelve-hour-marathon day of selecting art. There I discovered Harry Benjamin, a native of Silver City and a sophisticated painter who was knowledgeable about the art world beyond his hometown's borders. He is also the owner of What's a Pot Shop, which I had neglected on my first visit to Silver City. Benjamin drove me eight miles outside of town to Scott Nichols' house to see his painting *Love in America*. While most of the houses in Silver City are Craftsman or Victorian style, the Nichols' home is a neo-Greco palace, a surprise to this visitor and probably a landmark in the Silver City area. This morning visit to Silver City was productive. I ultimately selected two paintings by Harry Benjamin for the exhibition, *Love in America* and *The Marriage of Mr. and Mrs. Potato Head*, which have subtle references to his wit and political interests. I also made final selections of work by Richard Earnheart at his studio and by Carlene Roters, Karen Pritchett and Linda Brewer at the wonderful Blue Dome Gallery. I also went with Jason Willaford, artist and owner of the premier Galleri Urbane, to his studio to make a final selection from his accomplished new work.

In the afternoon Harry Benjamin offered to navigate me to the Mimbres River Valley, an offer I was only too happy to accept after the previous day's misadventures in the southern New Mexico desert. On Highway 152 we drove through green hills winding down to the small village of San Lorenzo to our first stop at photographer Michael Berman's studio, which was out of sight until I reached the end of his long driveway. After selecting some of his work for *SoQ*, we continued on in San Lorenzo, past several abandoned adobe houses to the steep, rocky driveway (with one treacherous horseshoe turn) that leads to the lovely home of Nancy Spencer and Eric Renner, set on 400 acres. Internationally known, Spencer and Renner are leading proponents of pinhole photography and publish *The Pinhole Journal*. It's always interesting to see what artists collect, and I was amazed to see Spencer and Renner's collection of 1,600 chalkware carnival figures. They not only photograph but make assemblages

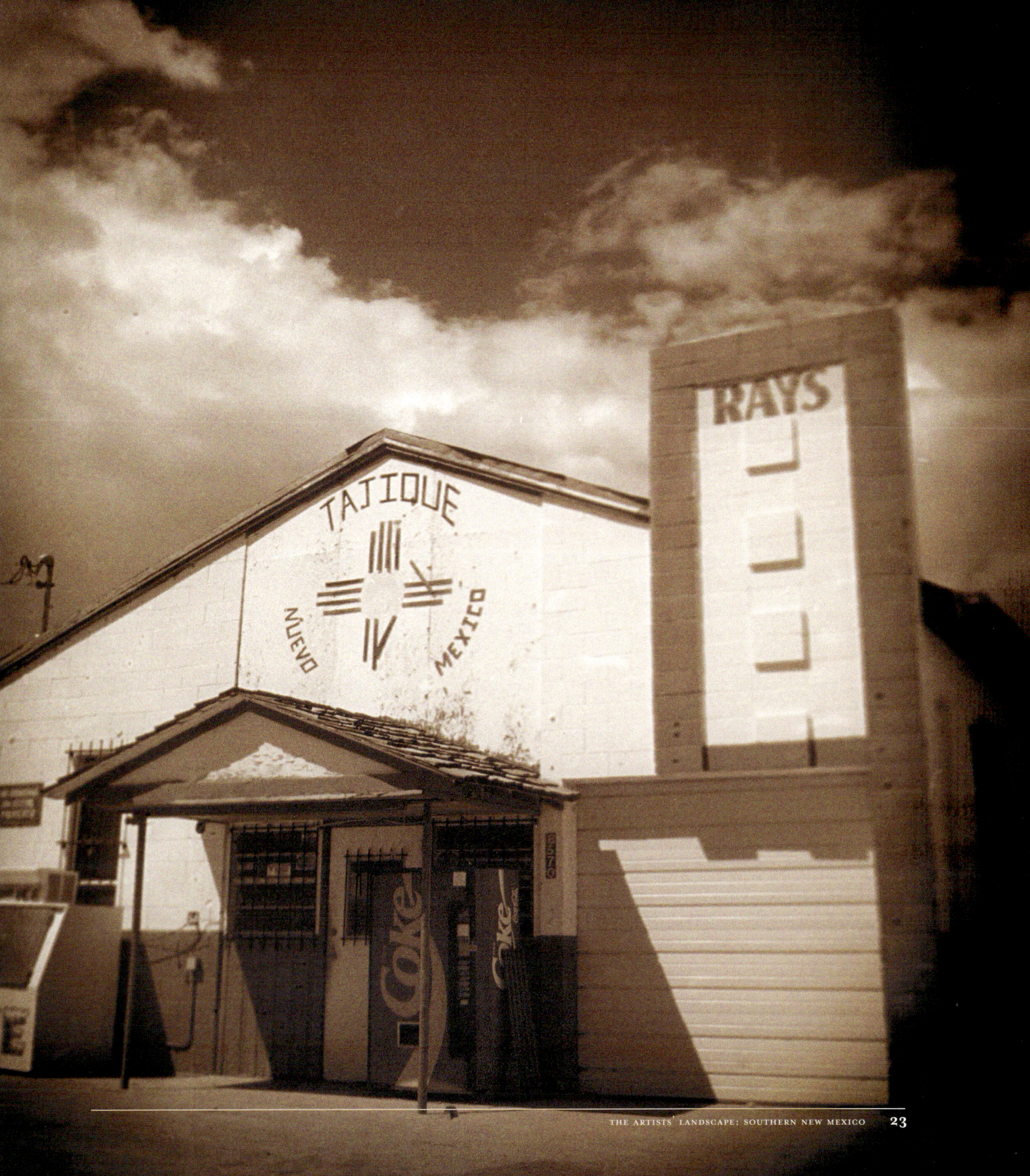
RAYS
TAJIQUE
NUEVO
MEXICO
Coke
Coke

as well. Their works in this exhibition are photographs of those assemblages. The last stop for the day was at the nearby pastoral village of Sherman (population 12) to make a final selection of work from Ann Lowe.

The next morning's trip was certainly a highlight of my southern New Mexico travels. Leaving Silver City, driving thirty-five miles past Deming on Route 11, I reached Columbus, a town of 1,700 people just four miles north of the Mexican border town of Palomas, the only 24-hour border crossing in New Mexico. Columbus is the site of Pancho Villa's infamous 1916 raid. Bullet holes can still be seen in the Hoover Hotel, one of the few buildings still standing that survived the raid. Columbus boasts a dinner theatre that draws people from as far away as El Paso, as well as a jail and a historical museum. Here I met with artist Tim McAndrews. After lunch at the Pancho Villa Cafe, I headed east on a desolate sixty-five-mile road to La Union. There I visited with Becky Hendrick and Ray Parish. I saw Parish's wonderful assemblage of an Airstream trailer with a piano attached to the roof. Unfortunately, the actual trailer wouldn't fit in the Museum of Fine Arts, but in order to acknowledge the work, it is represented by a photograph in this exhibition.

The drive from La Union to Las Cruces was an astonishing change from the flat, brown landscape of the drive from Columbus to La Union. The twenty-five-mile approach from the south to Las Cruces displayed an umbrella of towering pecan trees surrounded by lush fields of lettuce, onions and spinach. While in Las Cruces I visited the studios of Amanda Jaffe, David Taylor, Jackie Mitchell Edwards, Rachel Stevens, Jackie Mitchell and Georjeanna Feltha. I also saw Suzanne Kane's and Joshua Rose's work at the Branigan Cultural Center and at New Mexico State

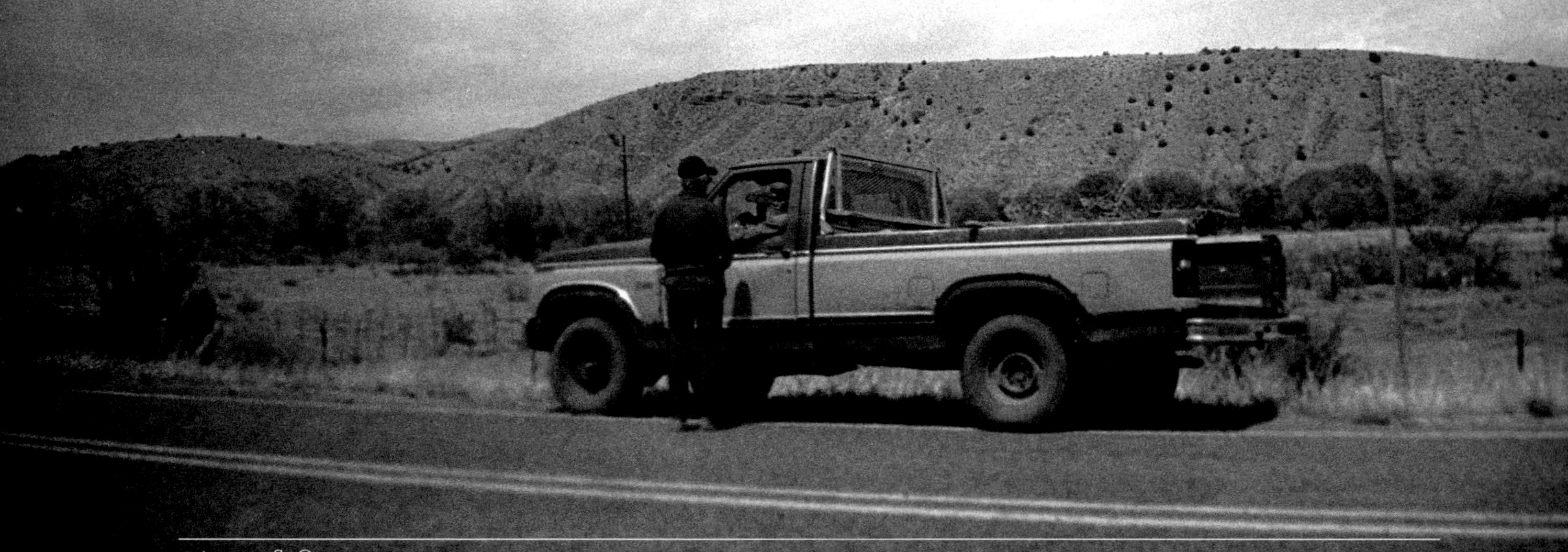

University, respectively. Heading back to Santa Fe the next day, I stopped at Truth or Consequences to make final selections from the Rio Bravo Fine Art gallery artists: Joe Waldrum, Dave Barnett, Danielle Auprix and Delmas Howe. Waldrum hosted a lunch at the Sierra Grande Lodge in T or C, which is owned by Serge Raoul, who also owns Raoul's, a landmark restaurant on Prince Street in New York's SoHo. After visiting with Delmas Howe at his home, I continued on to the tiny village of San Acacia to make a final selection of paintings from Fernando Mercado. I had planned to stop also at Veguita to see Iva Morris and Brian O'Connor again, but we had a misconnect, so I made a day trip to Veguita soon after my return.

My eighth trip focused on eastern New Mexico. I first went south through Roswell to Artesia to see Noel Márquez, a muralist who studied with Faith Ringgold and Italo Scagna at the University of California at San Diego. Márquez has lived in Artesia in a converted gas station for twenty-five years, directly across the street from an oil refinery, a view that is hard to reconcile with the human and landscape imagery in his work. Fifty miles south of Artesia is Carlsbad, where painter Helen Gwinn lives and where I stopped to visit the lively Carlsbad Museum and Art Center. Then it was on to Jal, the town which was the genesis for the scope of this exhibition. On the road into Jal, I finally saw *The Trail Ahead*, Brian Norwood's 400-foot sculpture, and met with the artist at the D and N Restaurant, a place where everyone seemed to know him. After a quick stop at the Chamber of Commerce, I drove north to the thriving city of Hobbs, where John Lathrop lives, and then to Lovington, where Carrie Swenson lives and where I visited the Lea County Museum to see a show of Brian Norwood's paintings.

The flat landscape of Lea County, which includes Jal, Hobbs and Lovington, is probably more like the landscape of western Texas, which it borders. The county is a major contributor to New Mexico's economy, producing oil and gas, and is home to a large agriculture, cattle and dairy industry. Highway 206 passes through this landscape as you drive north from Lovington to Portales, where photographer Greg Erf lives and teaches at Eastern New Mexico University. This was my last stop before I returned to Santa Fe to prepare for my ninth, and final, road trip.

This final trip took me down Route 14 to Estancia, where I turned west twelve miles to the charming village of Tajique, then five miles on a gravel road, where I was suddenly in the Manzano Mountains. Just a few more miles on a private road surrounded by a thick forest of pine trees, I came to the beautiful log house of wood turner Bud Latven. I would not have been surprised to find Little Red Riding Hood here, but when I got to Latven's workshop, after walking through the woods and over a wooden plank bridge, I was surprised to meet a renowned British computer czar who had come from London to Tajique for a weeklong private workshop with Latven.

Next I traveled south eighty miles to Carrizozo, where *santera* Polly Chavez lives, to Alamogordo to see the ceramic work of Lea Rano and then to Tularosa, a town of 2,500 residents with an especially interesting history. Settled first in 1860, Tularosa was so frequently invaded by Apache warriors from the Mescalero Apache Reservation that it was abandoned. In 1862, a hundred men from surrounding villages returned to Tularosa and established the original village in the neighborhood now called The 49 Blocks, the heart of Tularosa's historic district. The blocks were irrigated with acequias that operate to this day. Present-day homeowners are allocated water and are allowed to open the gate to the acequia once every two weeks to irrigate their property. The homes in the forty-nine-block area are seated on lots that are a minimum of a half-acre, and the district is filled with huge lawns, masses of towering trees and lush plantings of pampas grasses and reeds. Painter Tamiris Duke lives in one of the historic houses, where she paints Tai Chi- and Tibetan Buddhist-inspired work.

I didn't get to every one of the towns where *SoQ* artists live. Missing is the loop from Quemado down through Apache Creek, Reserve and Gila. Looking at the *SoQ* map, there is a distinct absence of art representing the area surrounding Vaughn. Vaughn is a town of 500 or so people, essentially abandoned, but where I had great hopes of finding an artist for this exhibition. It never happened—Vaughn is a railroad town, not an art village. The main lines of the Burlington Northern Santa Fe and Union Pacific Railways intersect here and railroad buffs come from all over the country to photograph the abundance of trains that can be found stacked up here at any given time.

So, lastly, I will salute the town of Vaughn for its trains, instead of its art, which I tried in vain to find.

Betty Gold, *Guest Curator*

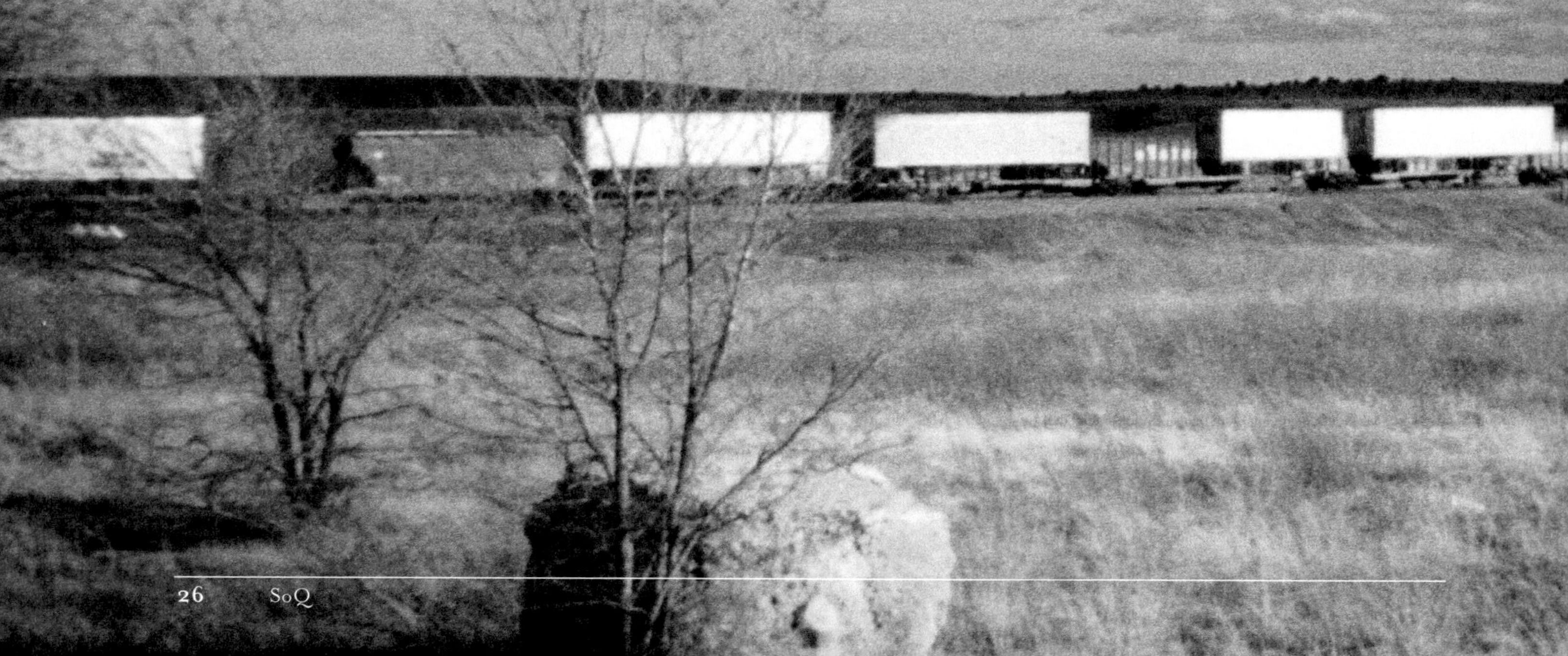

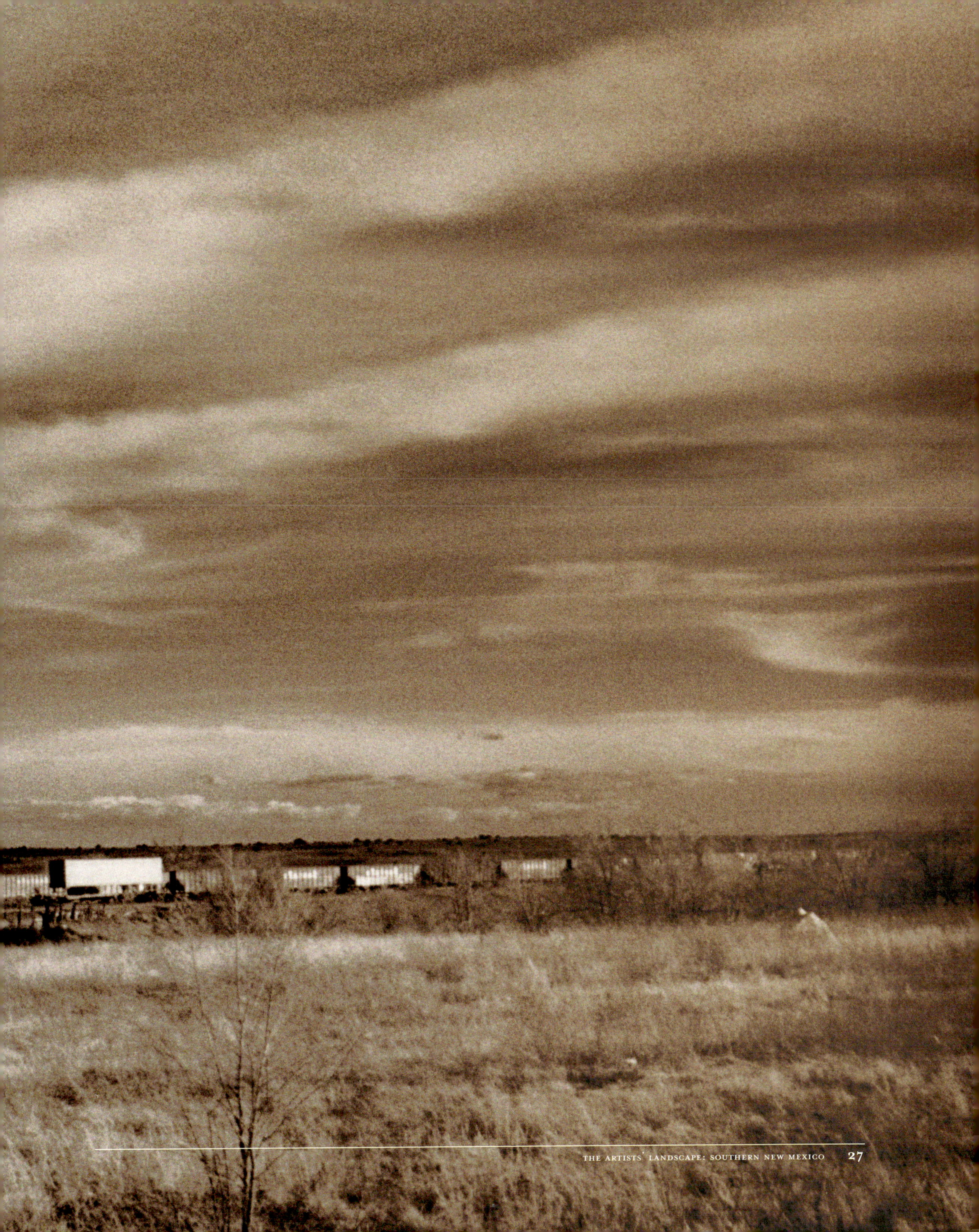

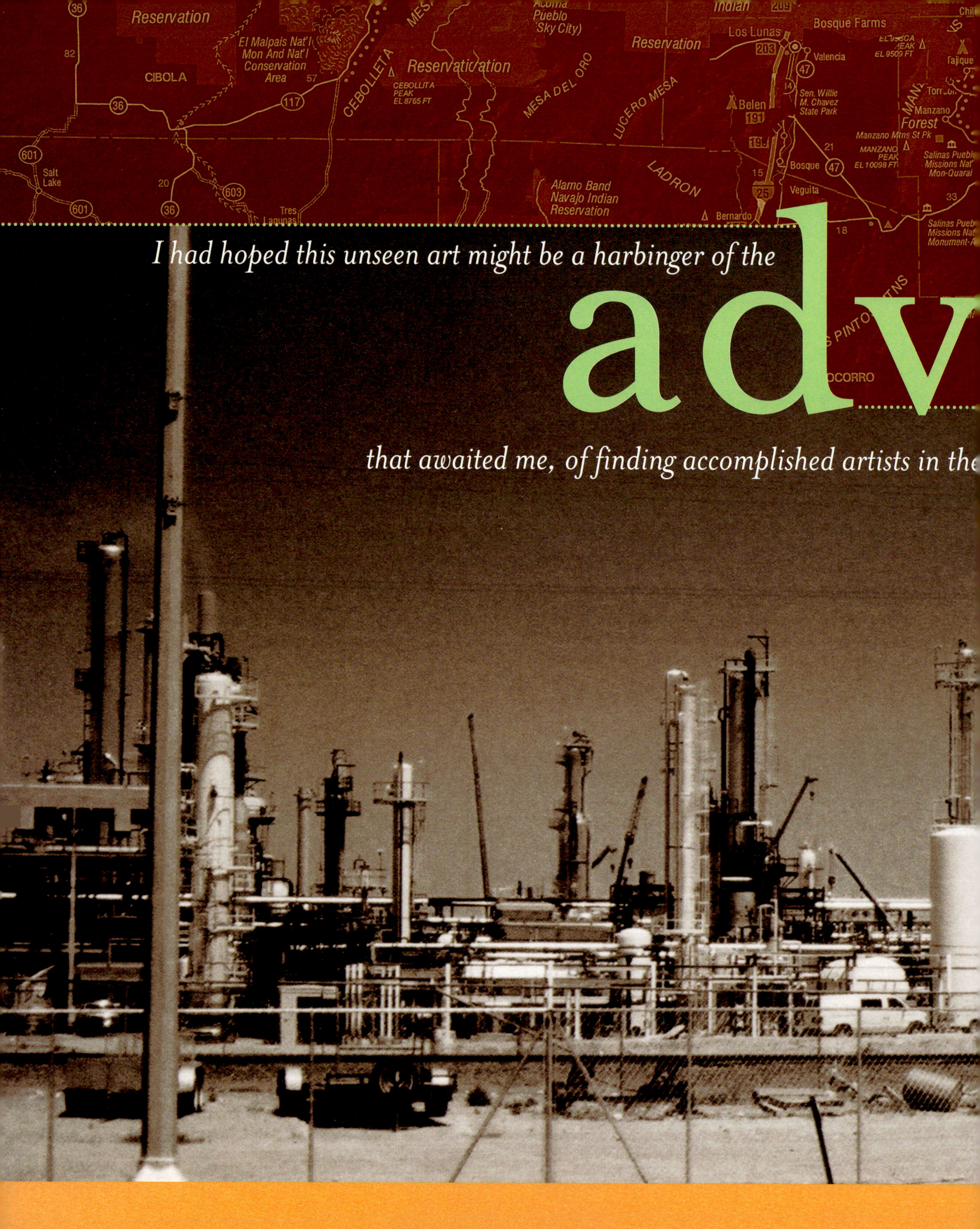

I had hoped this unseen art might be a harbinger of the

adv

that awaited me, of finding accomplished artists in the

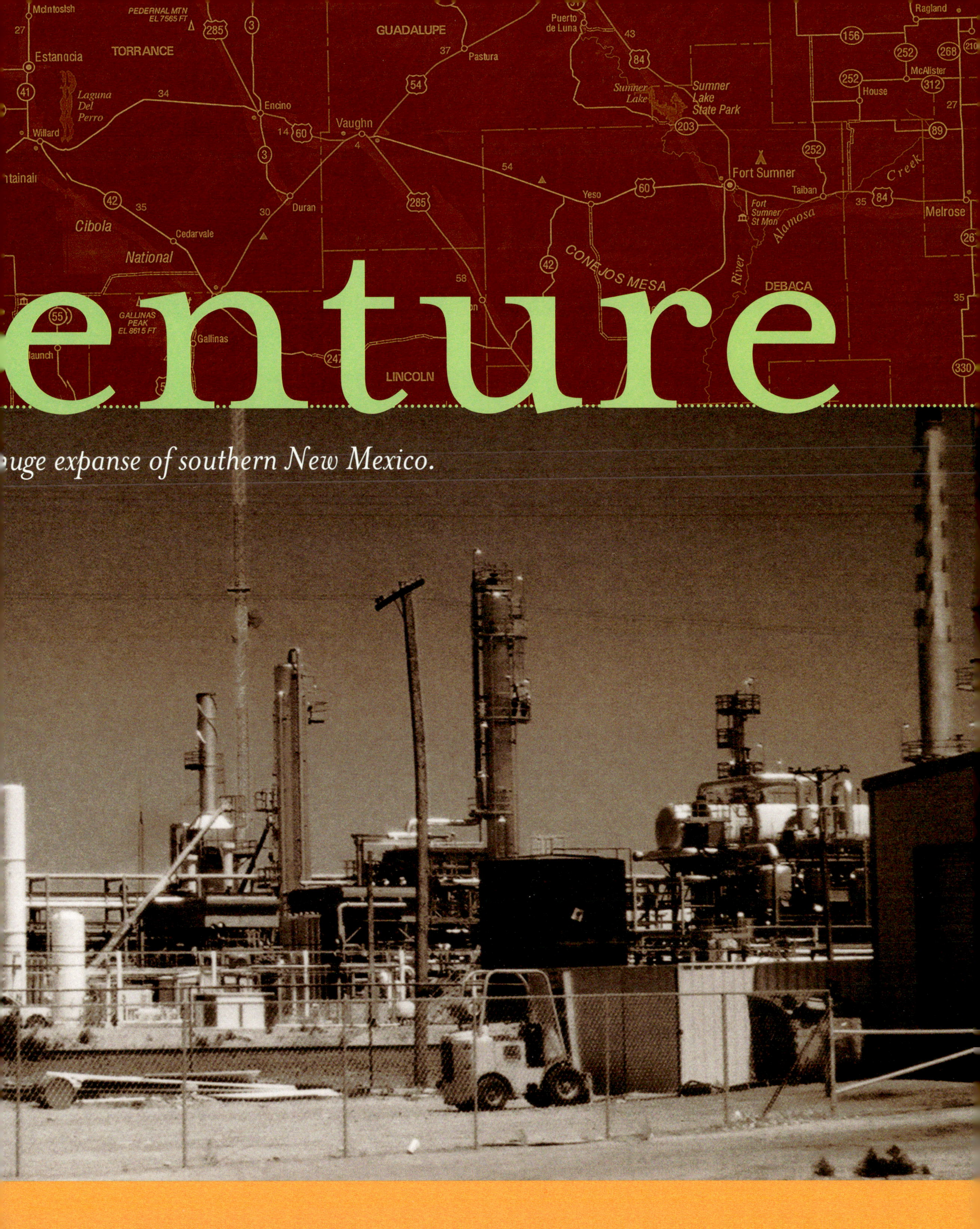

enture

uge expanse of southern New Mexico.

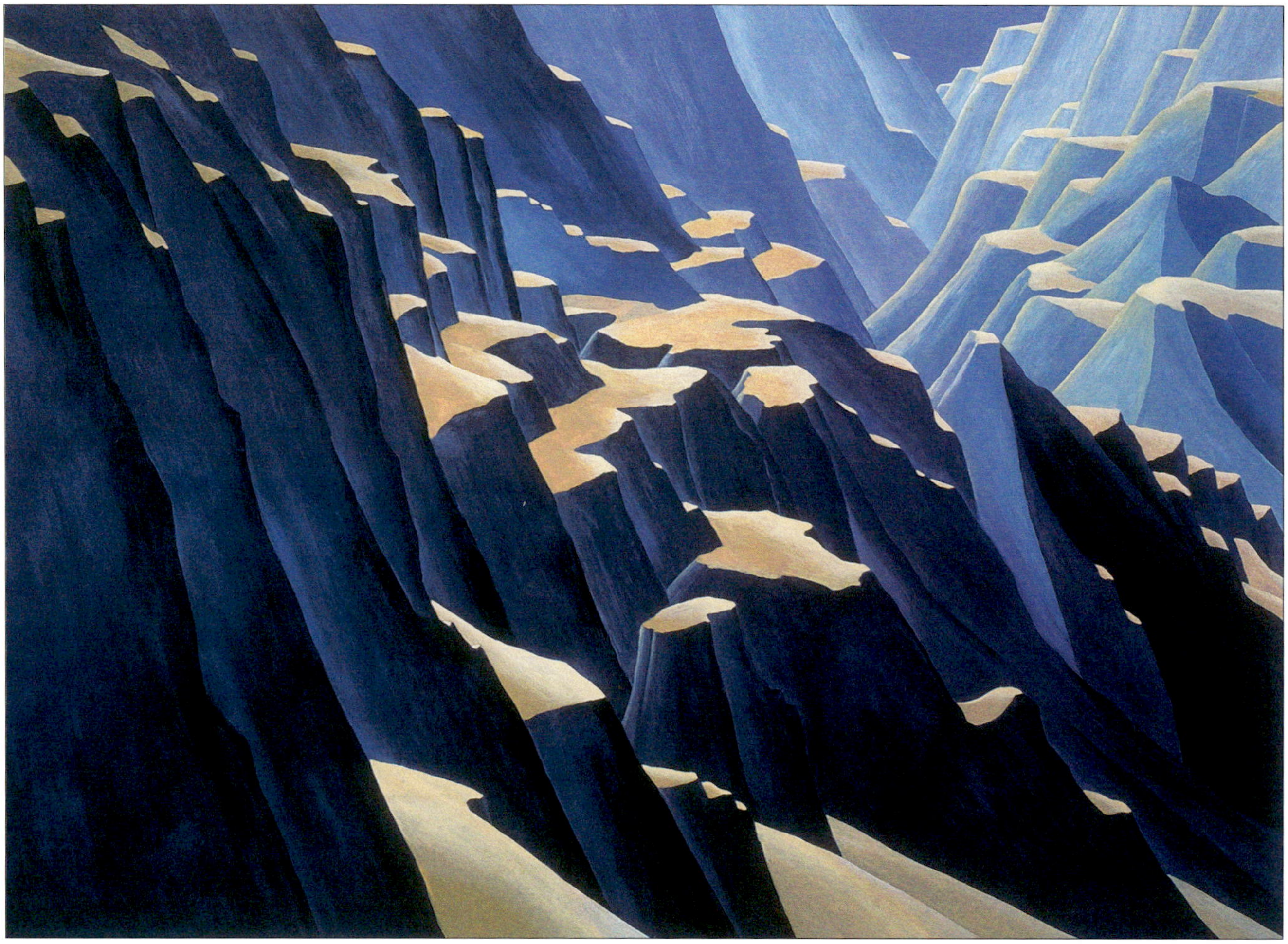

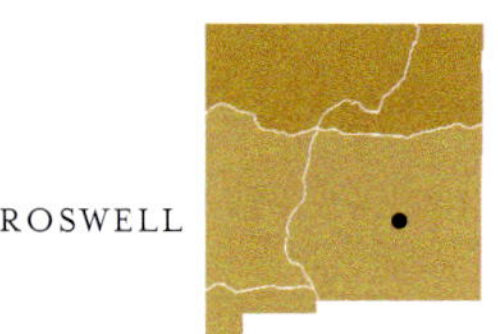

DONALD B. ANDERSON
Black Canyon
2002
Acrylic on canvas
72.5" x 100.5"

ROSWELL

STUART ARENDS
Unfolded A-11
2002
Oil on aluminum
4.5" x 7.5"
Lent by James Kelly Contemporary, Santa Fe, NM

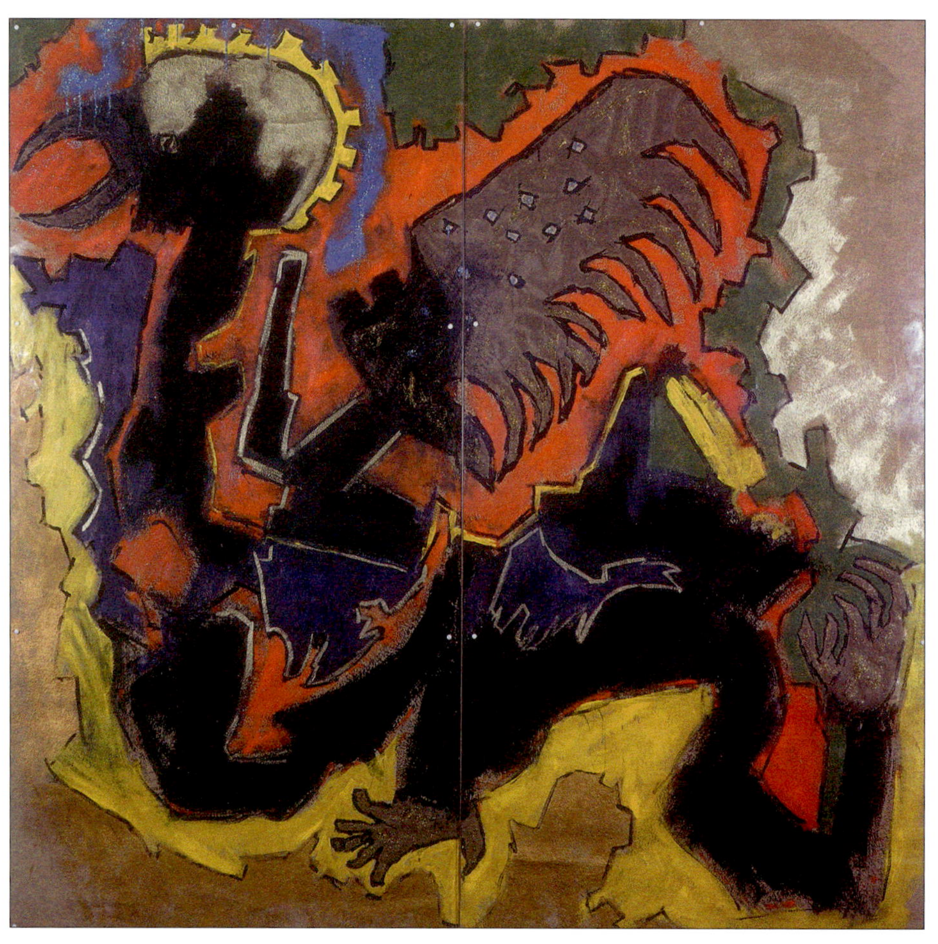

TRUTH OR CONSEQUENCES

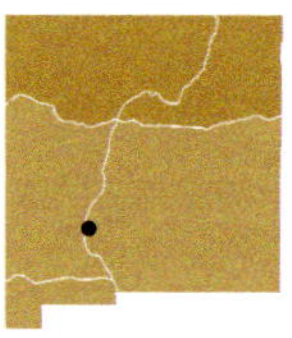

DANIELLE AUPRIX
Fiesta
2001
Acrylic on paper
72" x 72"
Lent by Rio Bravo Fine Art, Truth or Consequences, NM

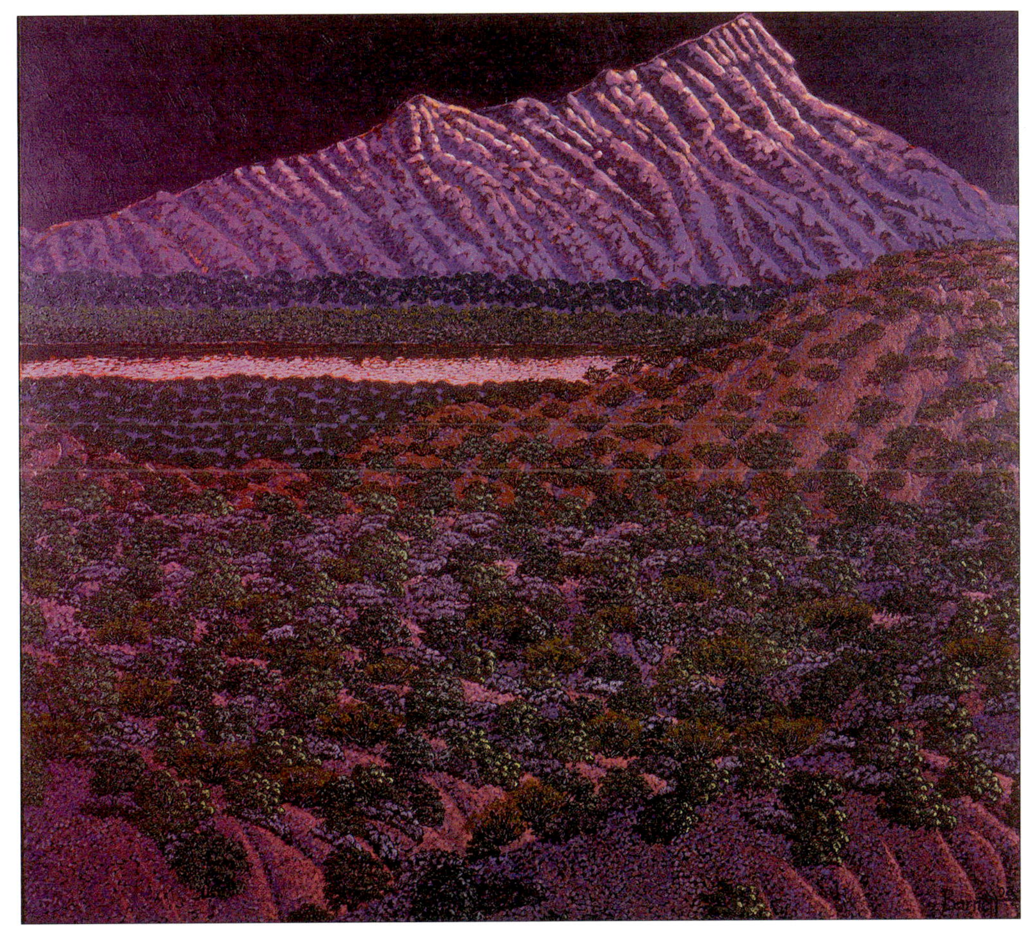

ELEPHANT BUTTE

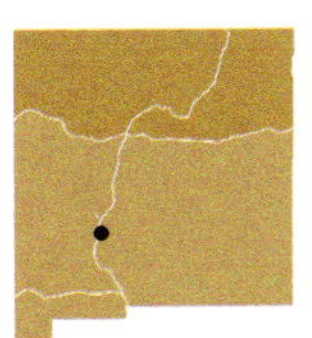

DAVE BARNETT
Turtleback Mountain
2002
Acrylic on canvas
44" x 48"
Lent by David G. Bullard, San Francisco, CA

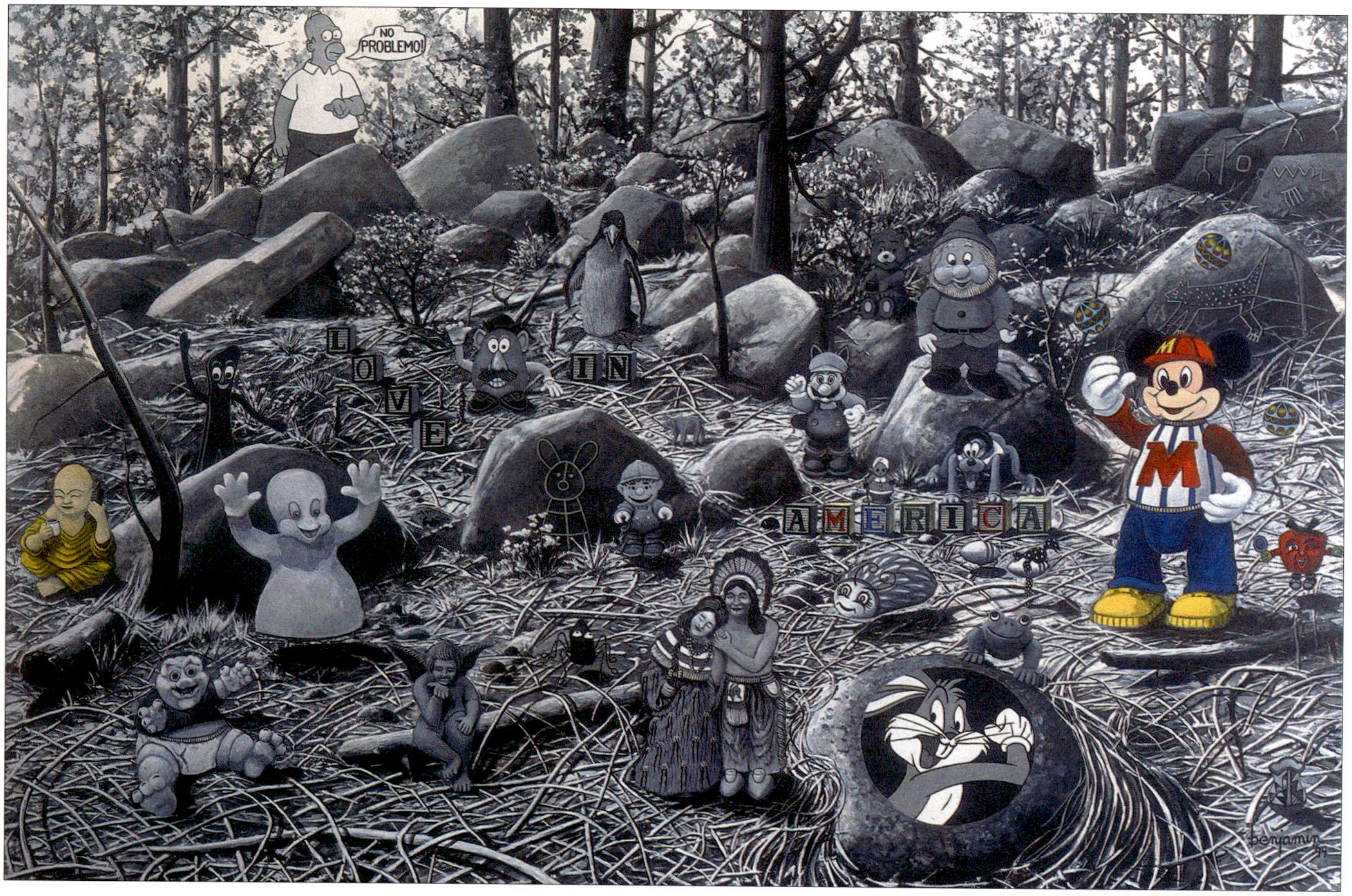

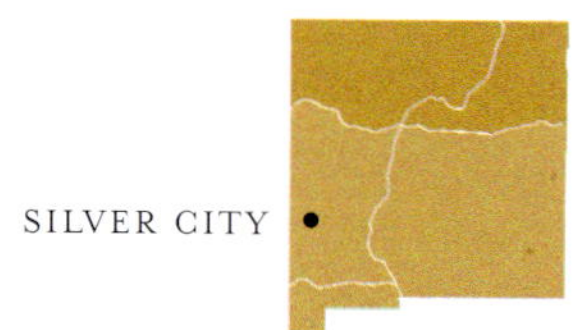

HARRY BENJAMIN
Love in America
2001
Acrylic on canvas
48" x 72"
Lent by Scott Nichols, Silver City, NM

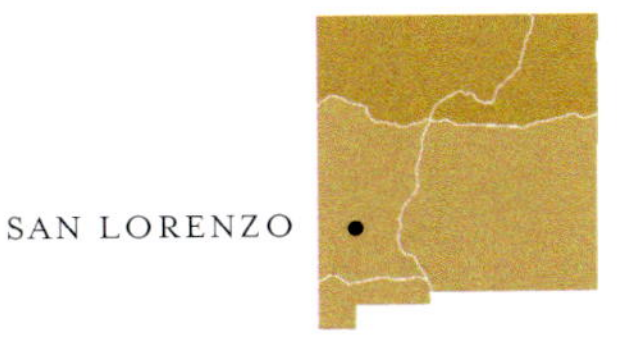

MICHAEL P. BERMAN
Dune, San Rosario
2001
Gelatin silver print
19" x 19"
Lent by Galleri Urbane, Silver City, NM, and Scheinbaum & Russek, Santa Fe, NM

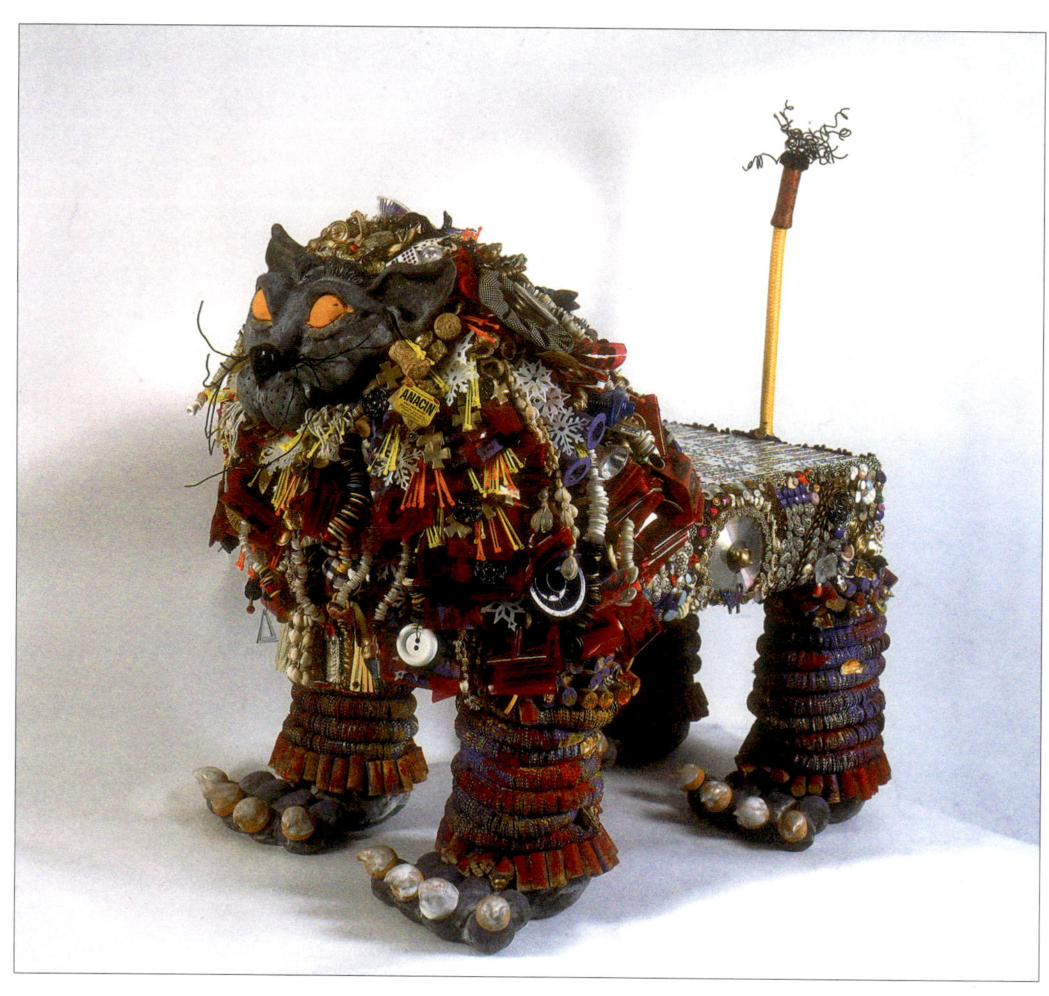

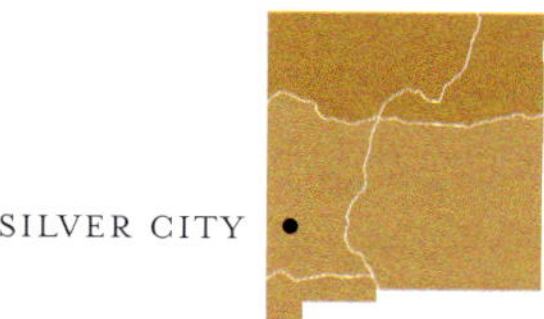

LINDA BREWER
The Lion Knew It Was the Tequila That Made Him Disappear
2001
Clay, bottle caps, tape, beads
33.5" x 33.5" x 18"
Lent by Blue Dome Gallery, Silver City, NM

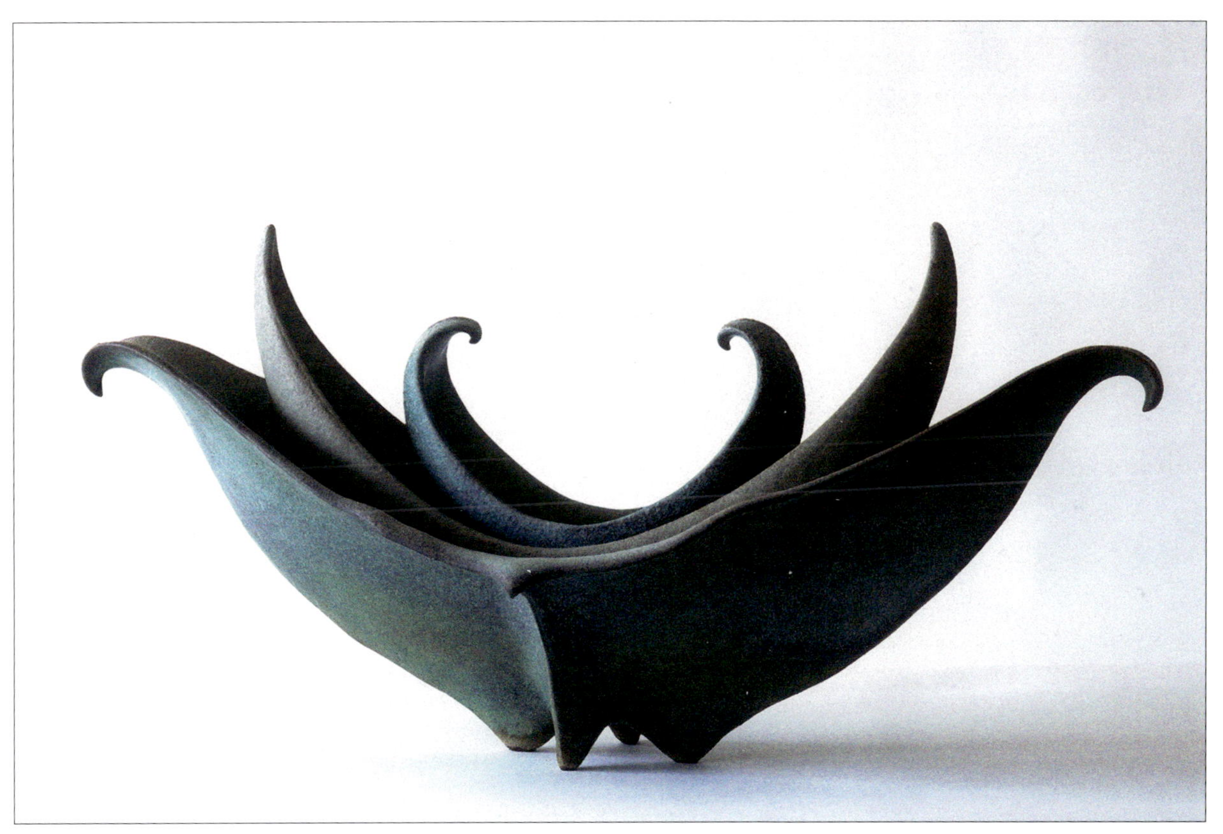

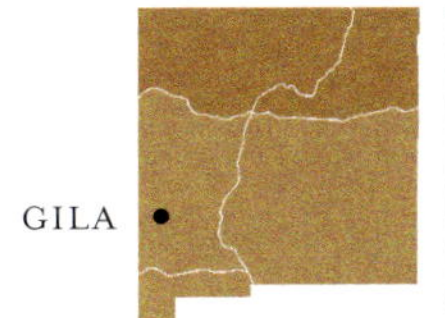

SHARON BRUSH
Leaf Spring
2001
Clay
13" x 23" x 10"

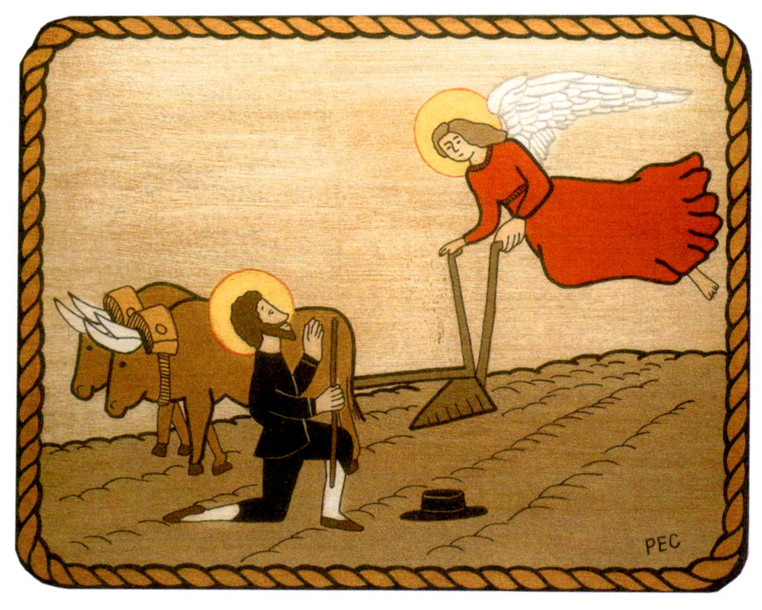

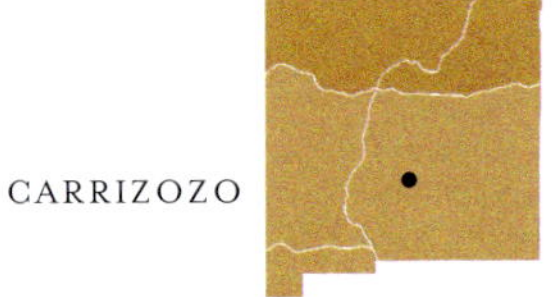

CARRIZOZO

POLLY E. CHAVEZ
San Ysidro, Patron Saint of Farmers
2002
Acrylic on wood
11" x 14"
Lent by Joseph and Doris Rini, Copley, OH

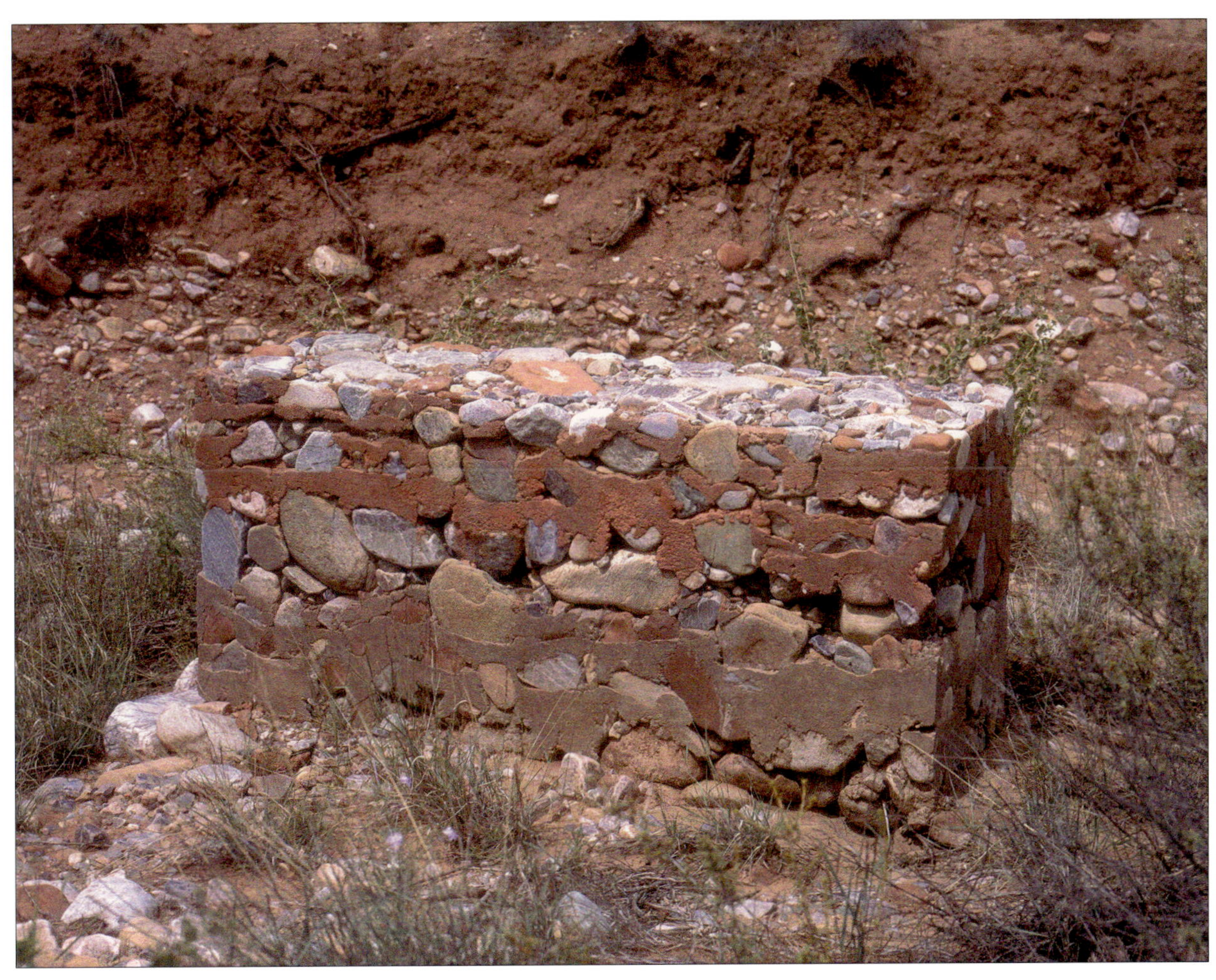

MOUNTAINAIR

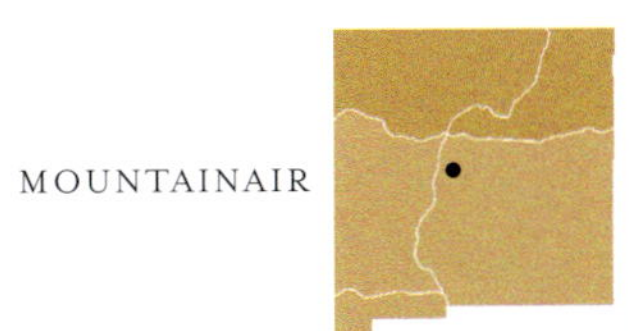

DANA CHODZKO
Sacrifice
Earthwork located in Mountainair, NM
1999
Earth, stone
40" x 68" x 30"

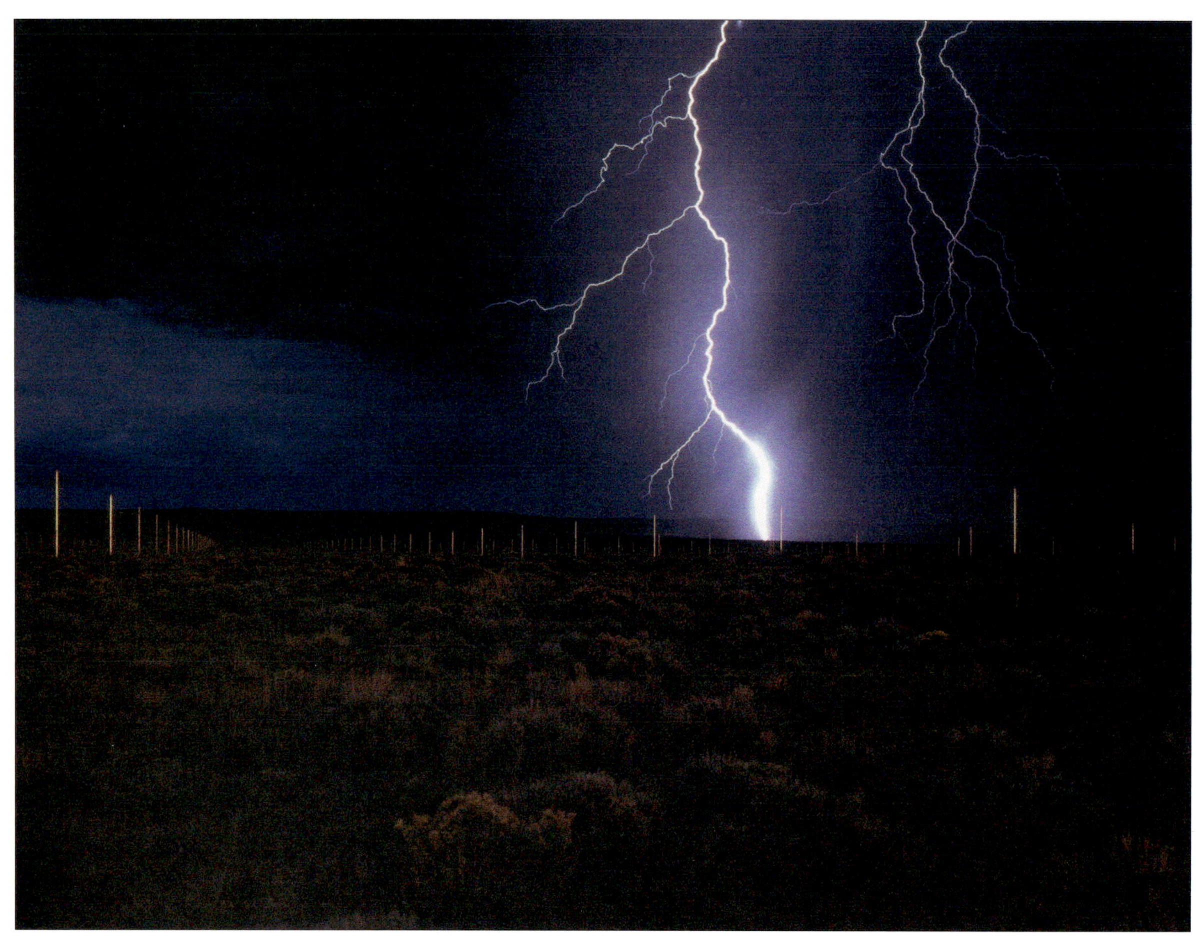

QUEMADO

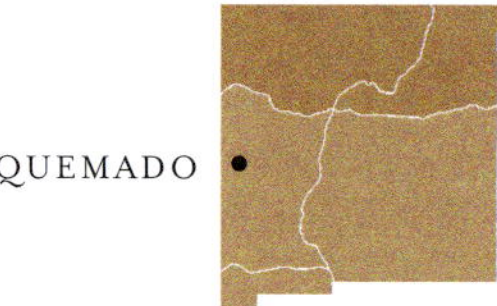

WALTER DE MARIA
The Lightning Field
Earthwork located in Quemado, NM
1977
1 mile x 1 kilometer
Photo by John Cliett © Dia Art Foundation

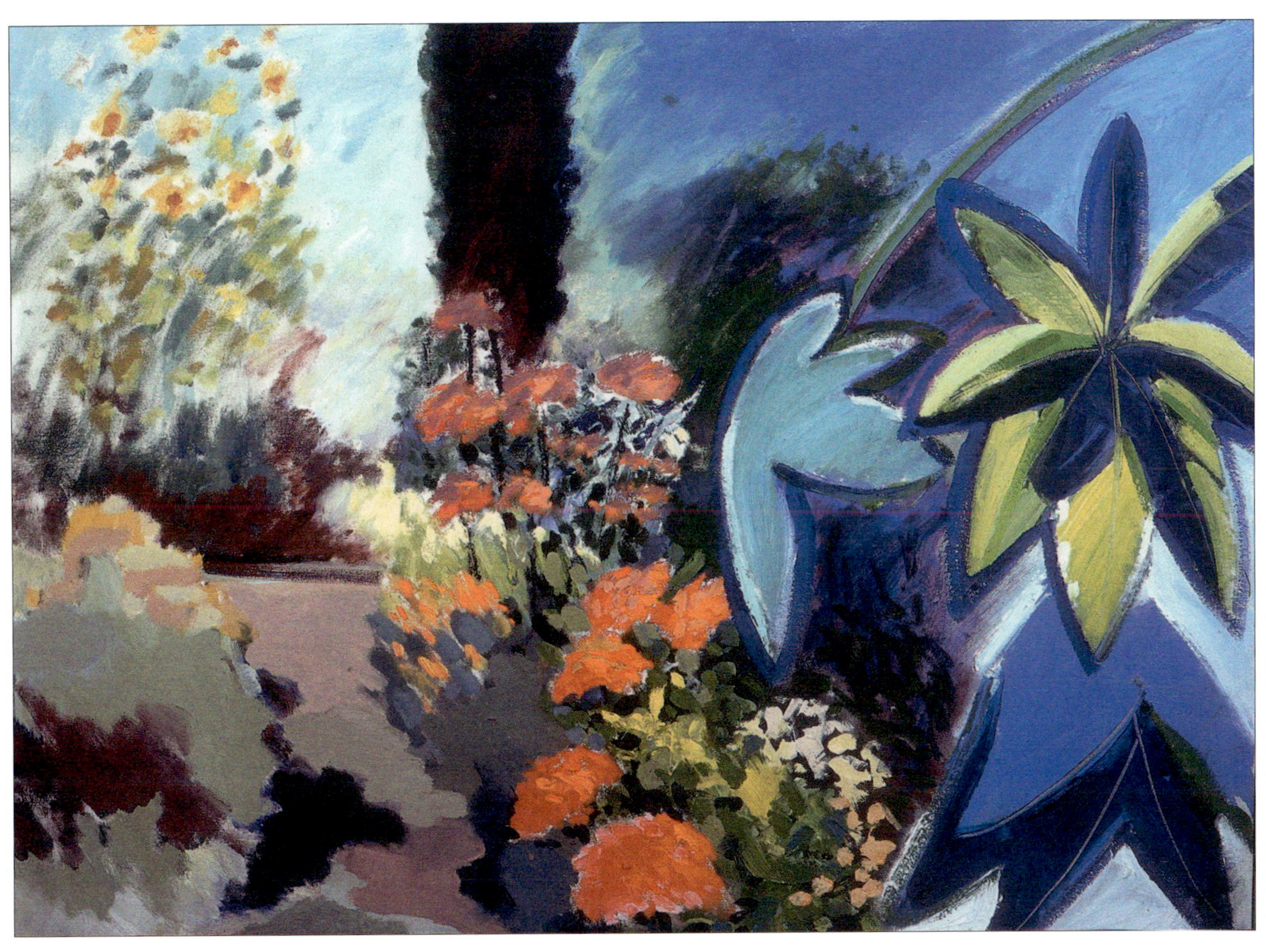

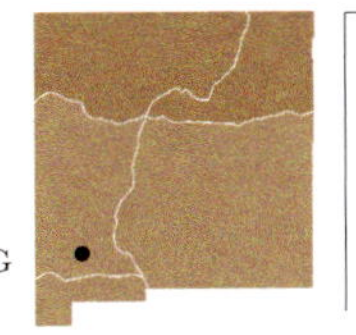

GORDON DIPPLE
Summer Garden
2001
Oil on canvas
36" x 48"

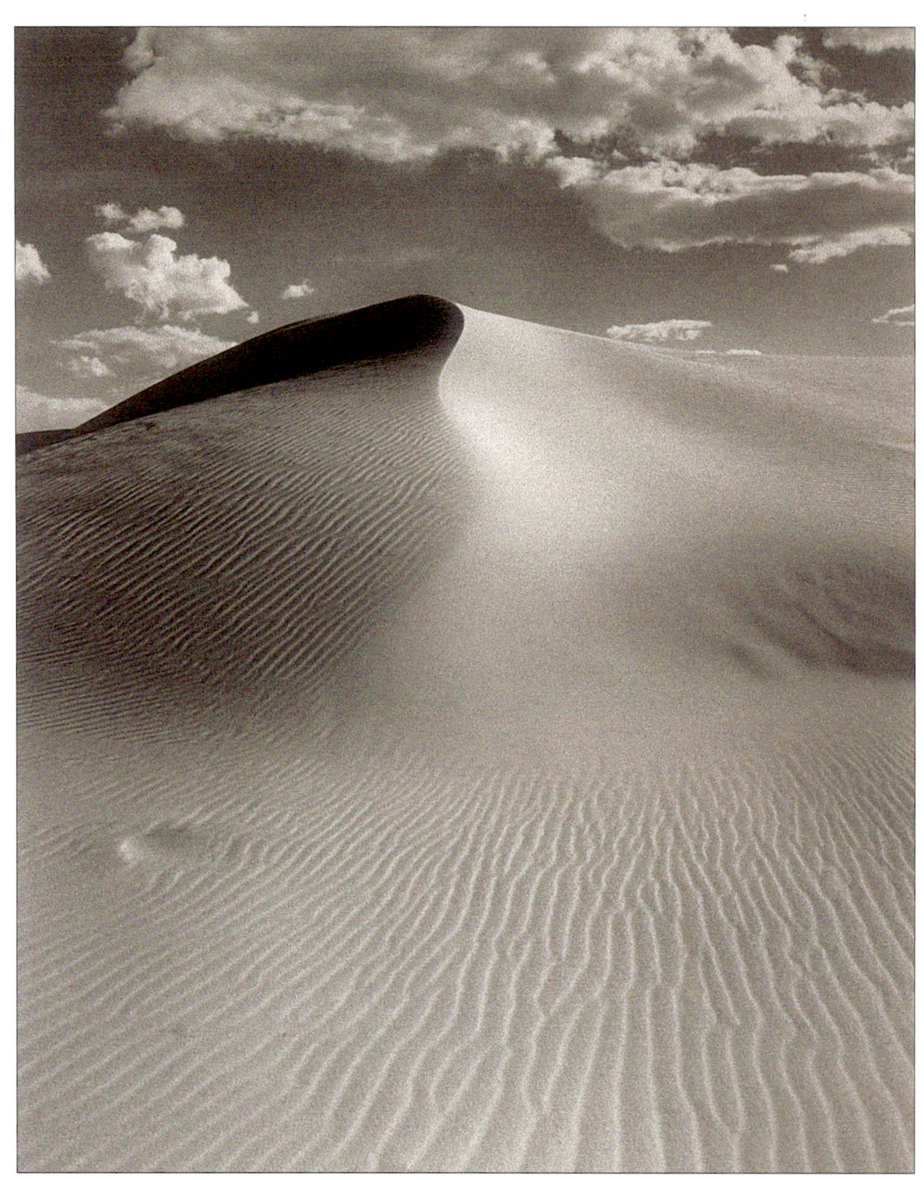

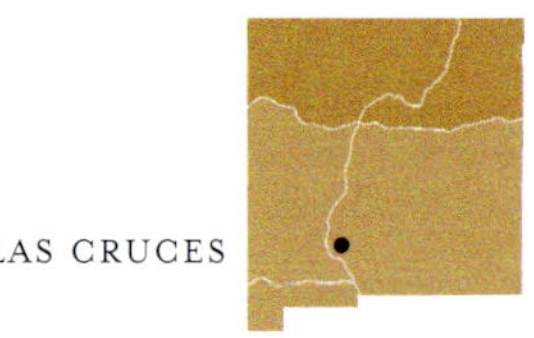

JOSEPH DOMINICK
Sand Dune, White Sands, NM
1995
Gelatin silver print
19" x 15"

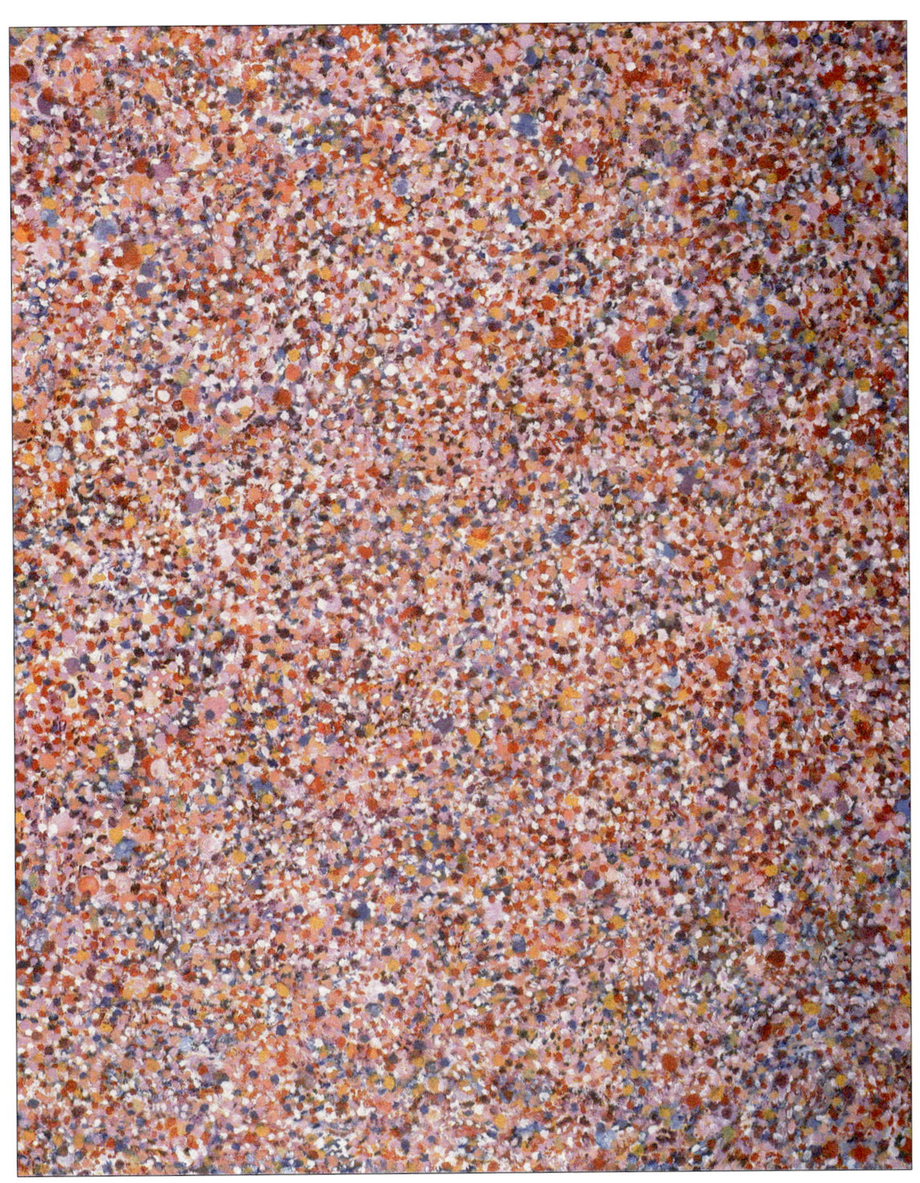

TULAROSA

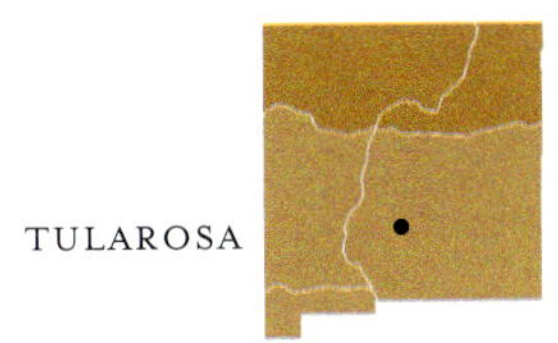

TAMIRIS DUKE
Dissolution or Approaching Dharma Kaya
2000
Acrylic on canvas
28" x 22"

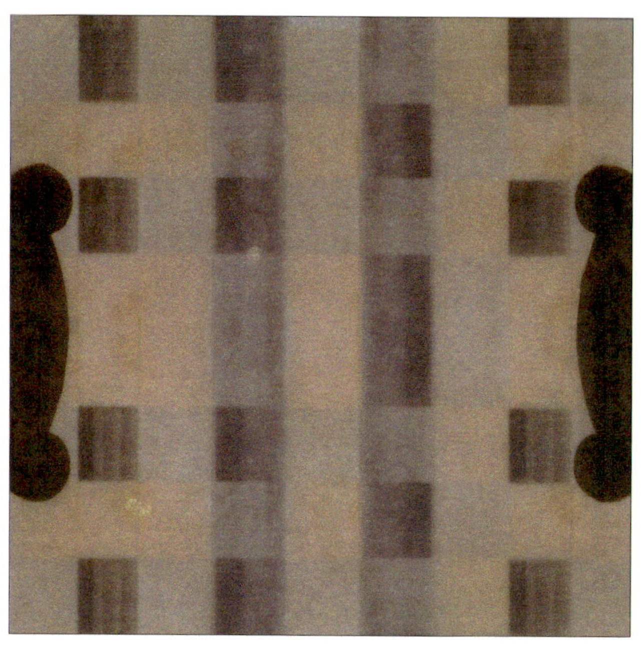

LAS CRUCES

JOHN DUNN
easure 3
2003
Paper, ink, encaustic on panel
8" x 8"

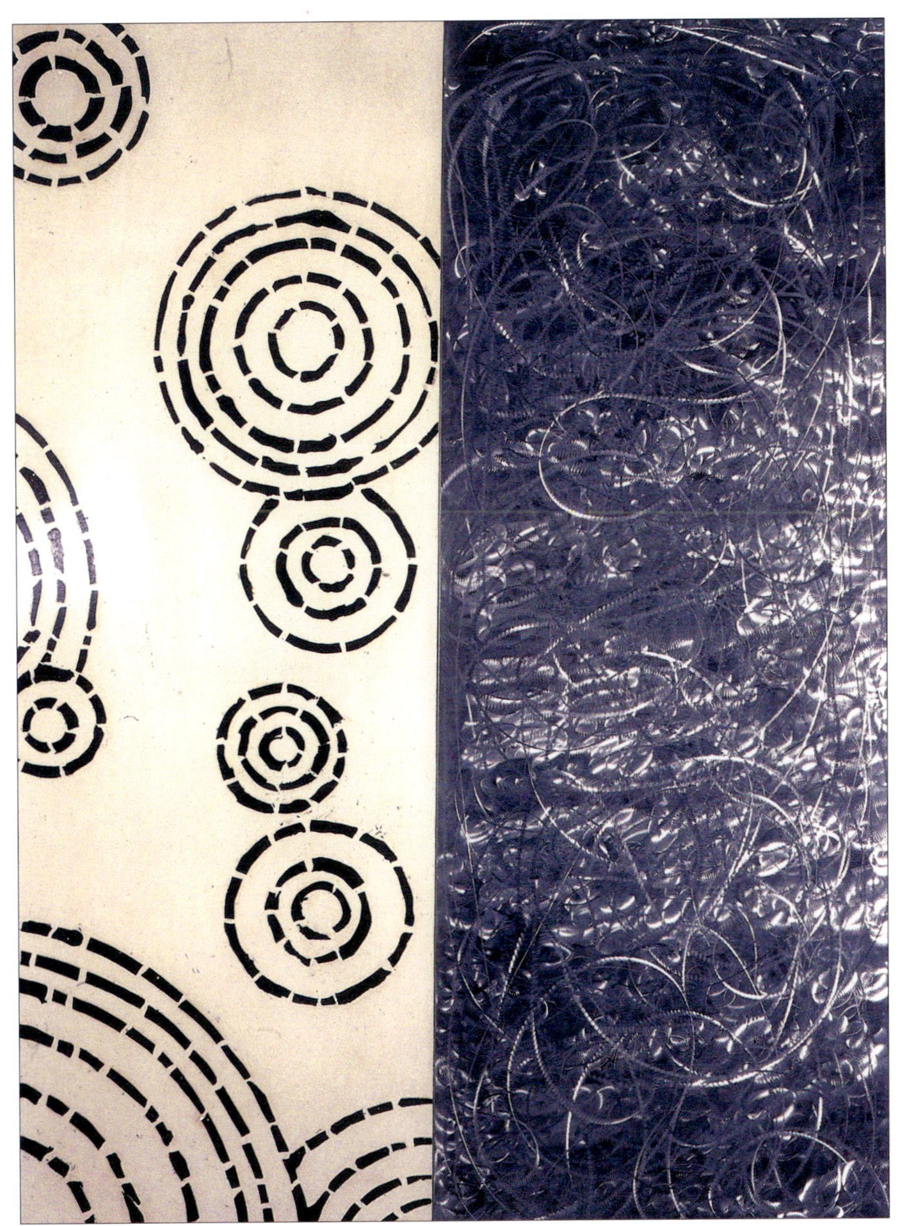

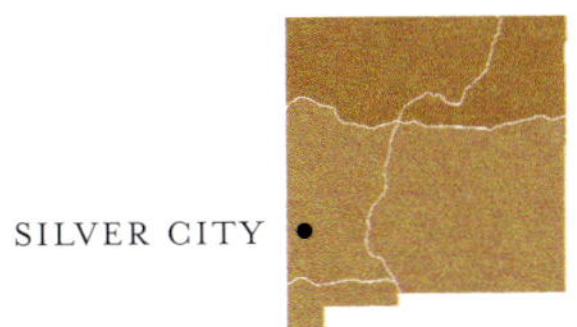

RICHARD EARNHEART
Tempux Rex
2003
Steel, plaster
66" x 48"

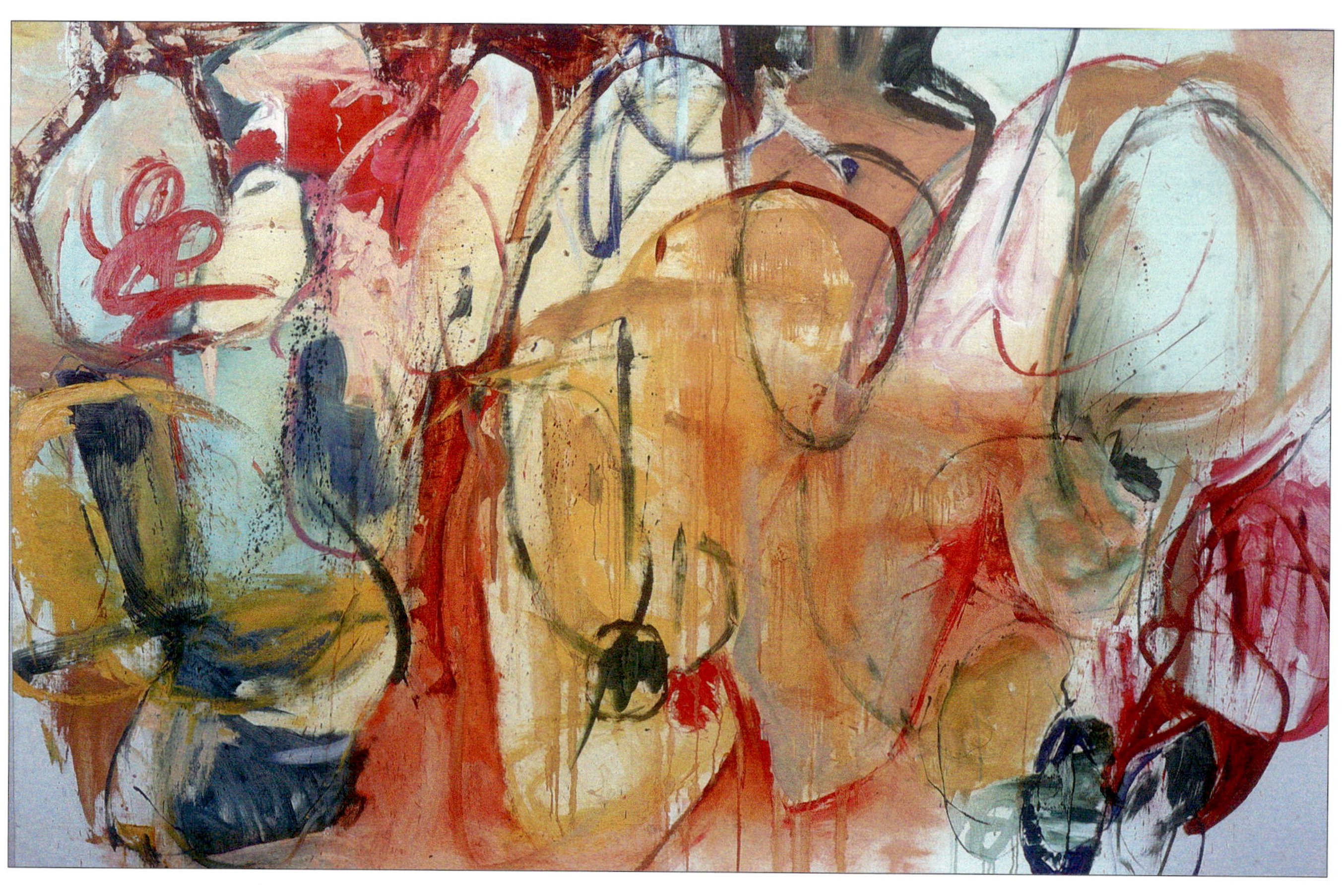

LAS CRUCES

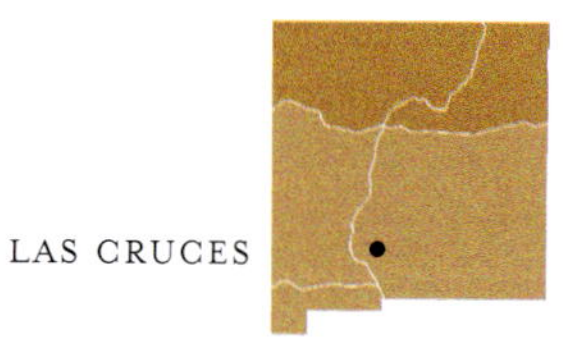

JACKIE MITCHELL EDWARDS
Prickly Pear #1
2000–2001
Oil on linen
49" x 75"

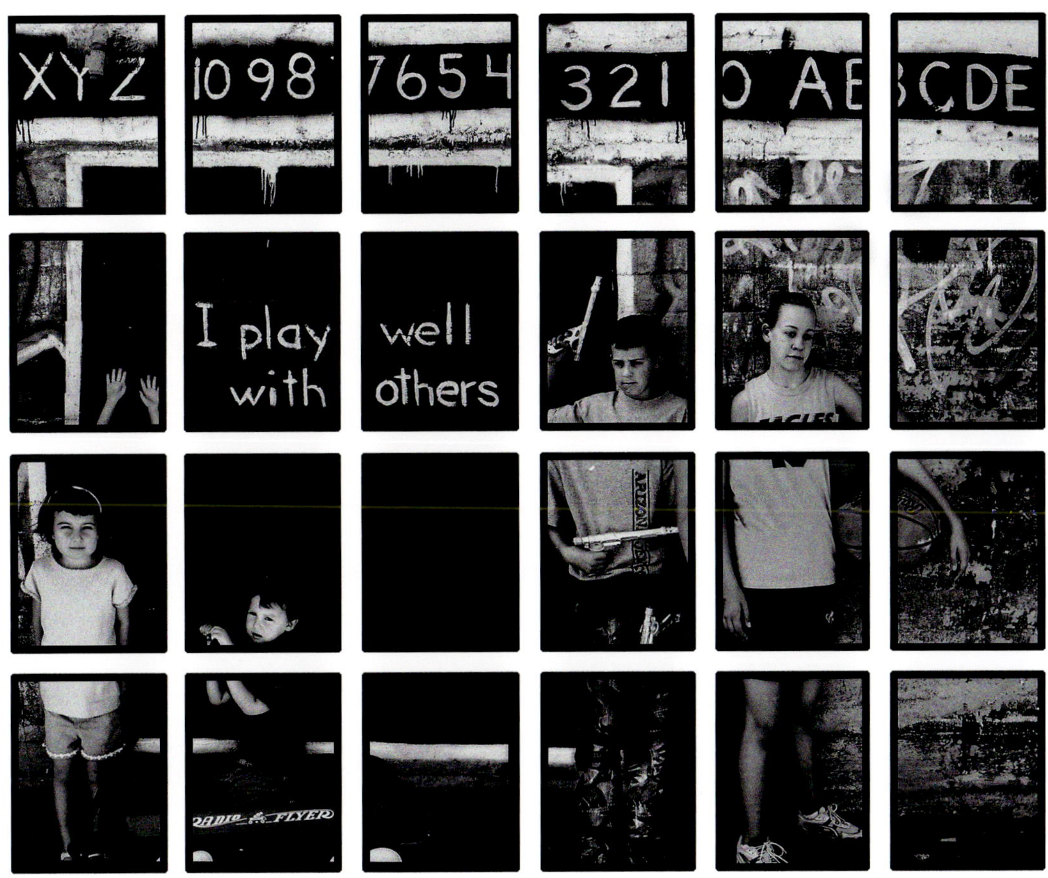

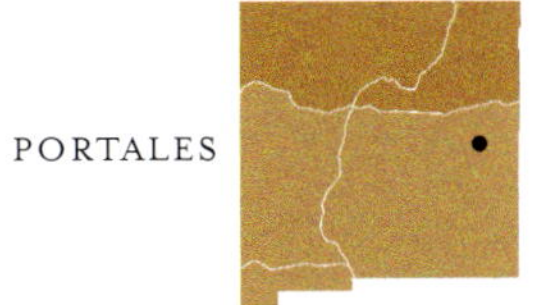

GREG ERF
I Play Well with Others
2002
Resin coated silver print
72" x 96"

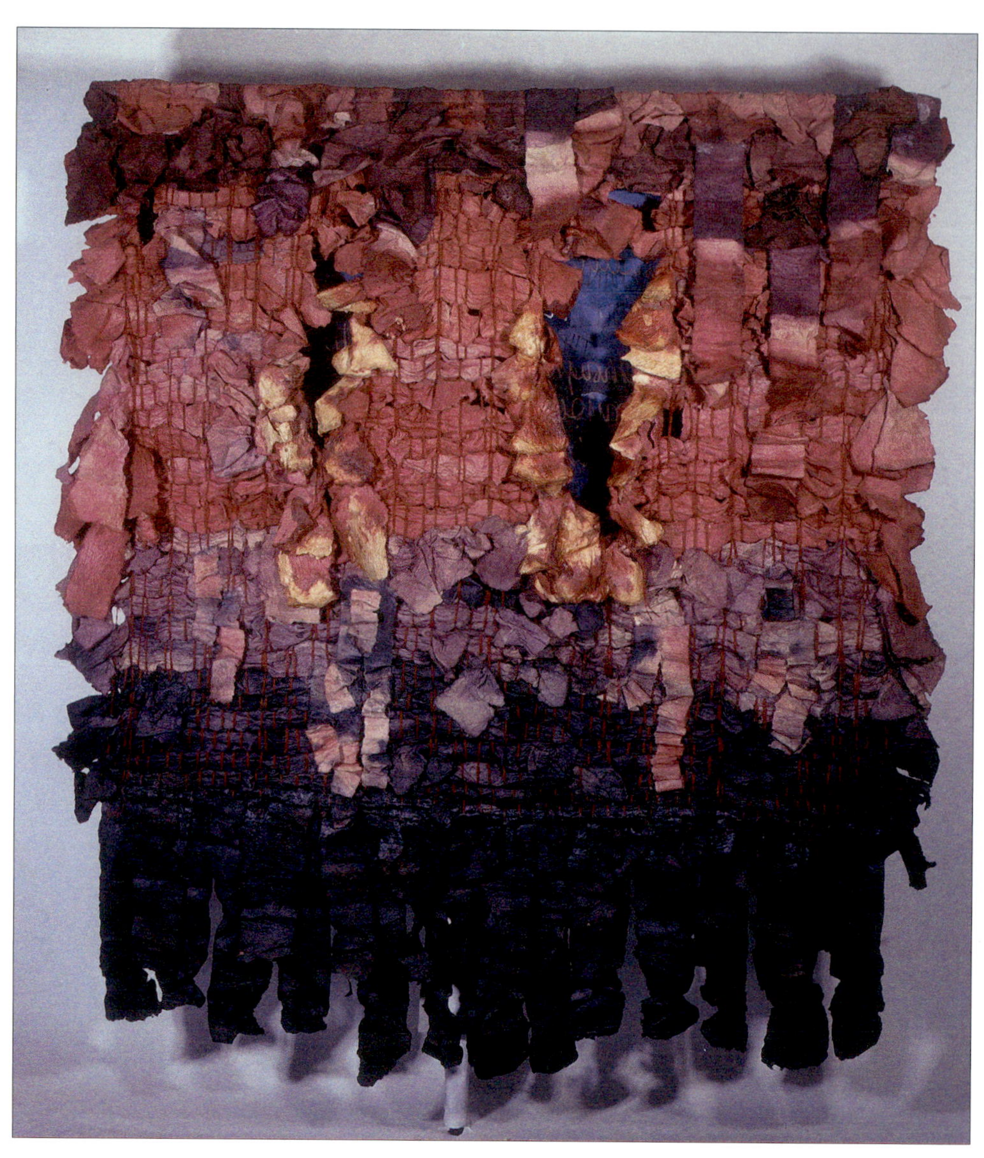

LAS CRUCES

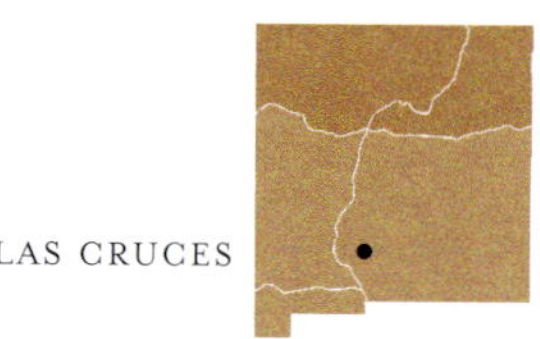

GEORJEANNA FELTHA

Passages

1999–2003

Woven dyed paper

54" x 60" x 12"

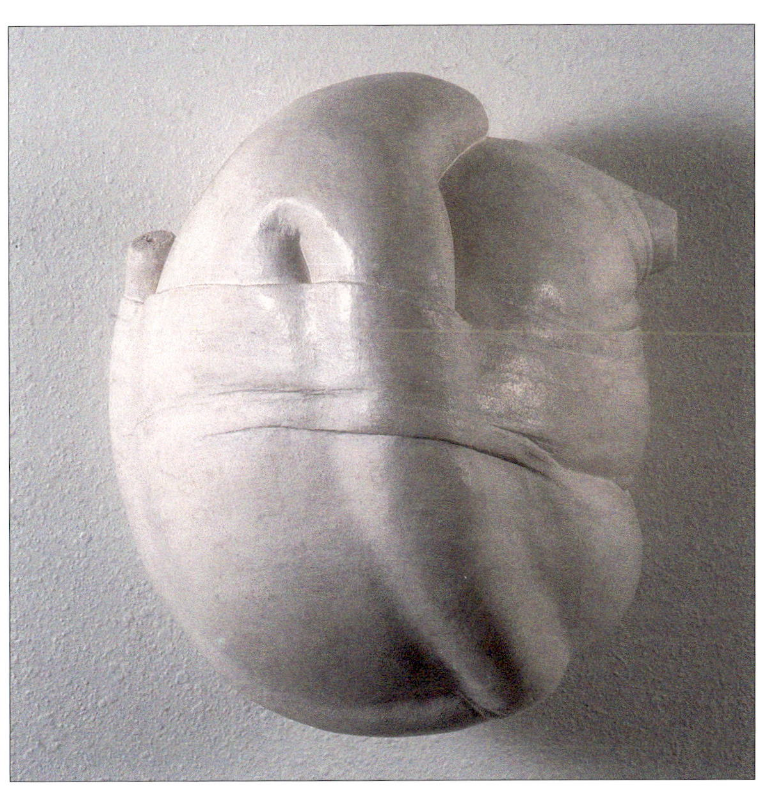

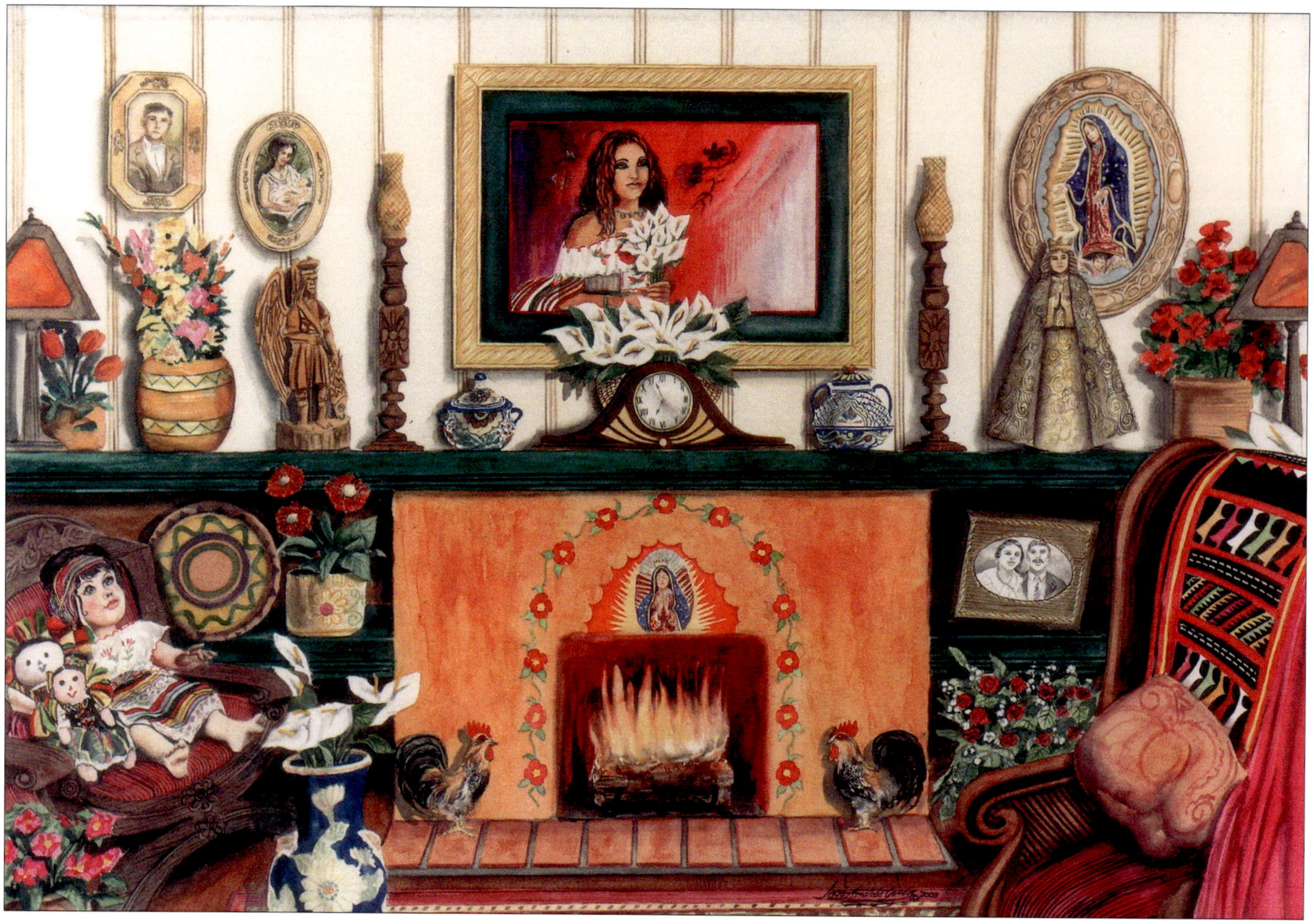

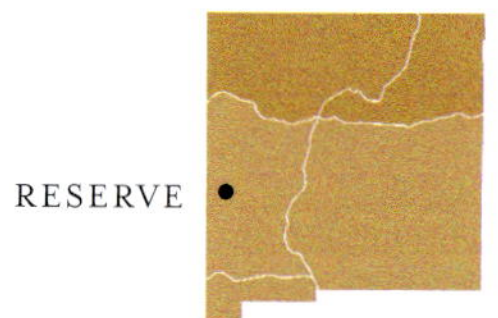

JOSÉ ANDRÉS GIRÓN
Mantel de Colores
2003
Watercolor
24" x 34"

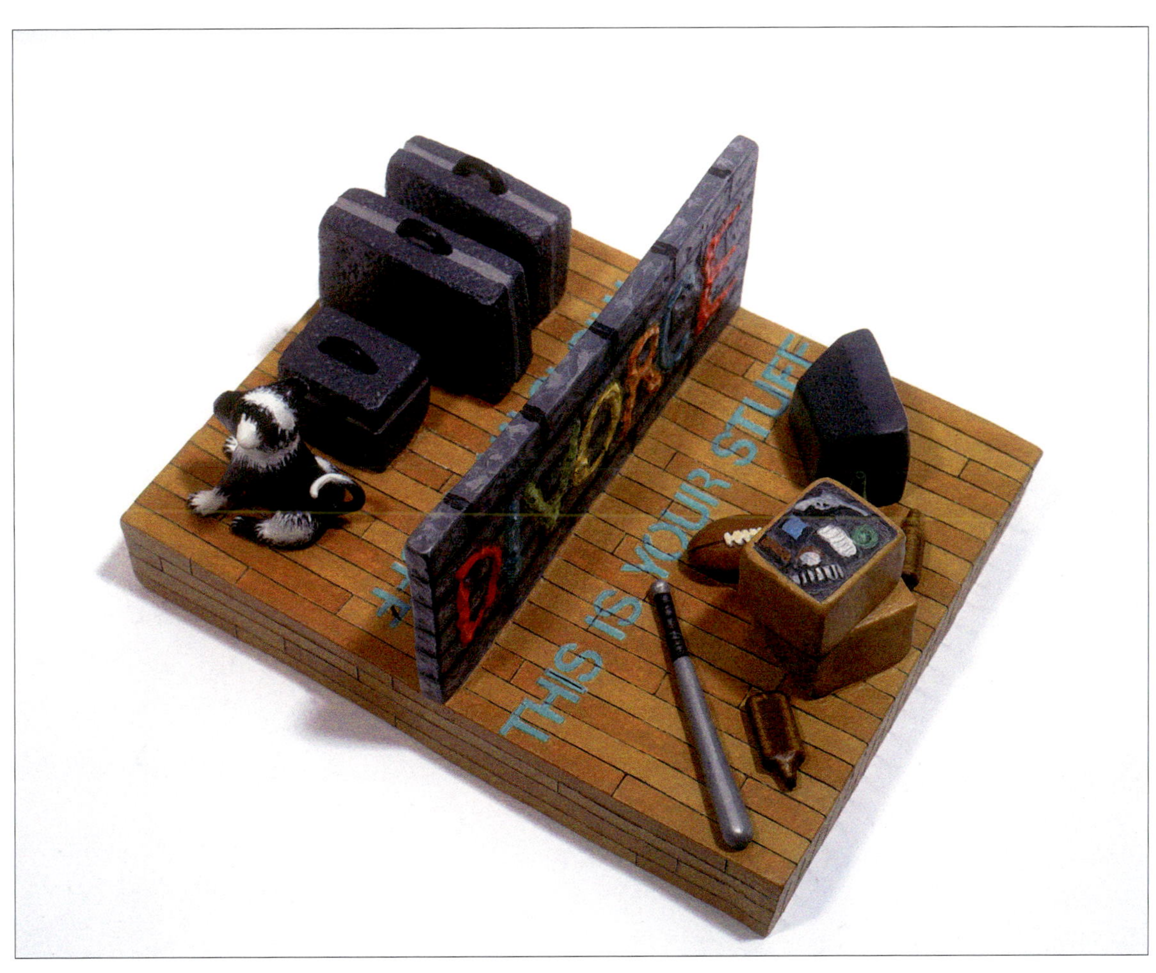

CLOUDCROFT

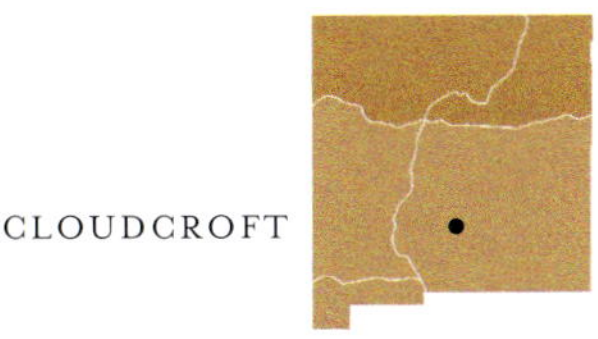

GEORGE GREEN
Divorce
2001
Ceramic, acrylic
6" x 9.5" x 12"

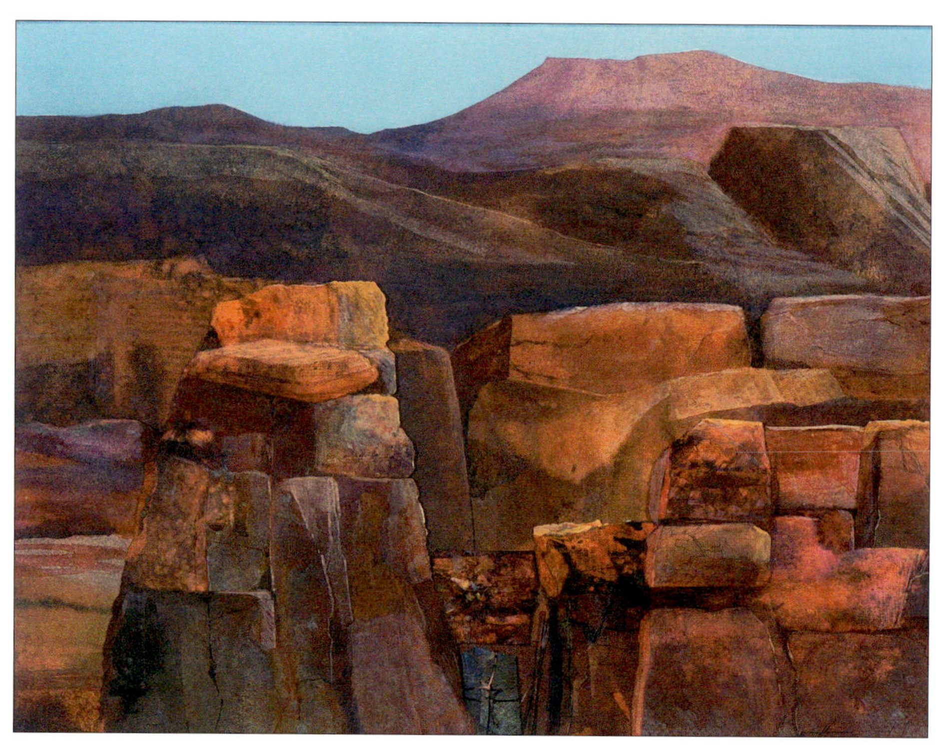

CARLSBAD

HELEN GWINN
Balanced Rock Canyon (Cliff Gifts Series)
2003
Watercolor, collage, assemblage
14" x 18"

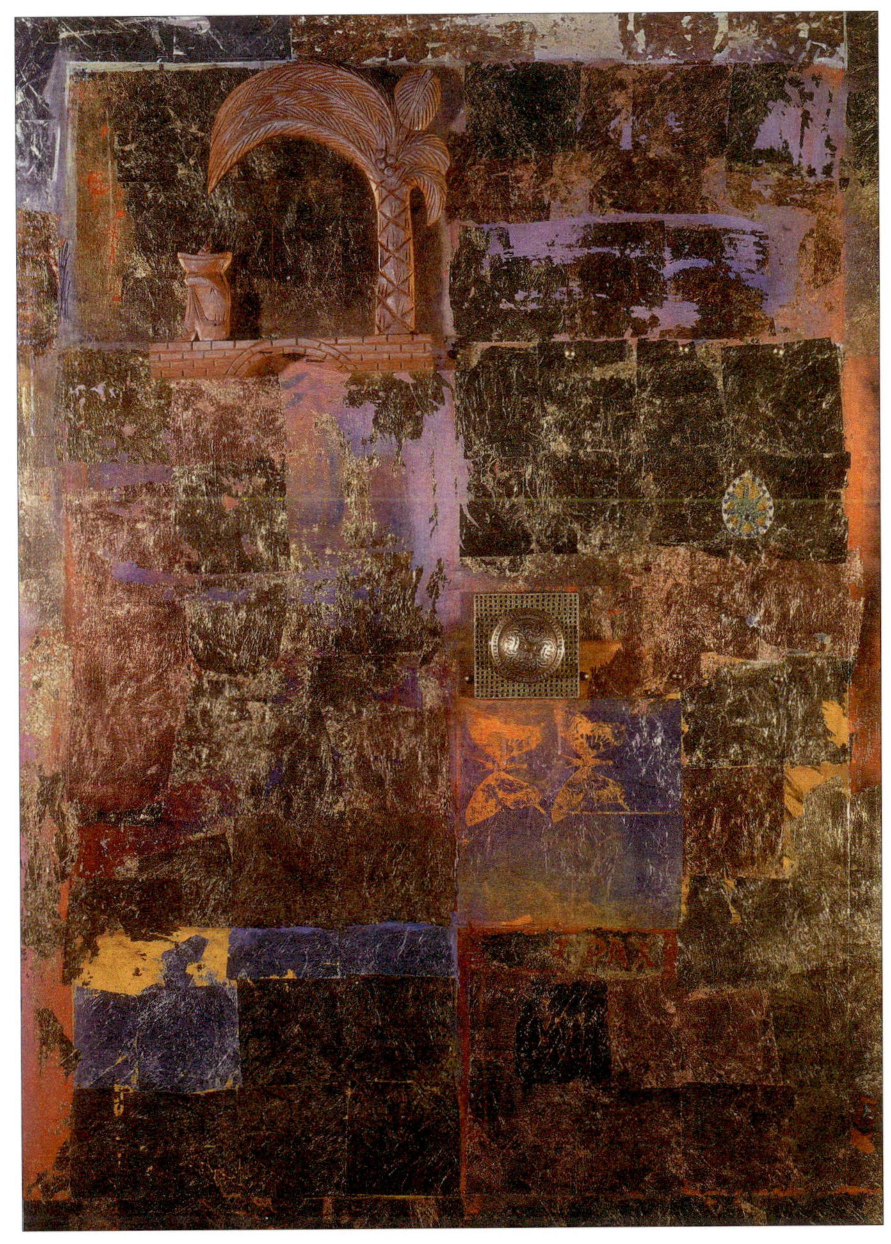

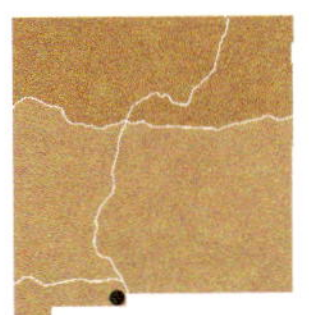

LA UNION

BECKY HENDRICK
Foment Peace
2003
Gold and metal leaf, enamel, beads, wood
60" x 42"

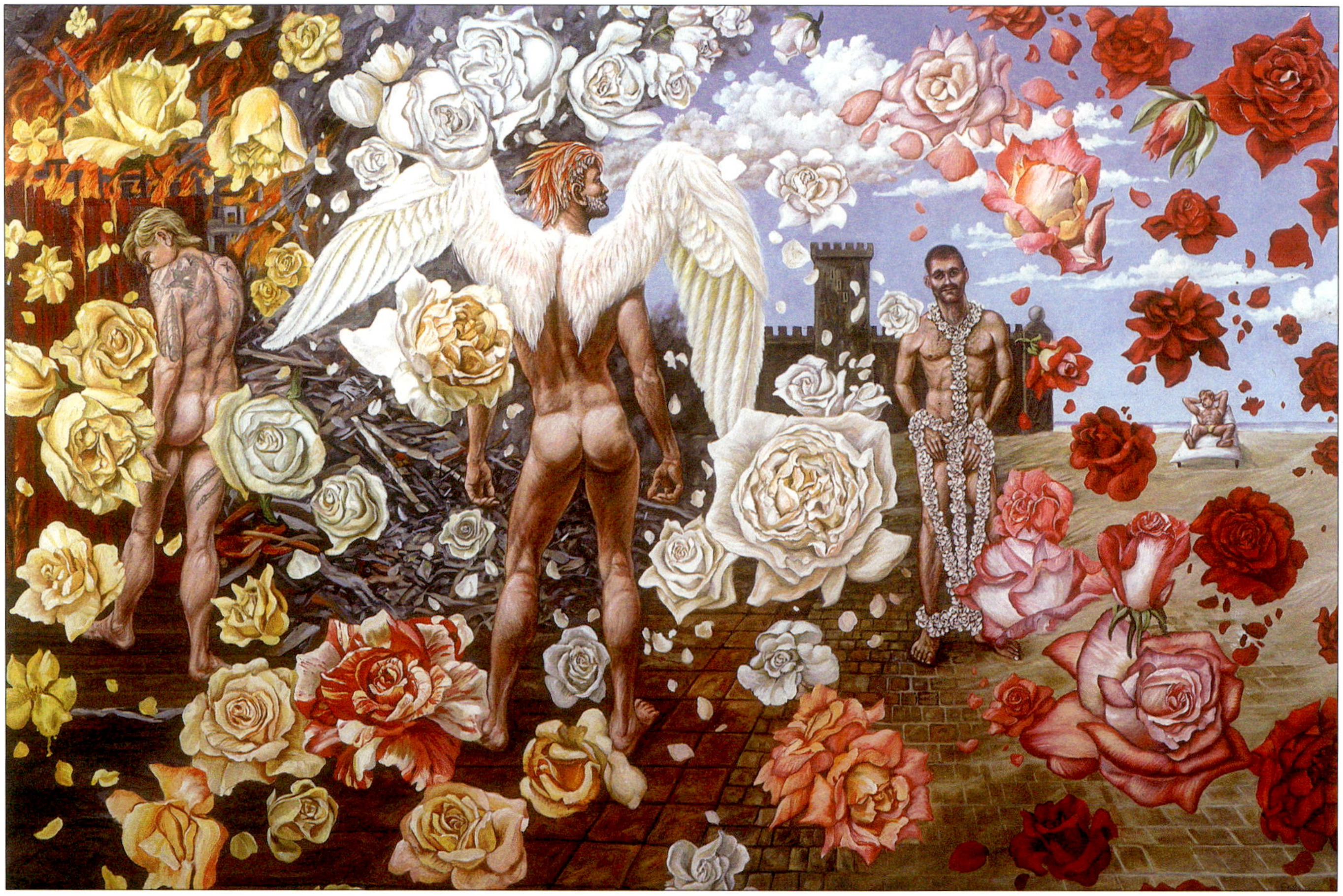

TRUTH OR CONSEQUENCES

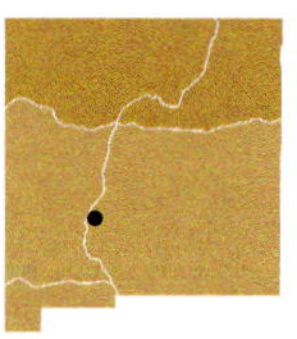

DELMAS HOWE
The Miracle (Genet's Dream)
2003
Oil on canvas
48" x 72"

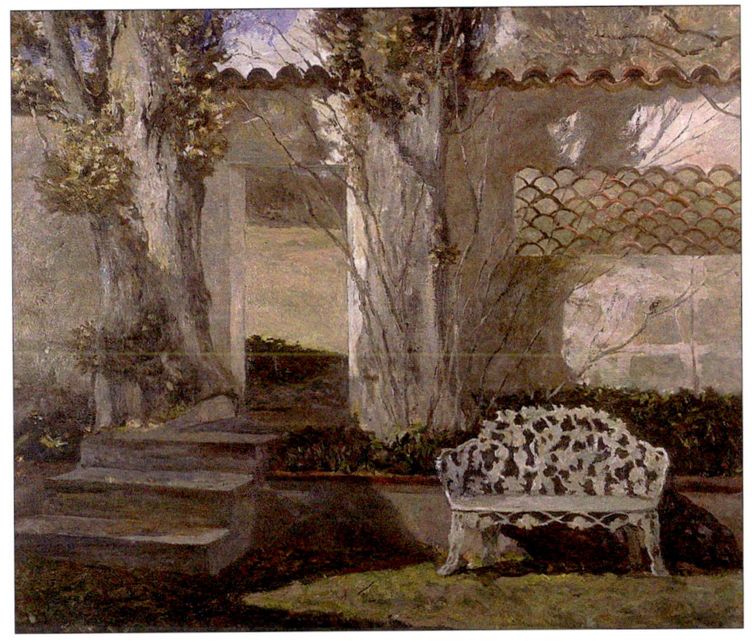

SAN PATRICIO

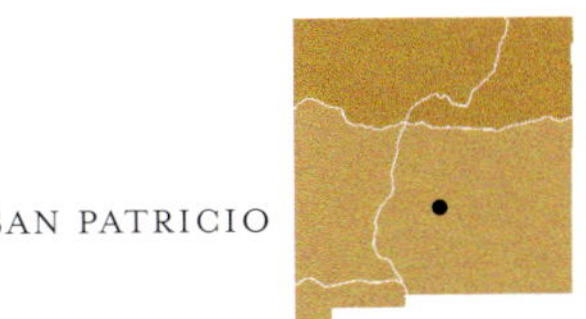

MICHAEL HURD

Loveseat

Oil on canvas

2002

24" x 28"

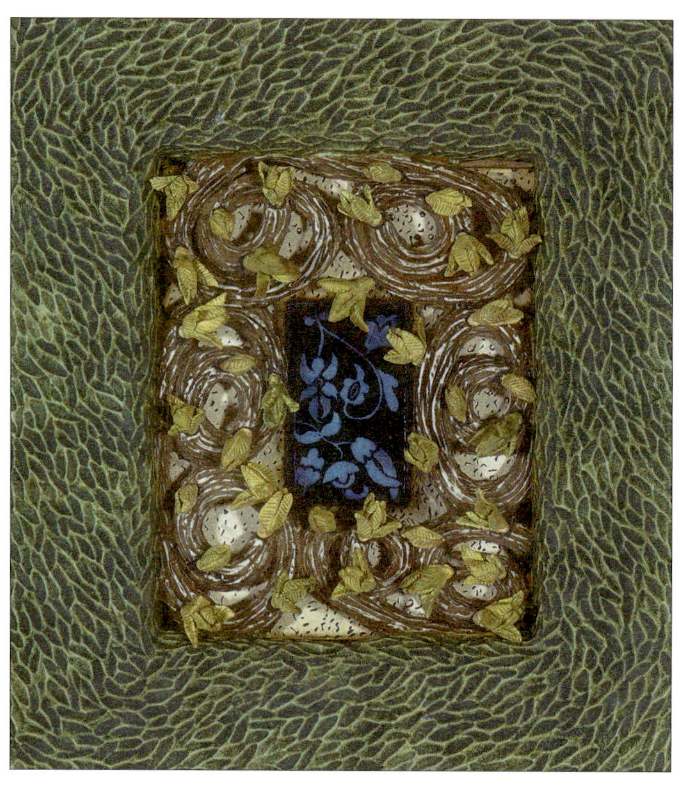

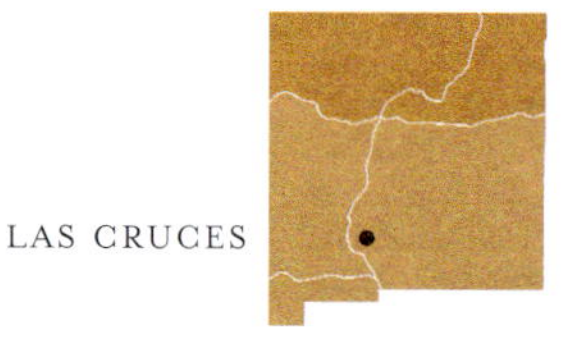

AMANDA JAFFE
Yellow Leaves III
2003
Clay
9" x 7.5" x 1.5"

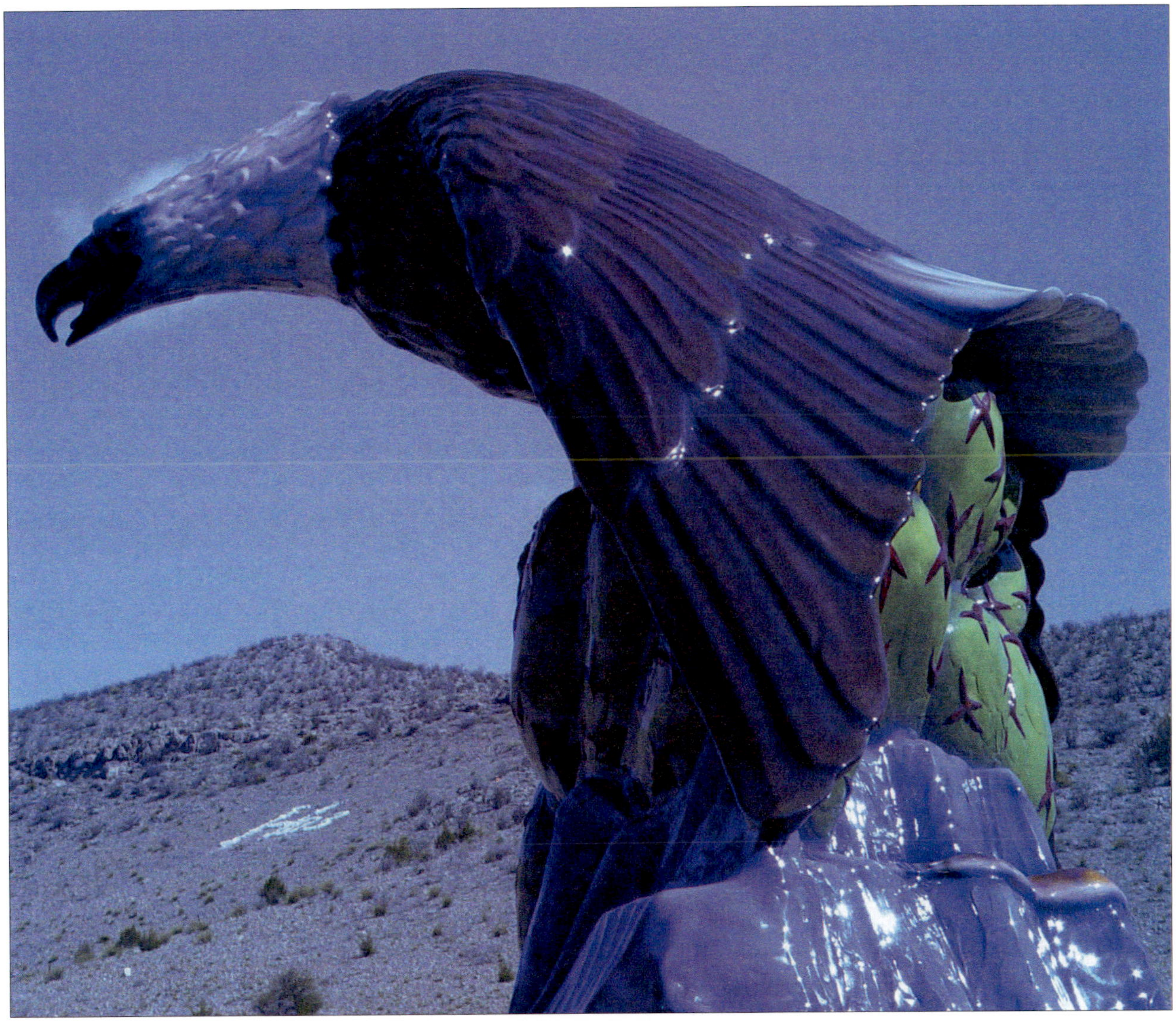

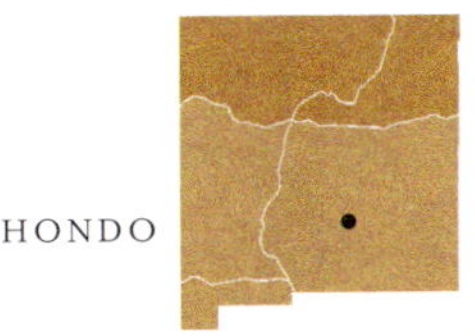

LUIS JIMENEZ

Eagle

2001–2002

Fiberglass

55" x 75" x 52.5"

Lent by Moody Gallery, Houston, TX

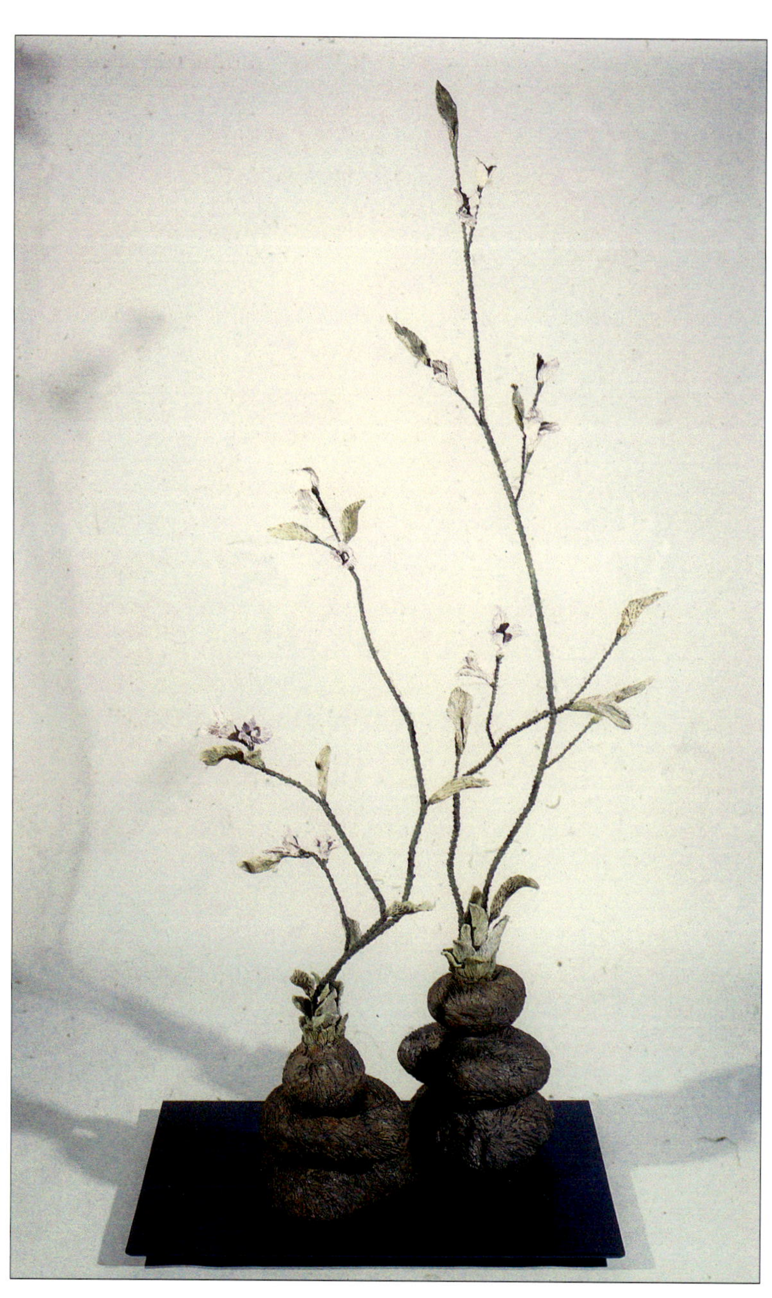

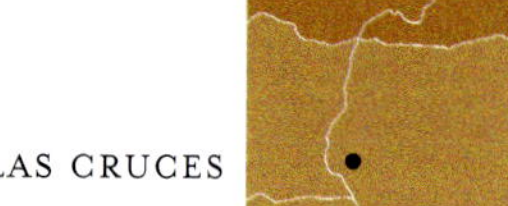

SUZANNE KANE
Two Lines in Space/Dona Ana
2003
Clay, steel
104" x 48" x 32"

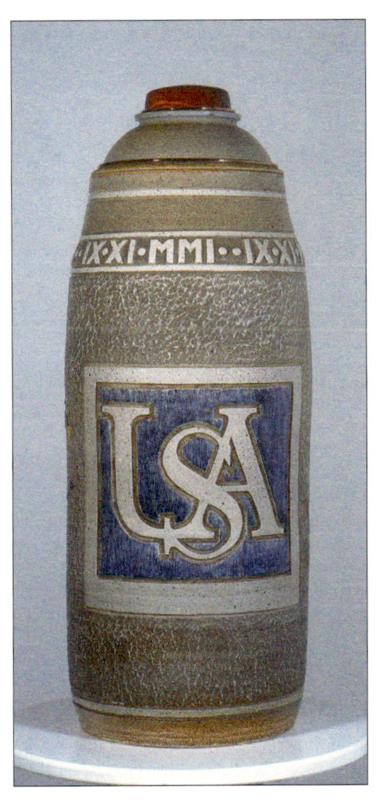

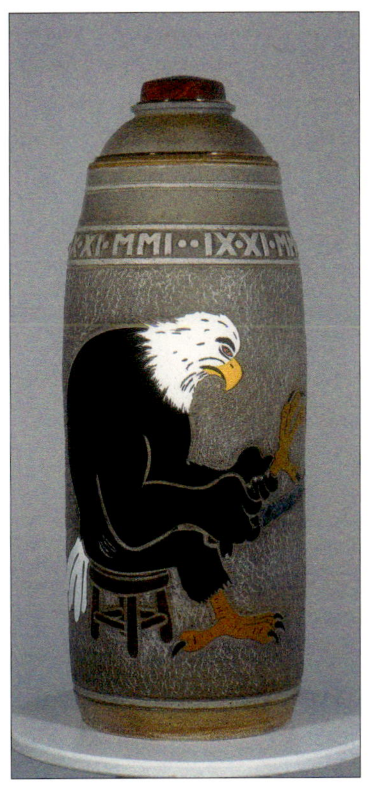

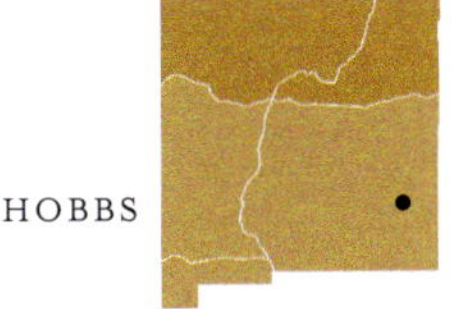

JOHN LATHROP
Getting Ready
2001
Clay, wood, copper, glaze, acrylic
32" x 13" diameter

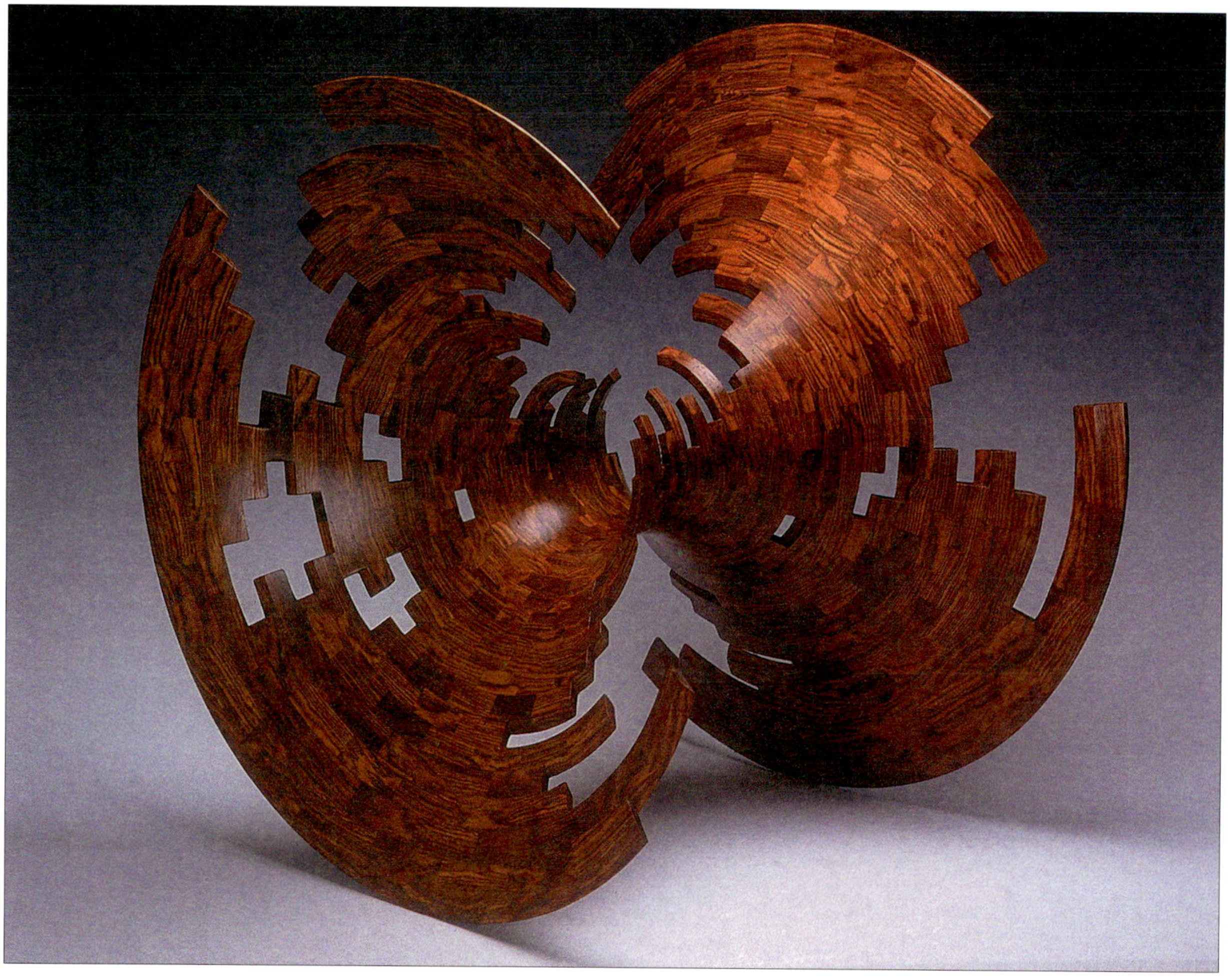

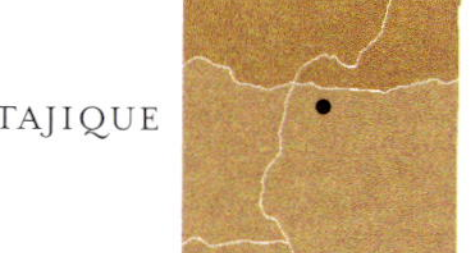

BUD LATVEN
Torsion (Torsion Series #8)
2002
Tulipwood
20" x 20" x 14"
Lent by Patina Gallery, Santa Fe, NM

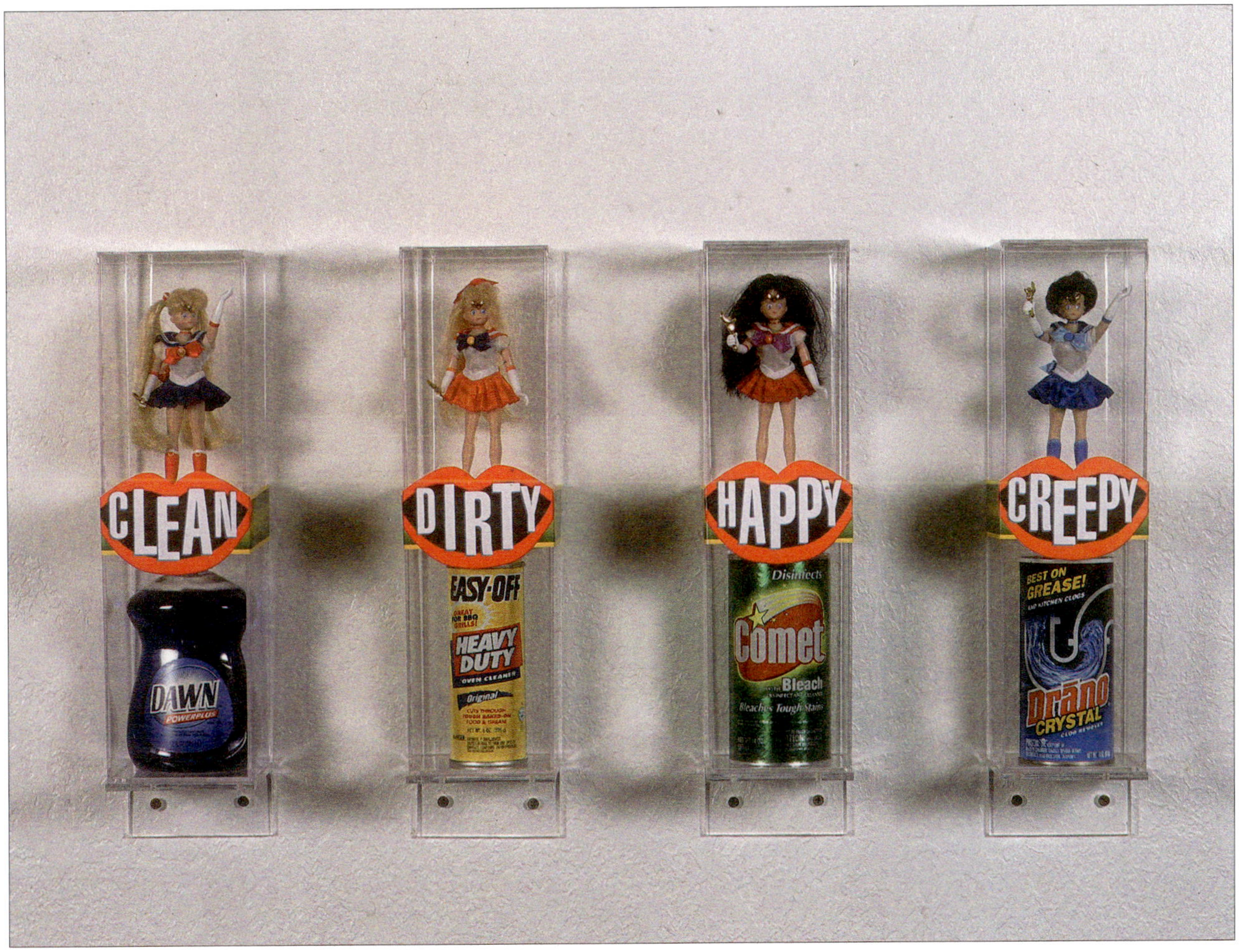

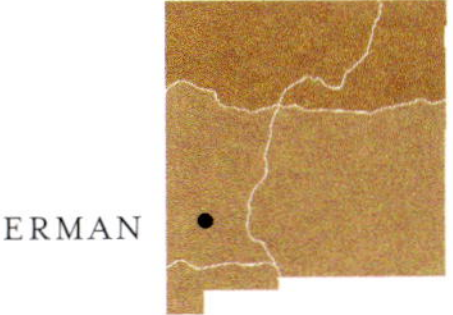

ANN LOWE

Clean, Dirty, Happy, Creepy

2001

Plexiglas, dolls, cleaning products, computer labels

16.5" x 28" x 4"

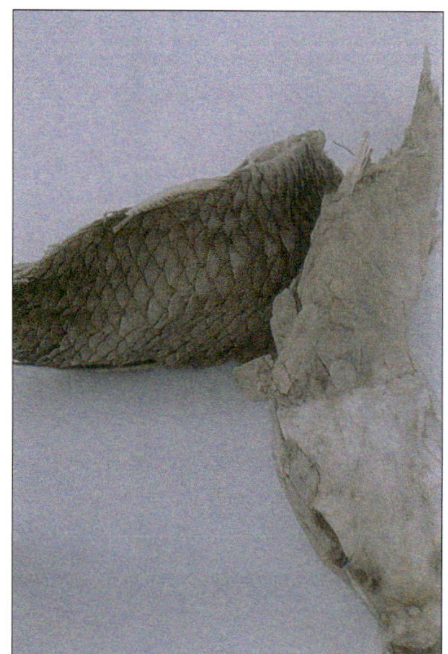
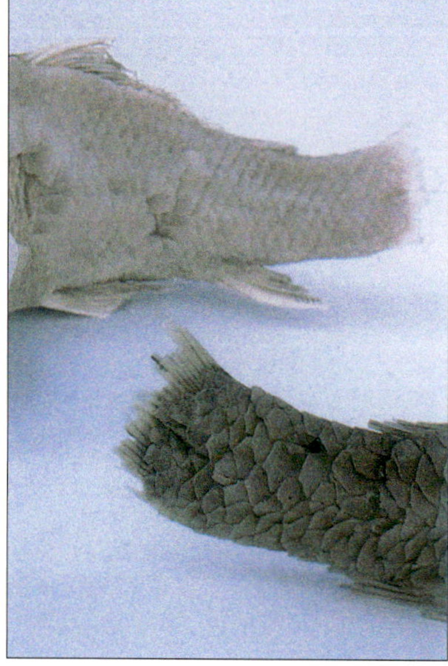
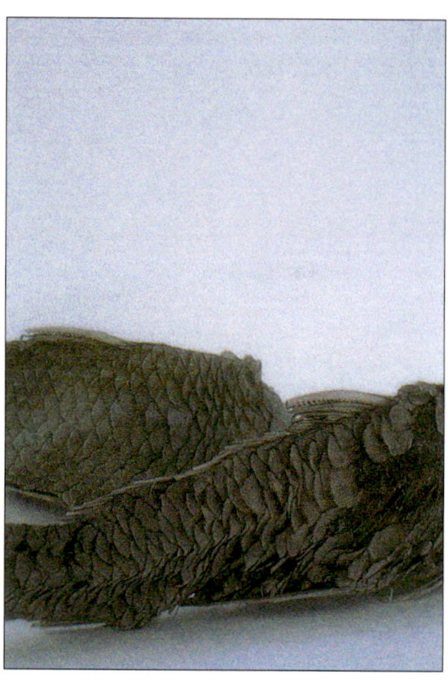

SOCORRO

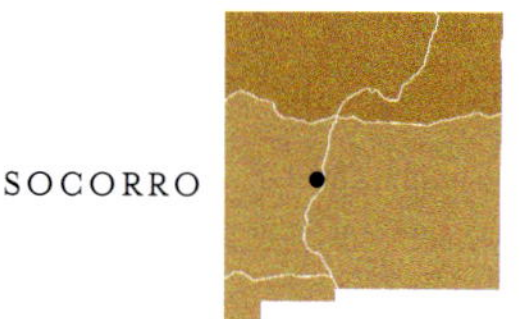

LORETTA LOWMAN

Fish Out of Water I, II, III

2001

Digital photographs

22.5" X 15"; 21" X 14"; 22.5" X 15"

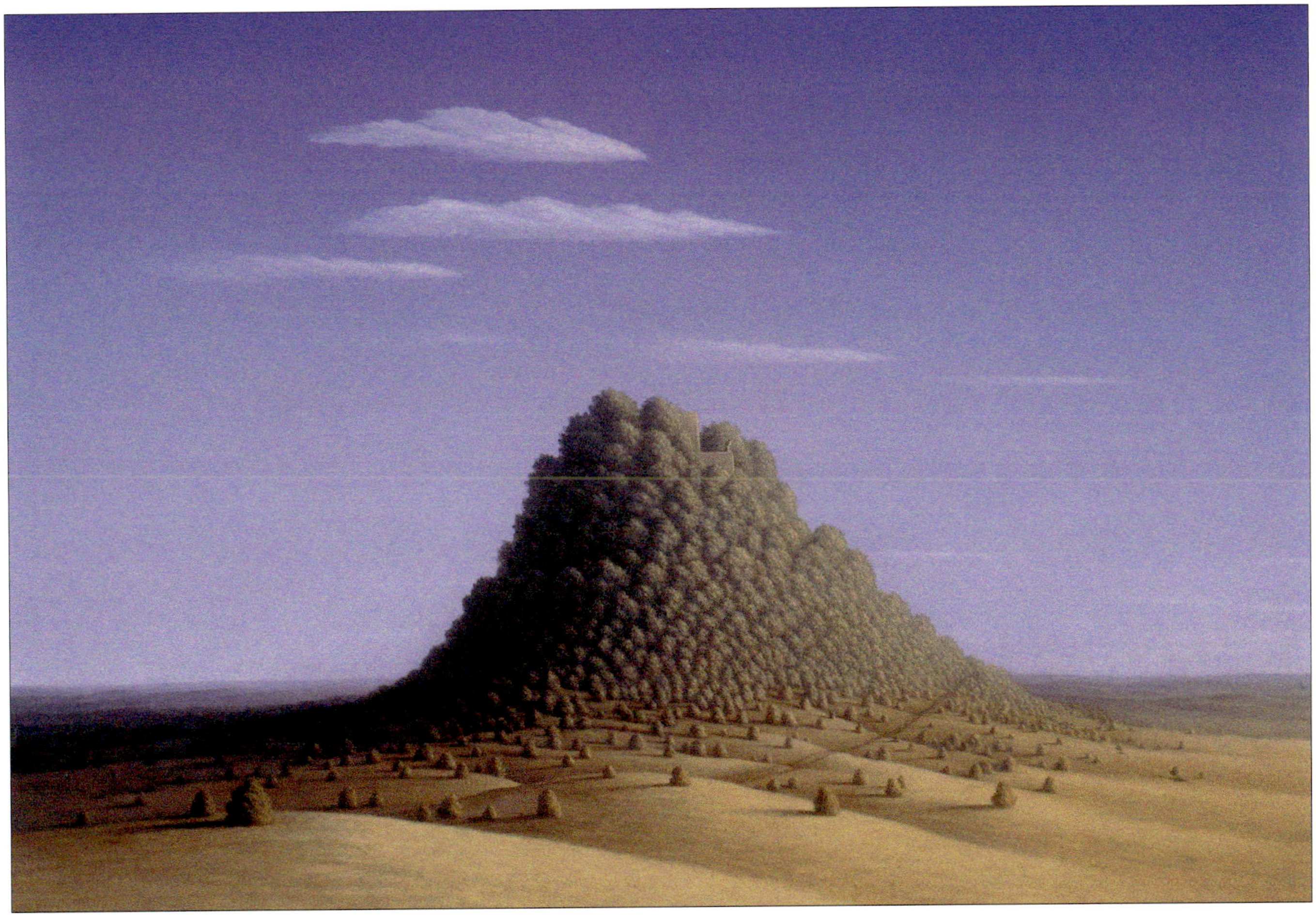

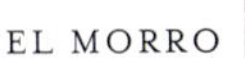

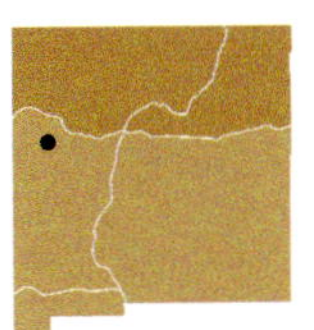

BRUCE LOWNEY
The Hermitage
2002
Oil on canvas
38" x 54"

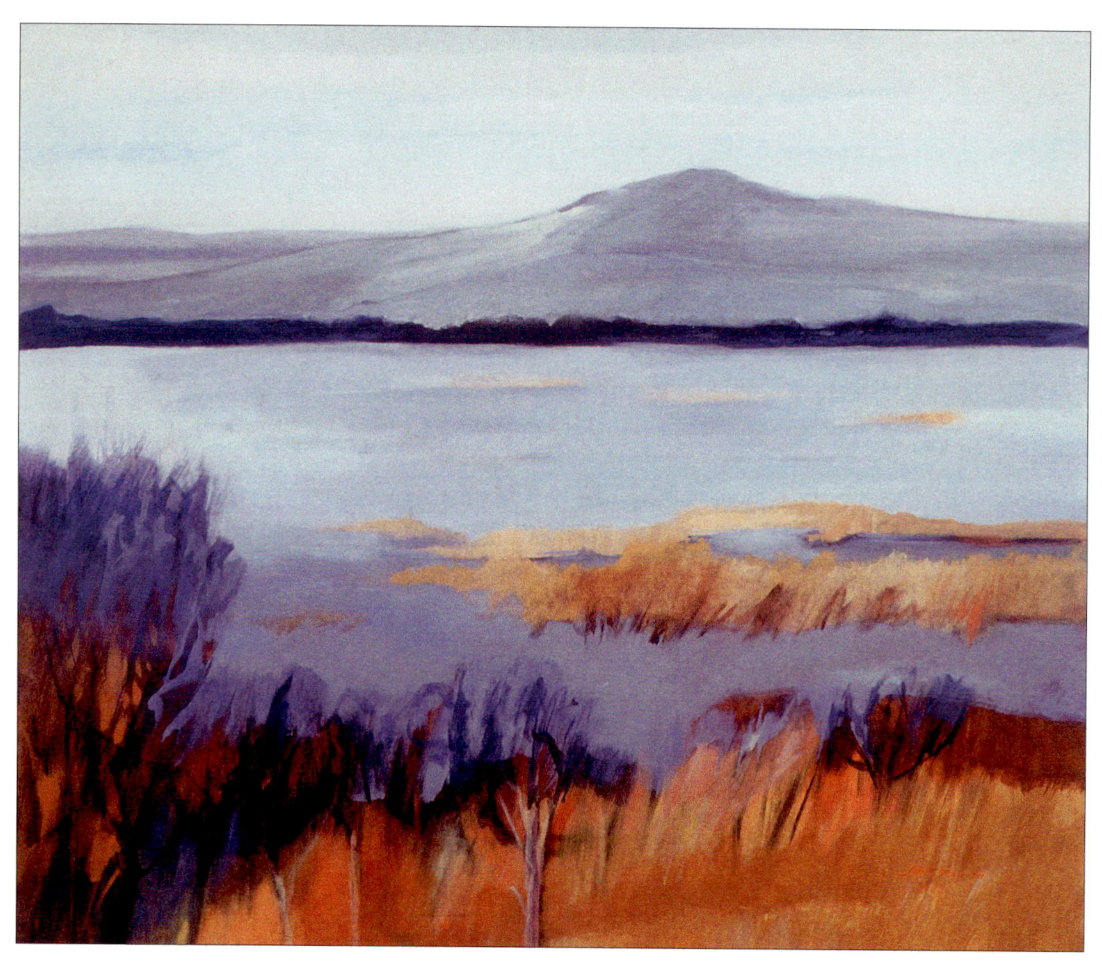

LAS CRUCES

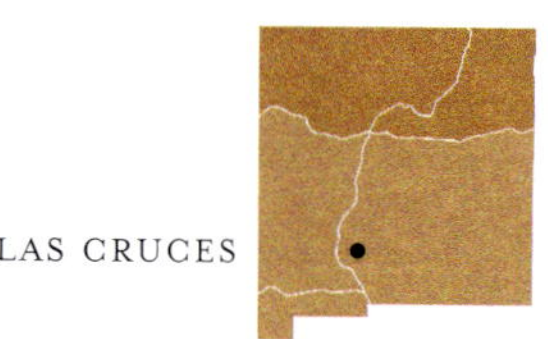

JOYCE T. MACRORIE
Before Rain - Bosque del Apache
2002
Acrylic on canvas
40" x 46"

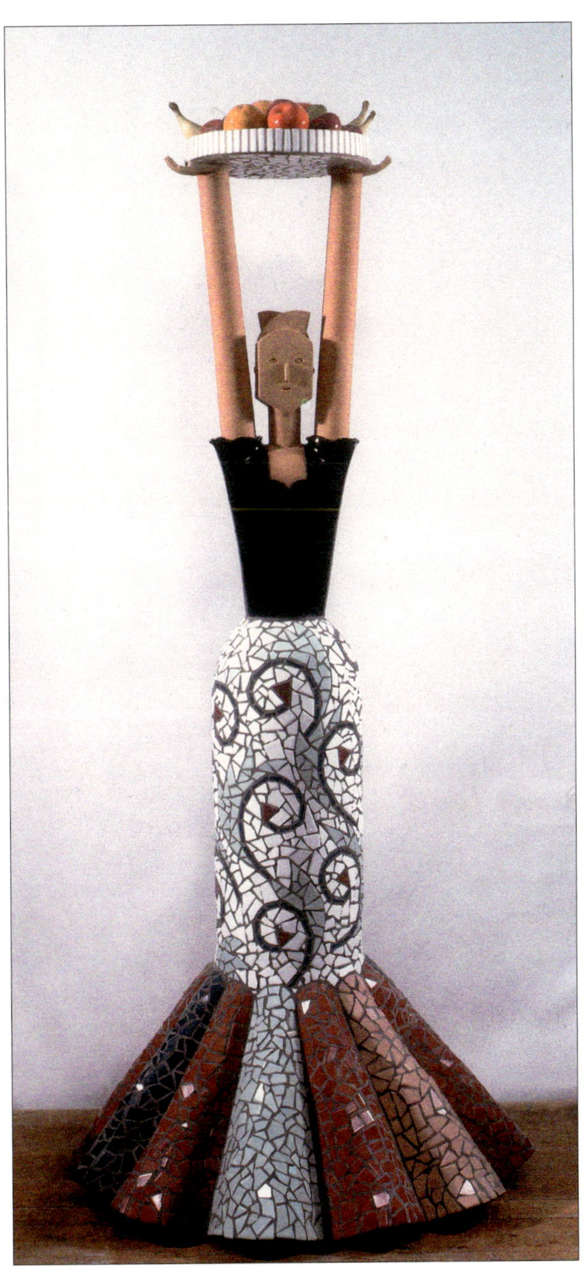

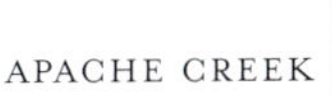

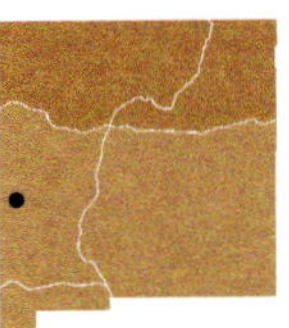

BEVERLY MAGENNIS
Garden Lady
1995
Clay, cement
60" x 32" diameter
Lent by the Albuquerque Museum, NM
Gift of The Fund at the Albuquerque Community Foundation

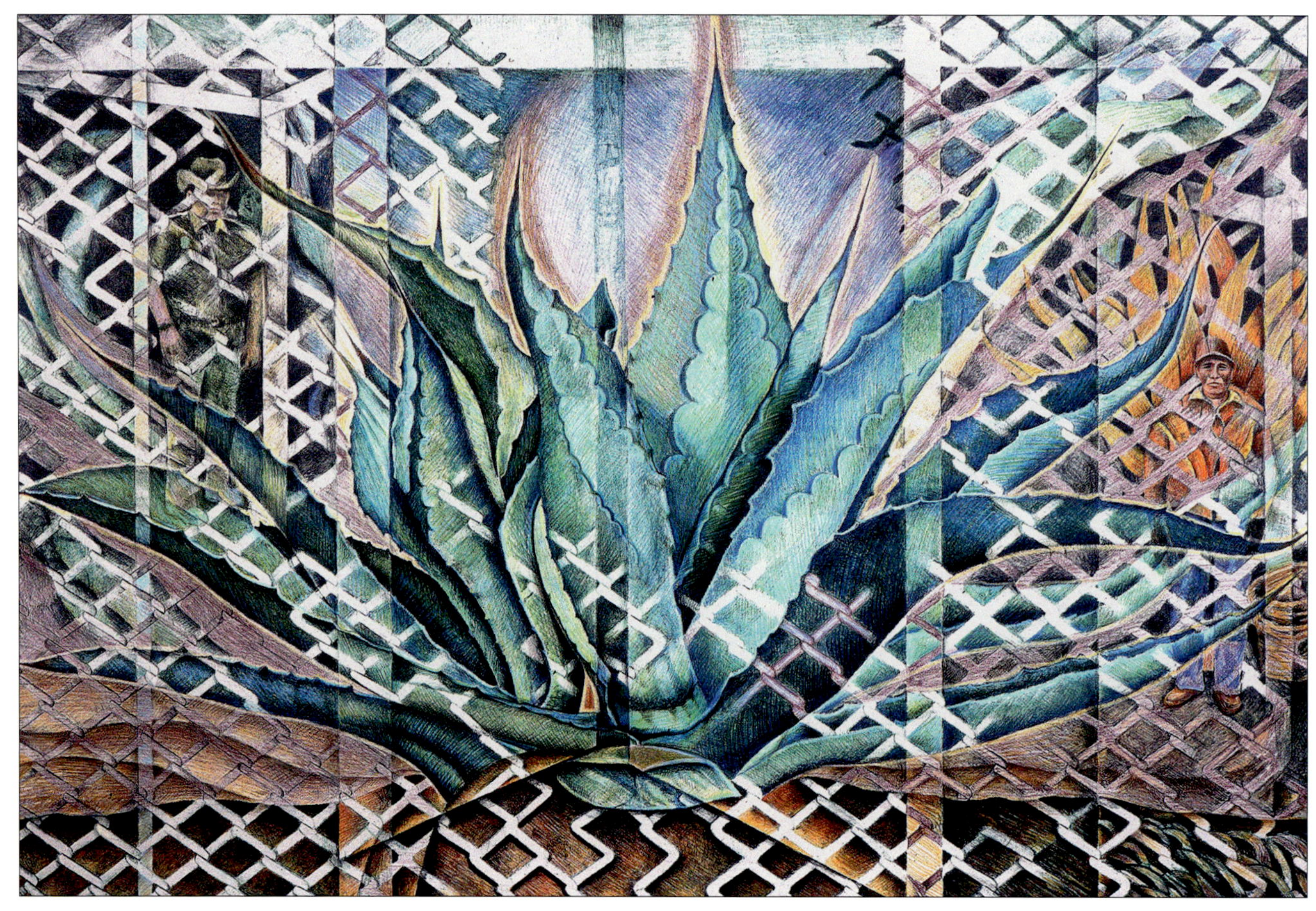

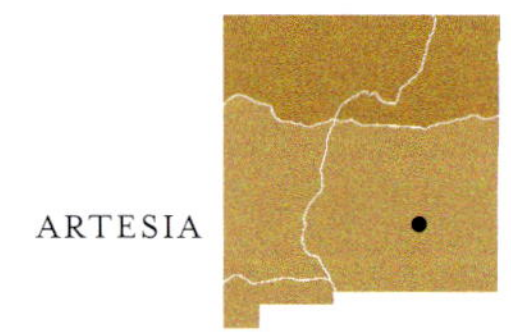

ARTESIA

NOEL MÁRQUEZ
Agave #1
1990, 2003
Lithograph
30" x 41"

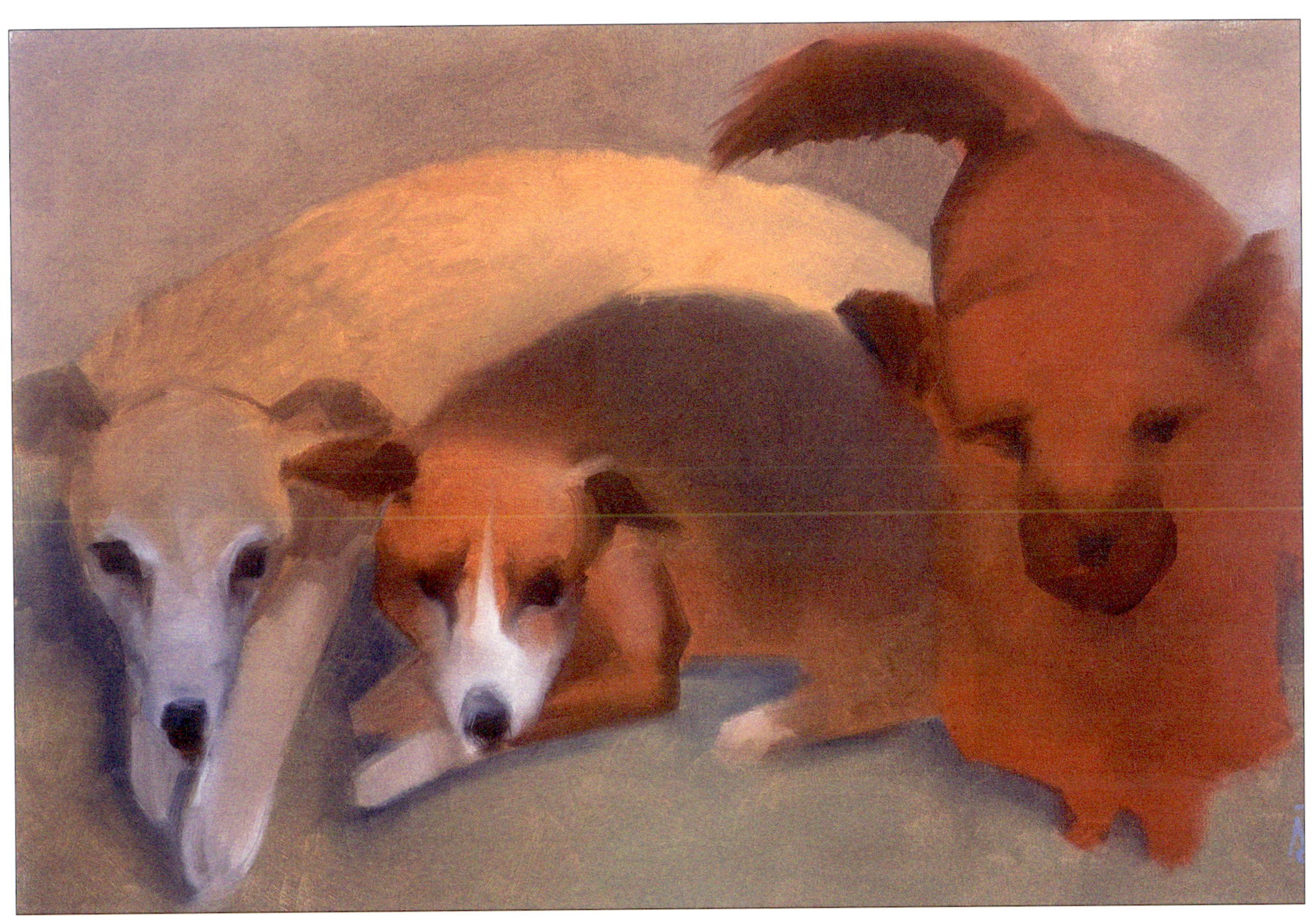

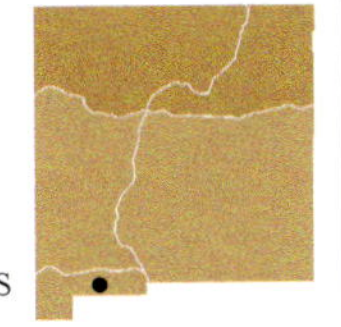

TIMOTHY McANDREWS
Dogs
2000
Oil on canvas
20" x 30"

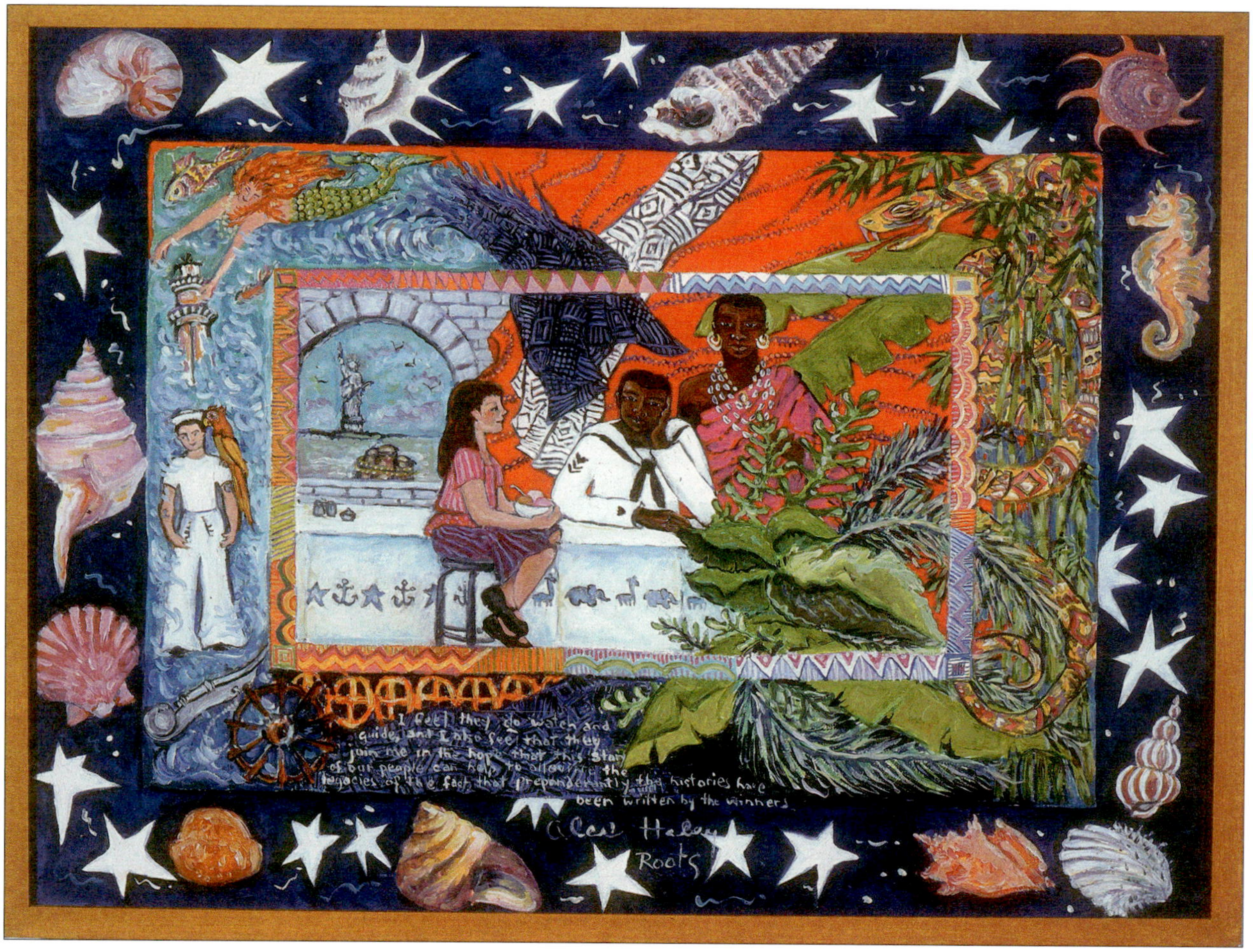

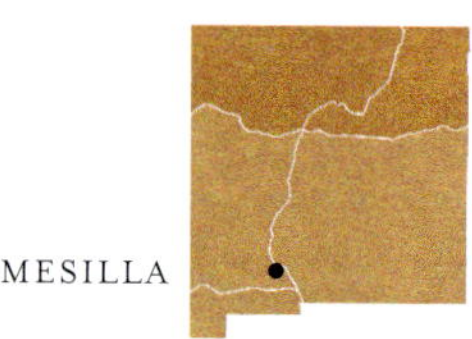

ROSEMARY McLOUGHLIN
Ice Cream and Alex Haley
2002
Oil on canvas
18" x 24"
Lent by John and Susan Meier, Las Cruces, NM

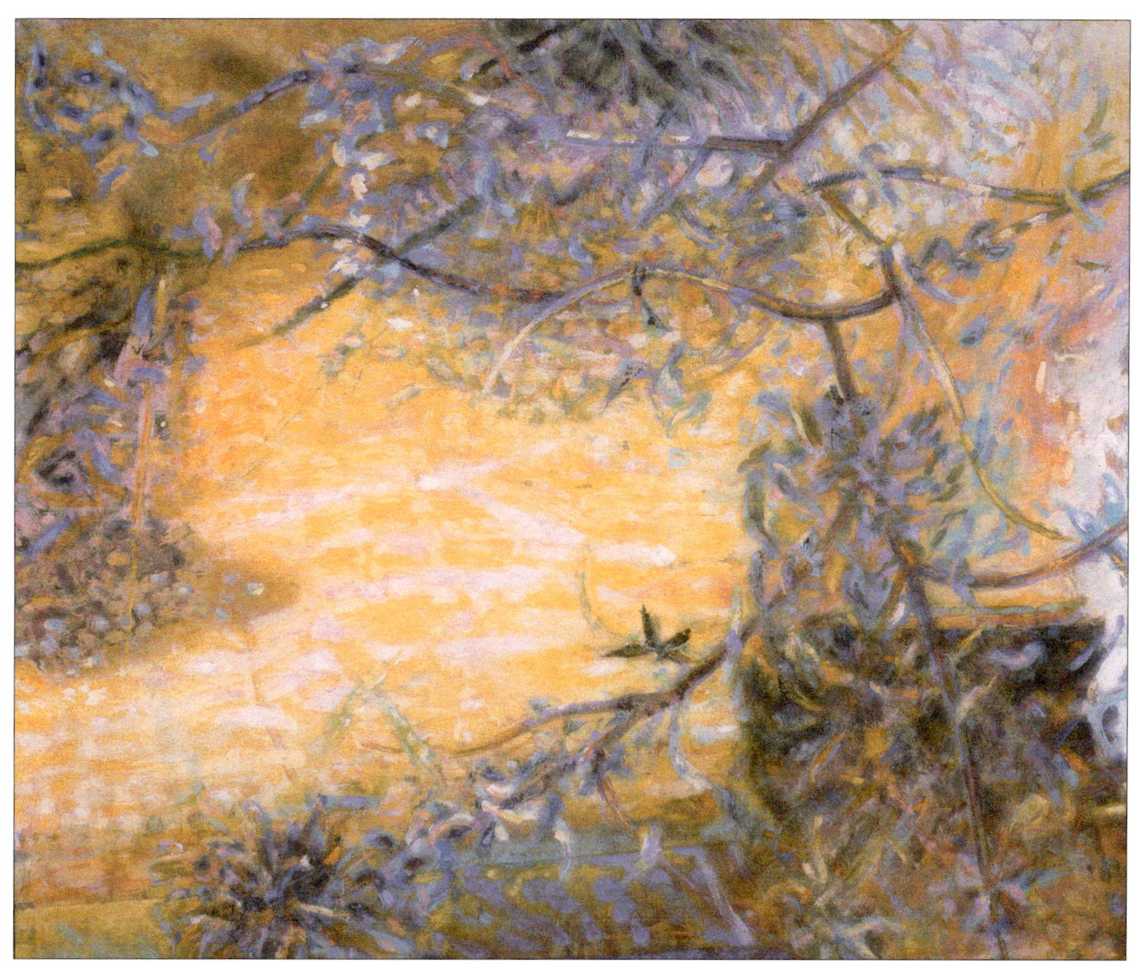

SAN ACACIA

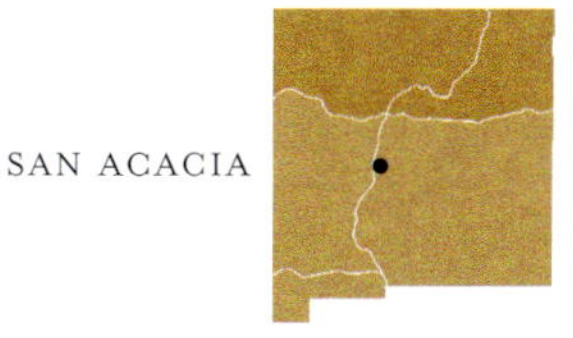

FERNANDO MERCADO

Summer Light - San Acacia

2002

Oil, oil stick, pastel on linen

49" x 62"

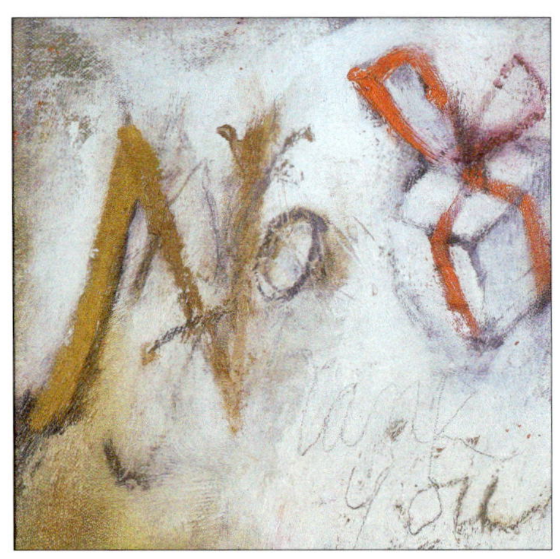

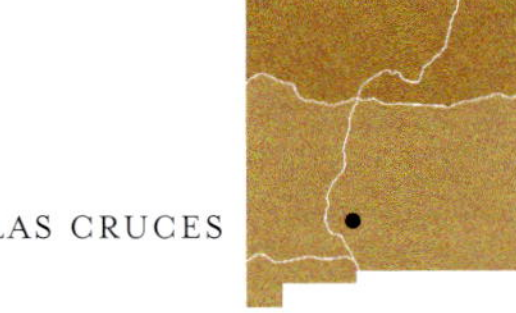

JACKIE MITCHELL
No Thank-You
2001
Oil, oil stick, pencil on canvas
7.75" x 7.75"

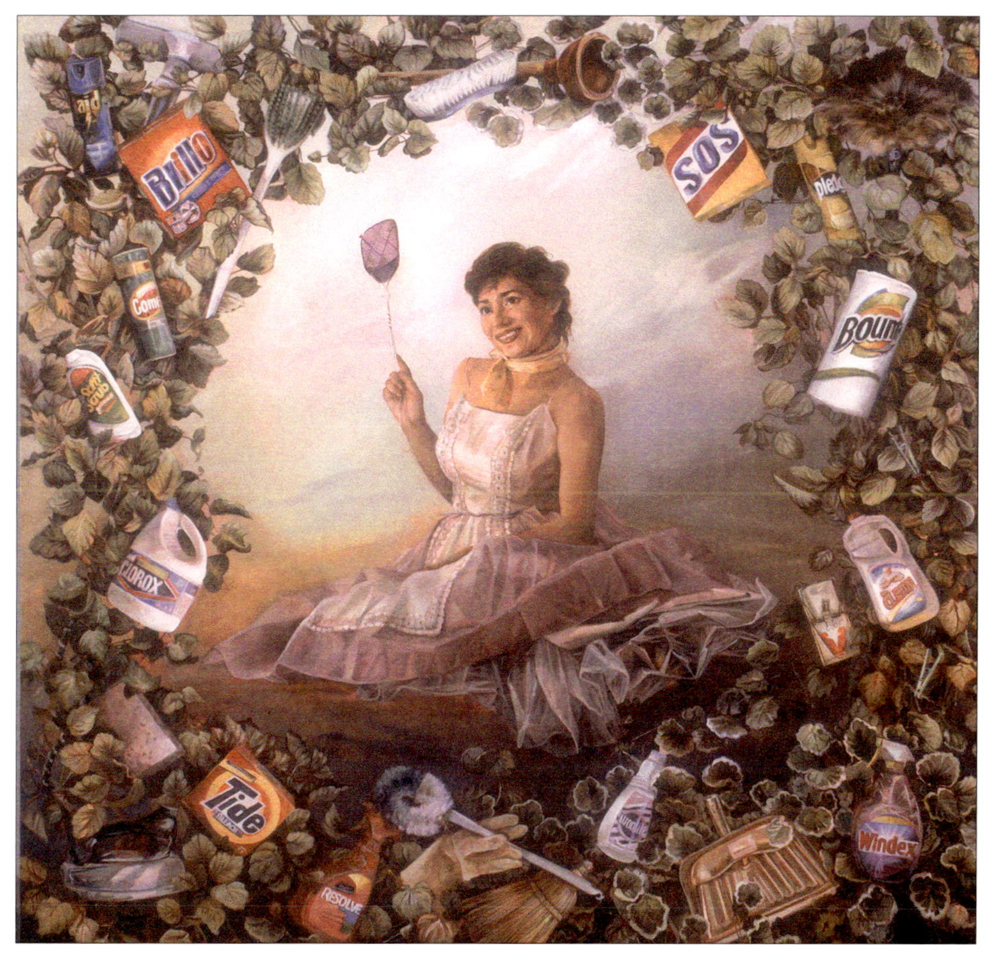

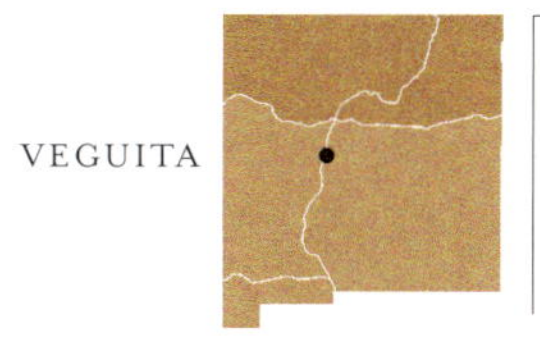

IVA MORRIS

Our Lady of Perpetual Housework

2002

Oil on canvas

67" x 67"

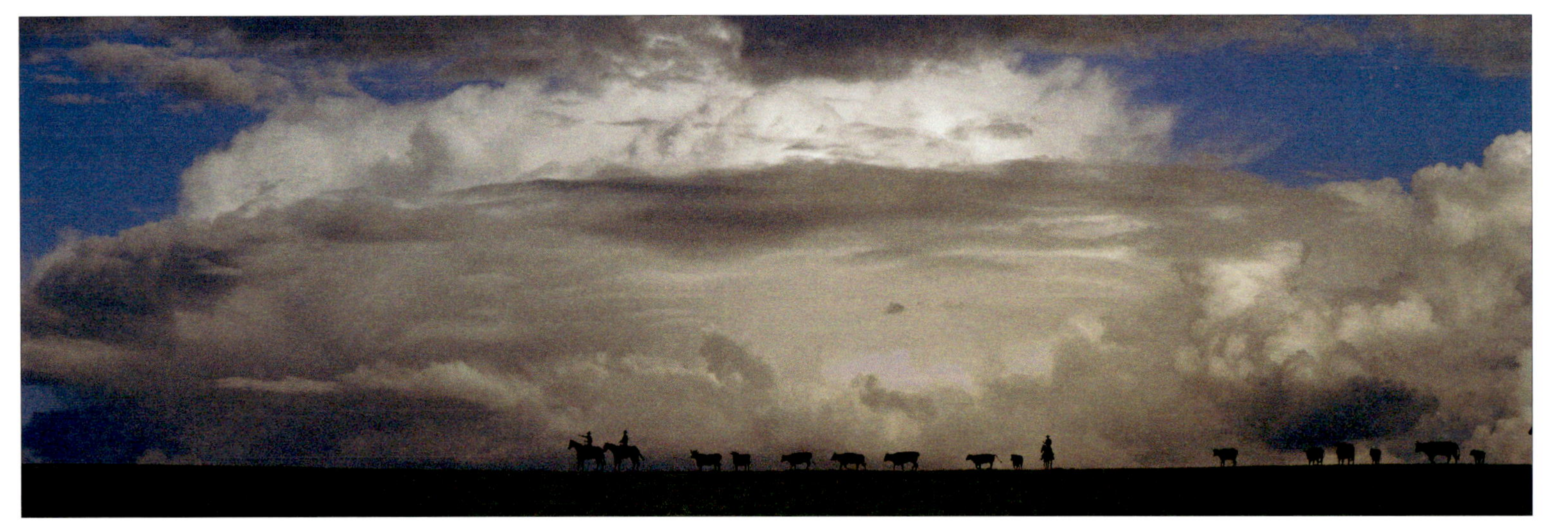

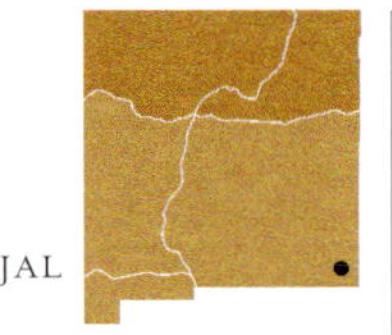

BRIAN NORWOOD
The Trail Ahead
Sculpture located in Jal, NM
2000
Steel
20 feet x 400 feet

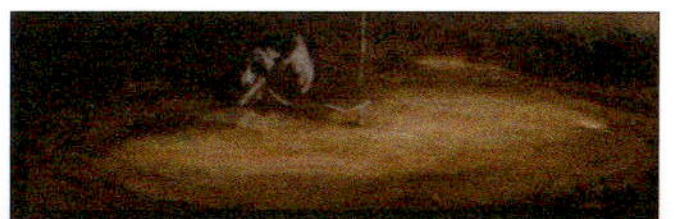

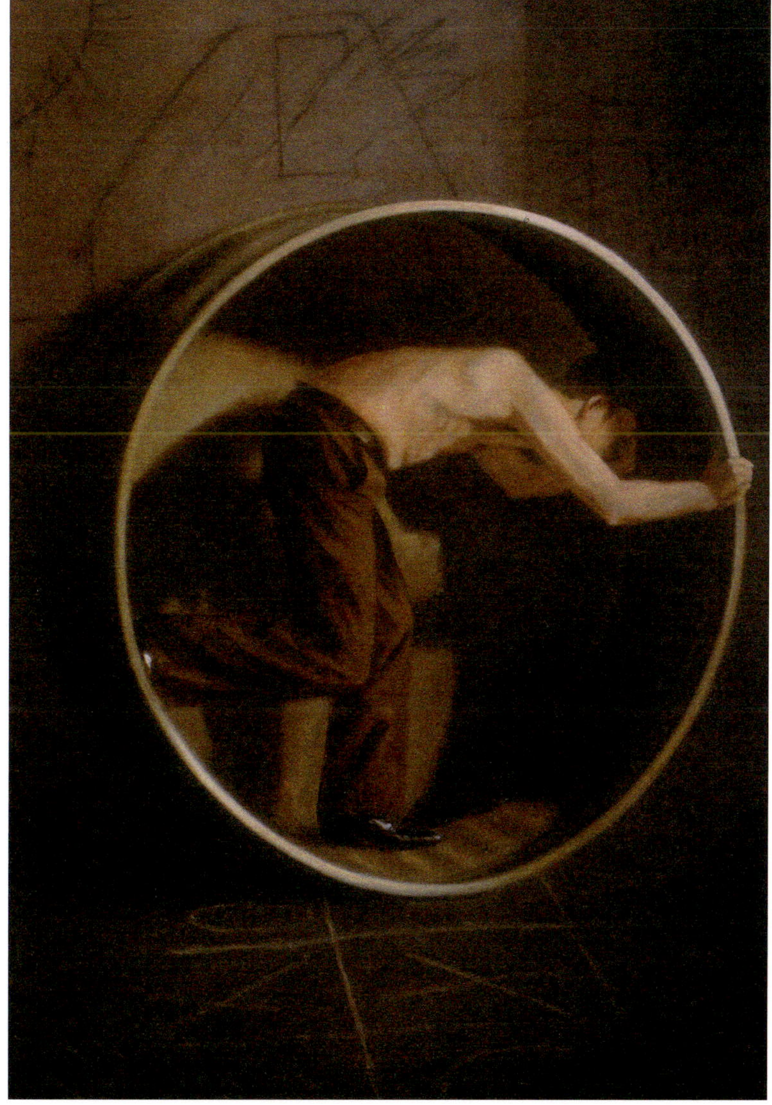

VEGUITA

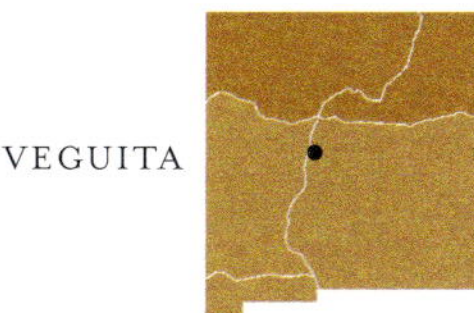

BRIAN O'CONNOR
Perfect Circle
2000
Oil on canvas on panel/oil on linen
73" x 48"
Collection of the Museum of Fine Arts, Museum of New Mexico
Purchased with funds donated by the Herzstein Family Acquisitions Endowment Fund, Lynn Marchand and George Goldstein, and Christopher Han

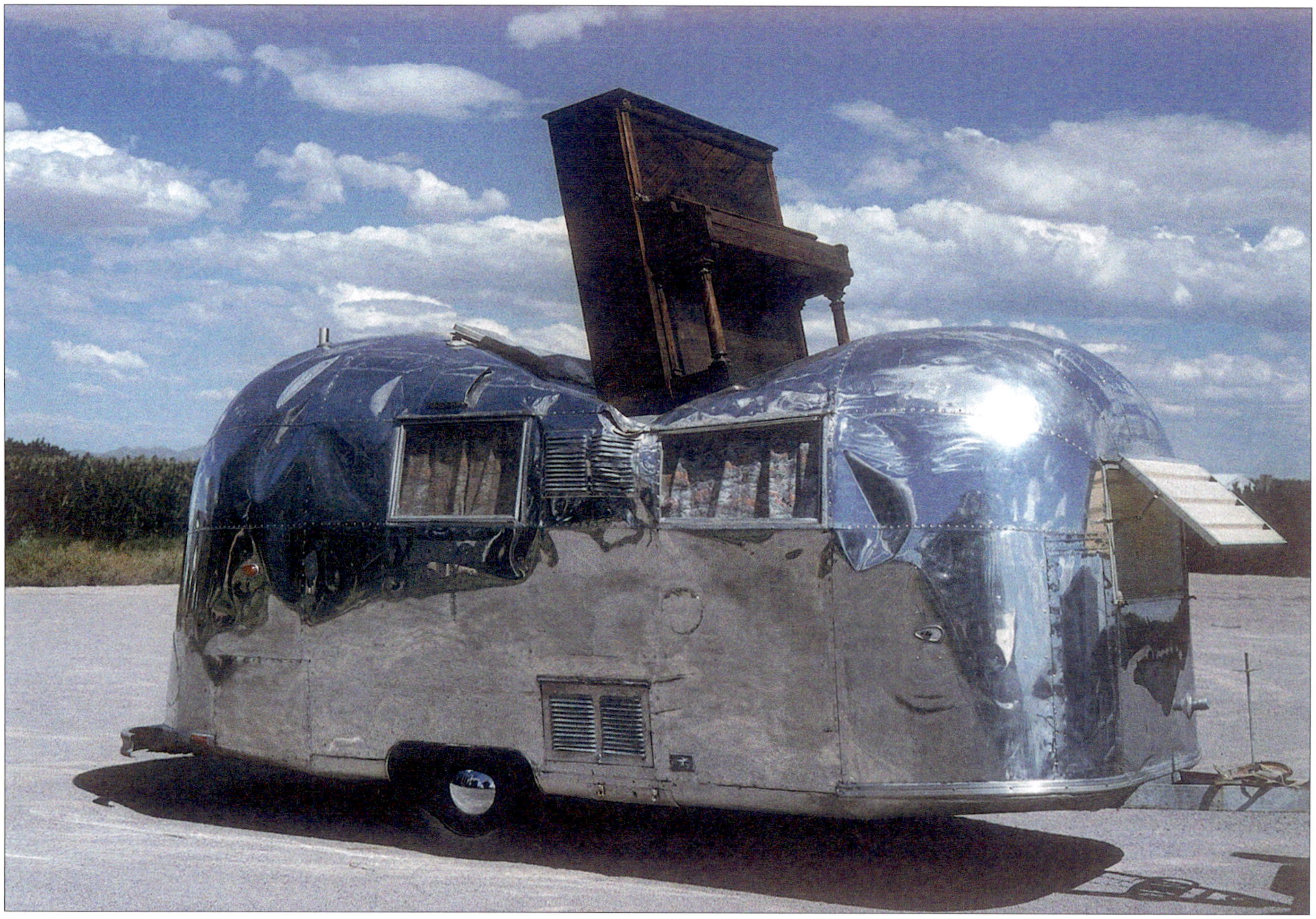

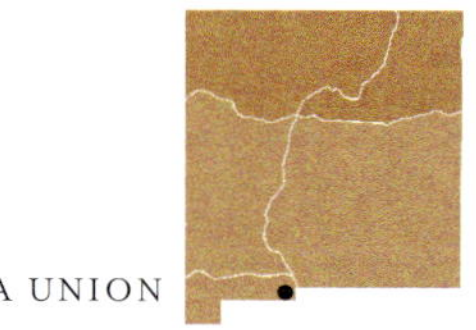

WILLIE RAY PARISH

Undeterred, They Continued Driving South

2000

Steel, wood

12' x 18' x 7'

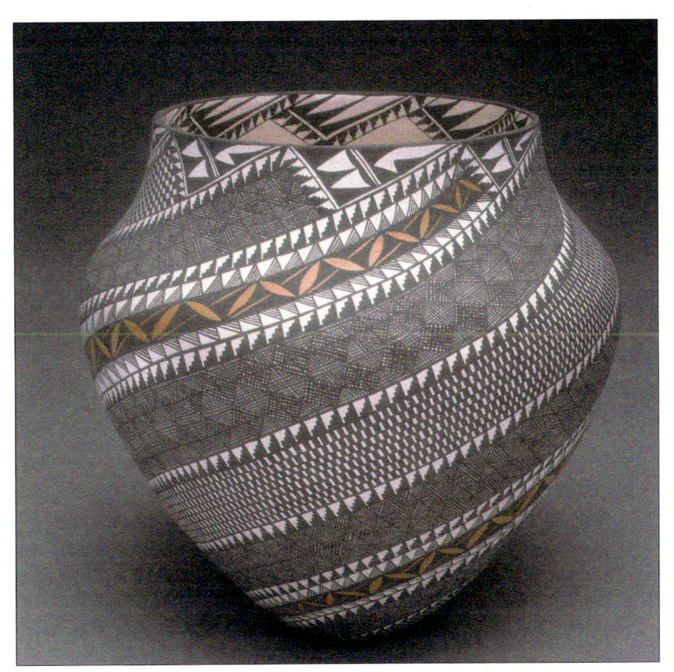

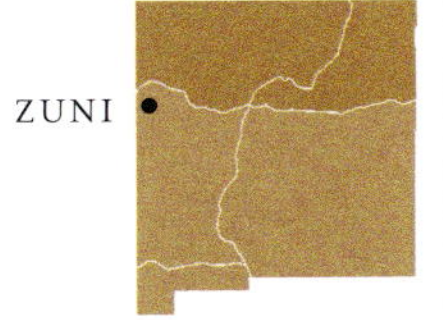

PRISCILLA PEYNETSA
Untitled
2003
Clay
11.25" x 11.25" diameter
Lent by Andrea Fisher Fine Pottery, Santa Fe, NM

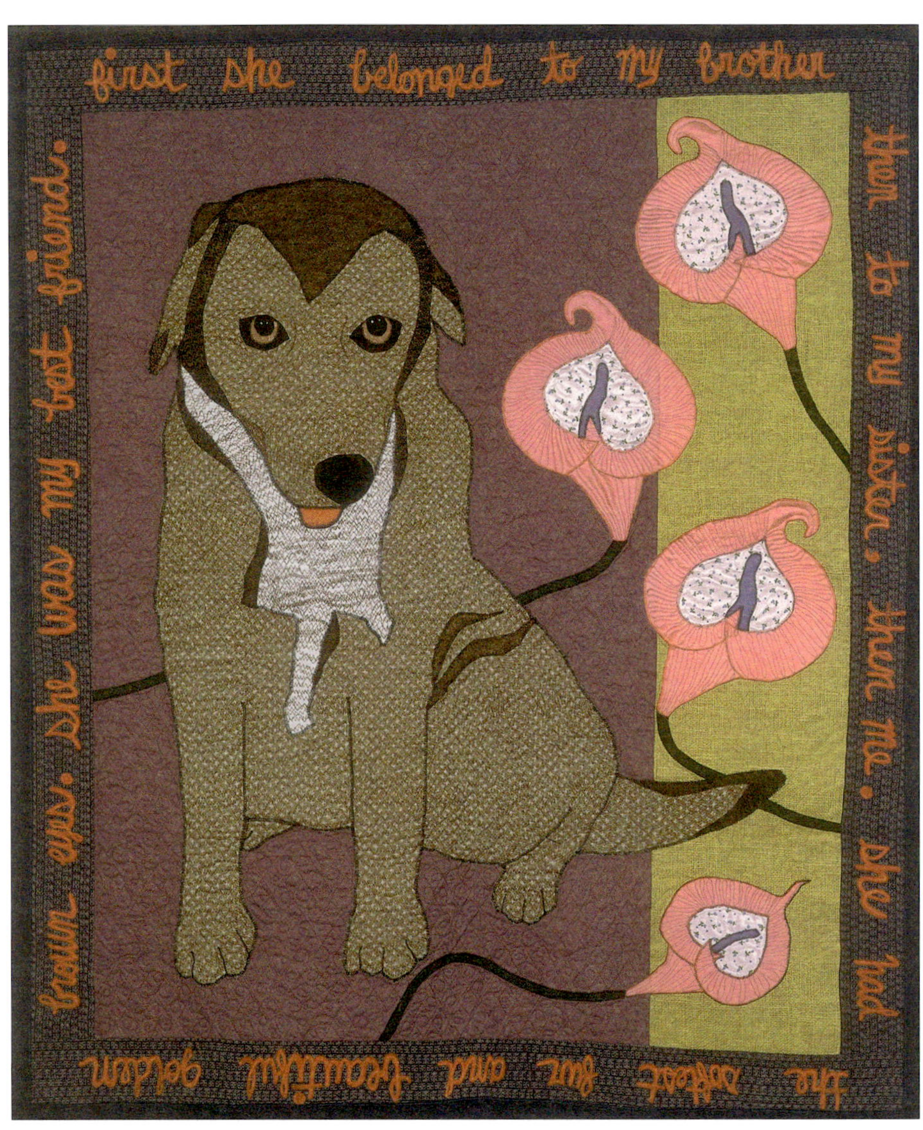

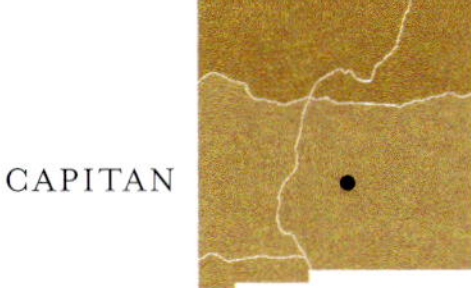

KAREN PRITCHETT
Lassie, My Last Dog
2002
Hand sewn quilted fabric
48" x 38"
Lent by Blue Dome Gallery, Silver City, NM

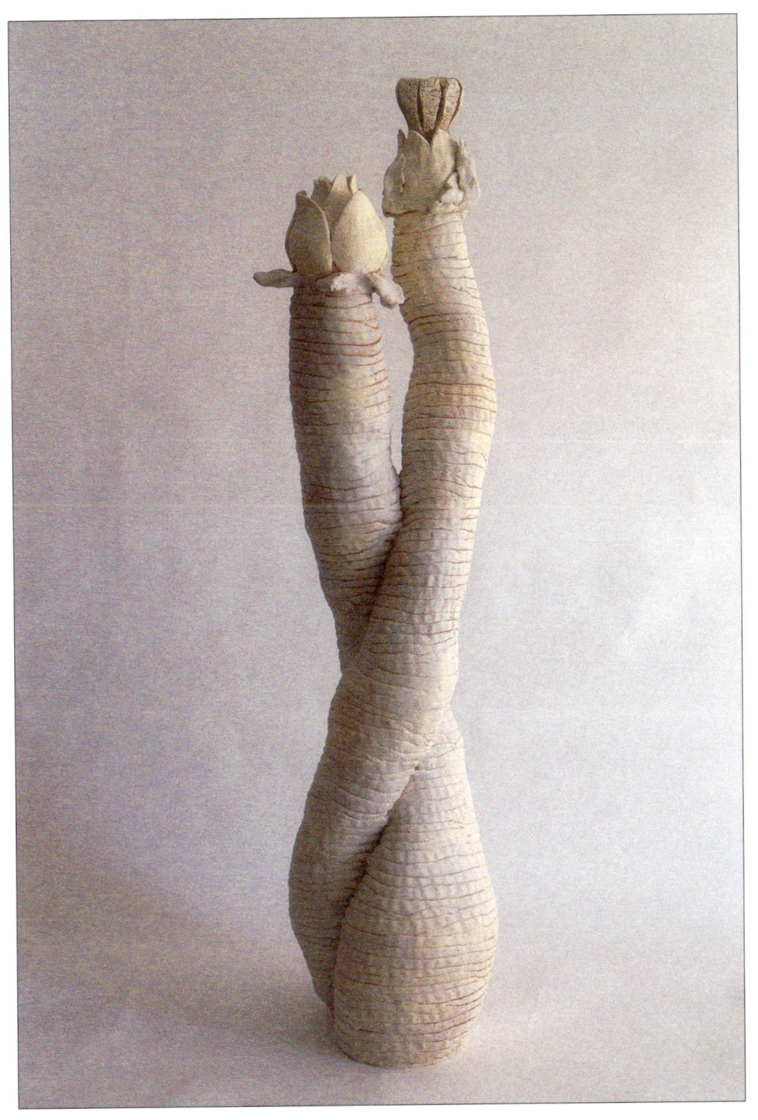

ALAMOGORDO

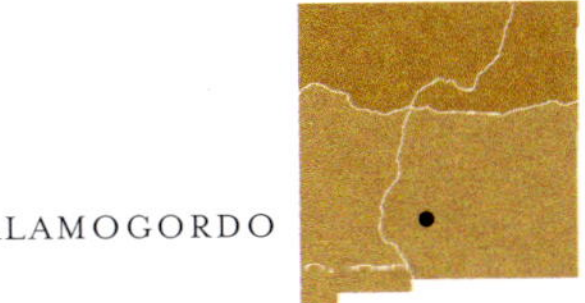

LEA RANO
Embrace
2002
Clay
49.5" x 11" diameter

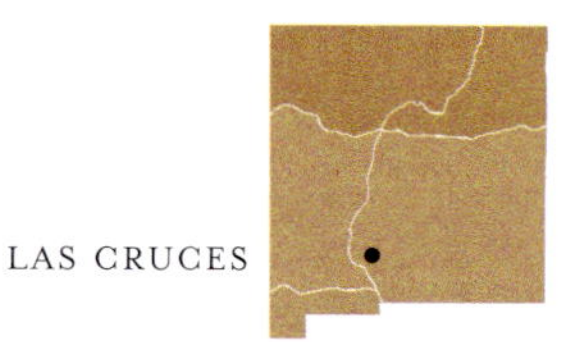

JOSHUA ROSE
Winter
2002
Acrylic on paper
30" x 22"

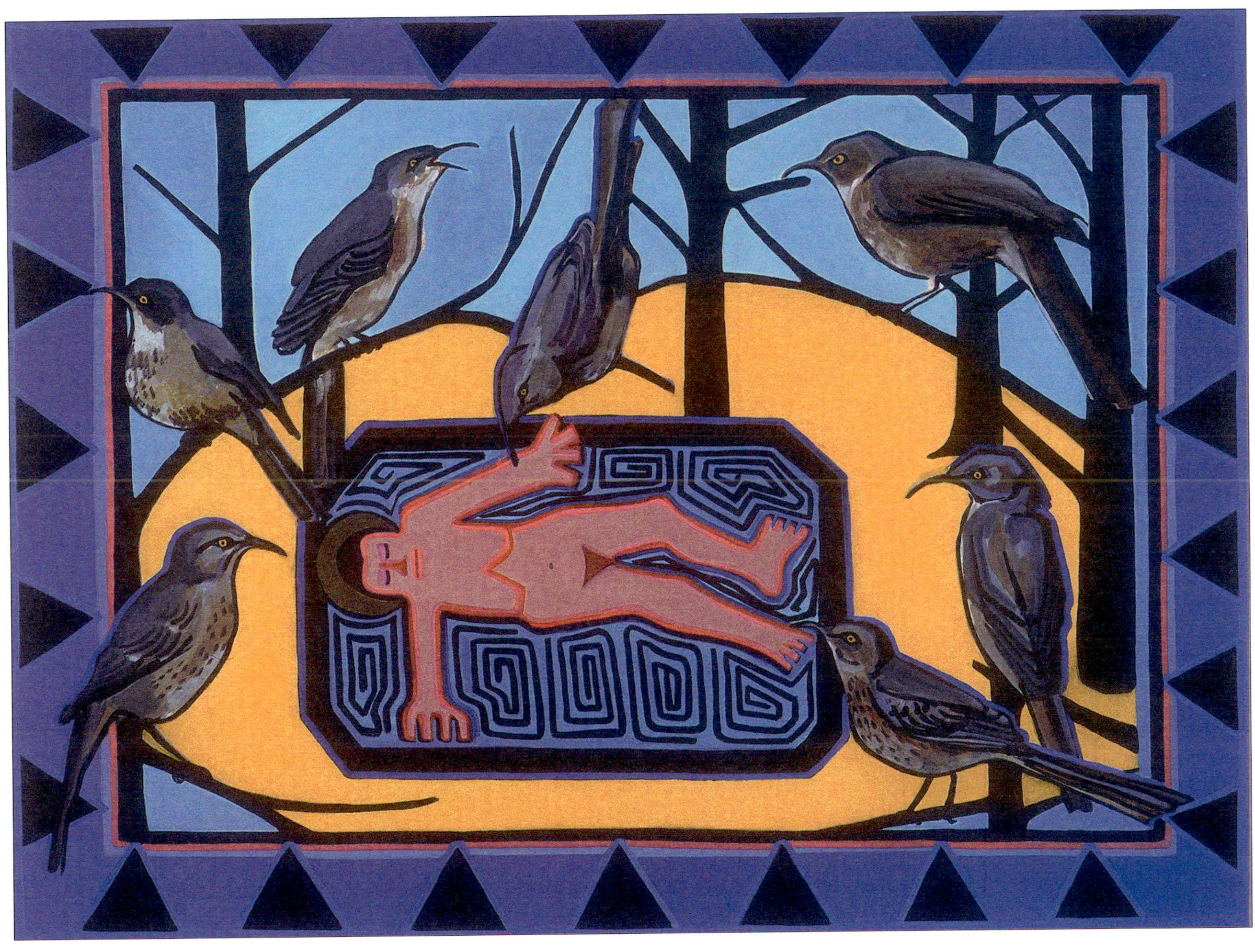

SILVER CITY

CARLENE ROTERS
Serenade of the Thrashers
2002
Oil on canvas
36" x 48"
Lent by Blue Dome Gallery, Silver City, NM

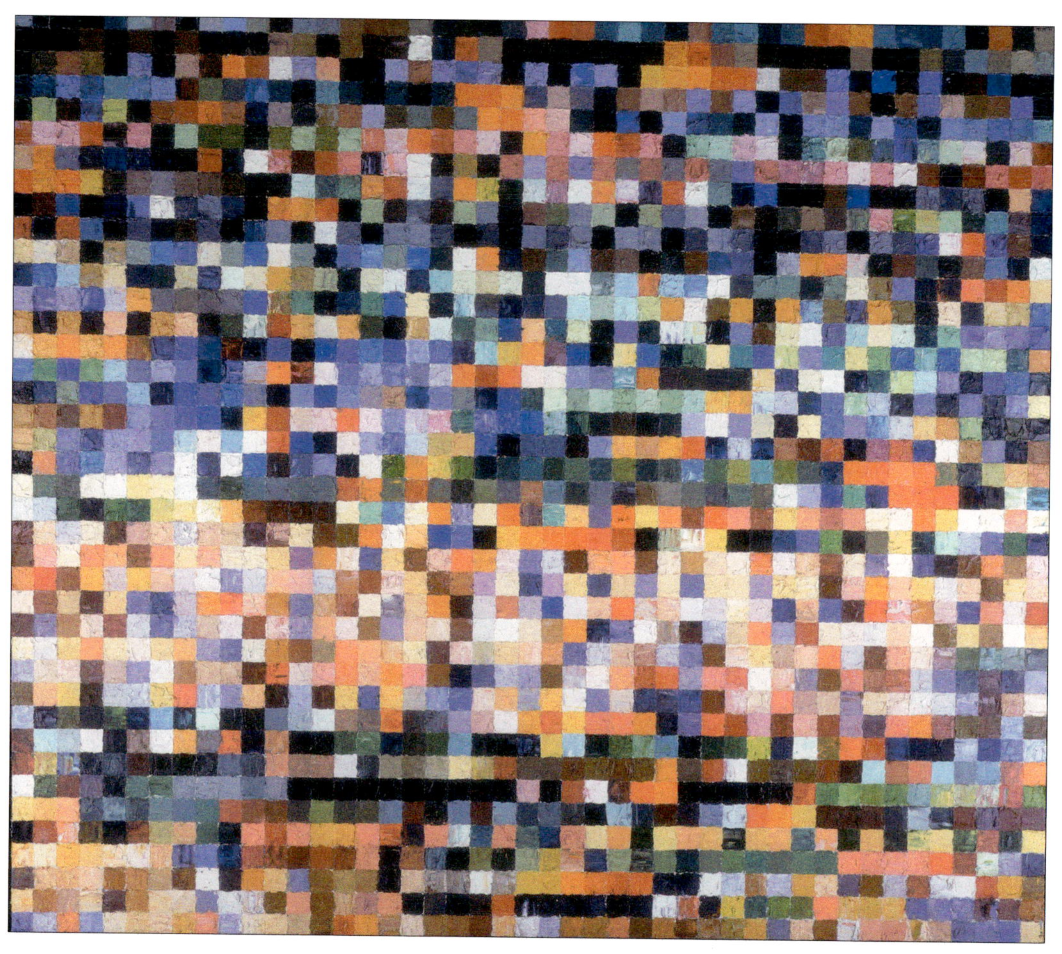

ROSWELL

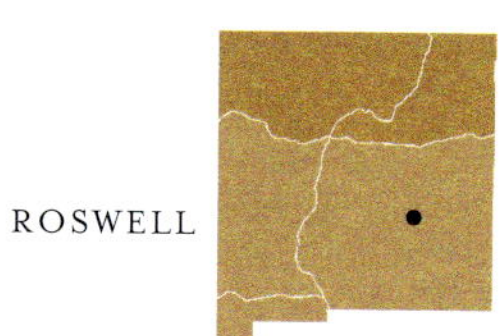

ELMER SCHOOLEY
Freedom and Responsibility
1989
Oil on canvas
80" x 90"
Lent by The Munson Gallery, Santa Fe, NM

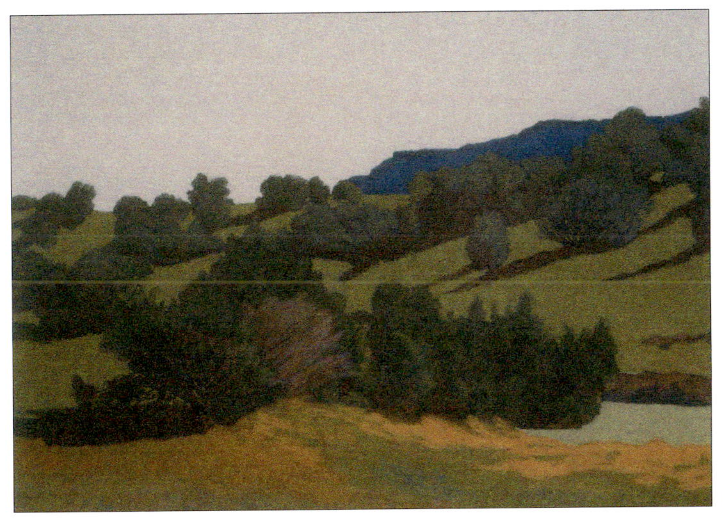

BELEN

MARY SILVERWOOD
Yellow Bird Wash
2000
Pastel on paper
27 x 38"
Lent by Joyce Robins Gallery, Santa Fe, NM

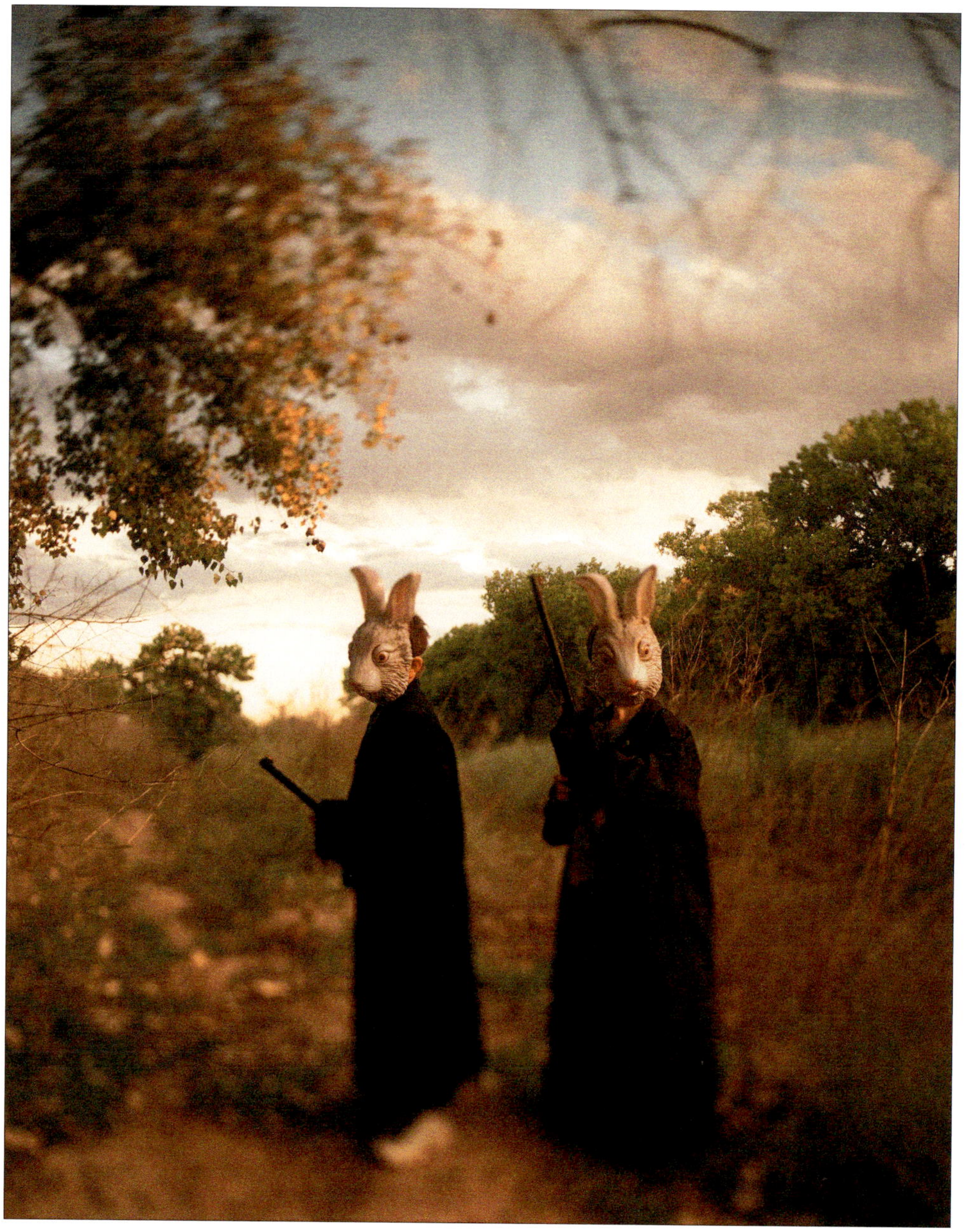

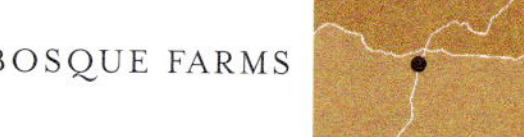

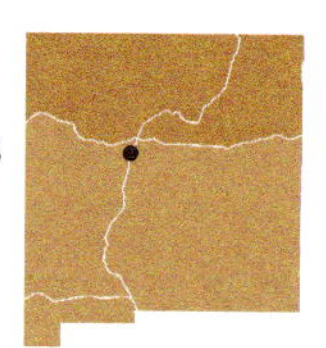

CHIP SIMONS
Bunnies
2002
Iris print
20" x 16"

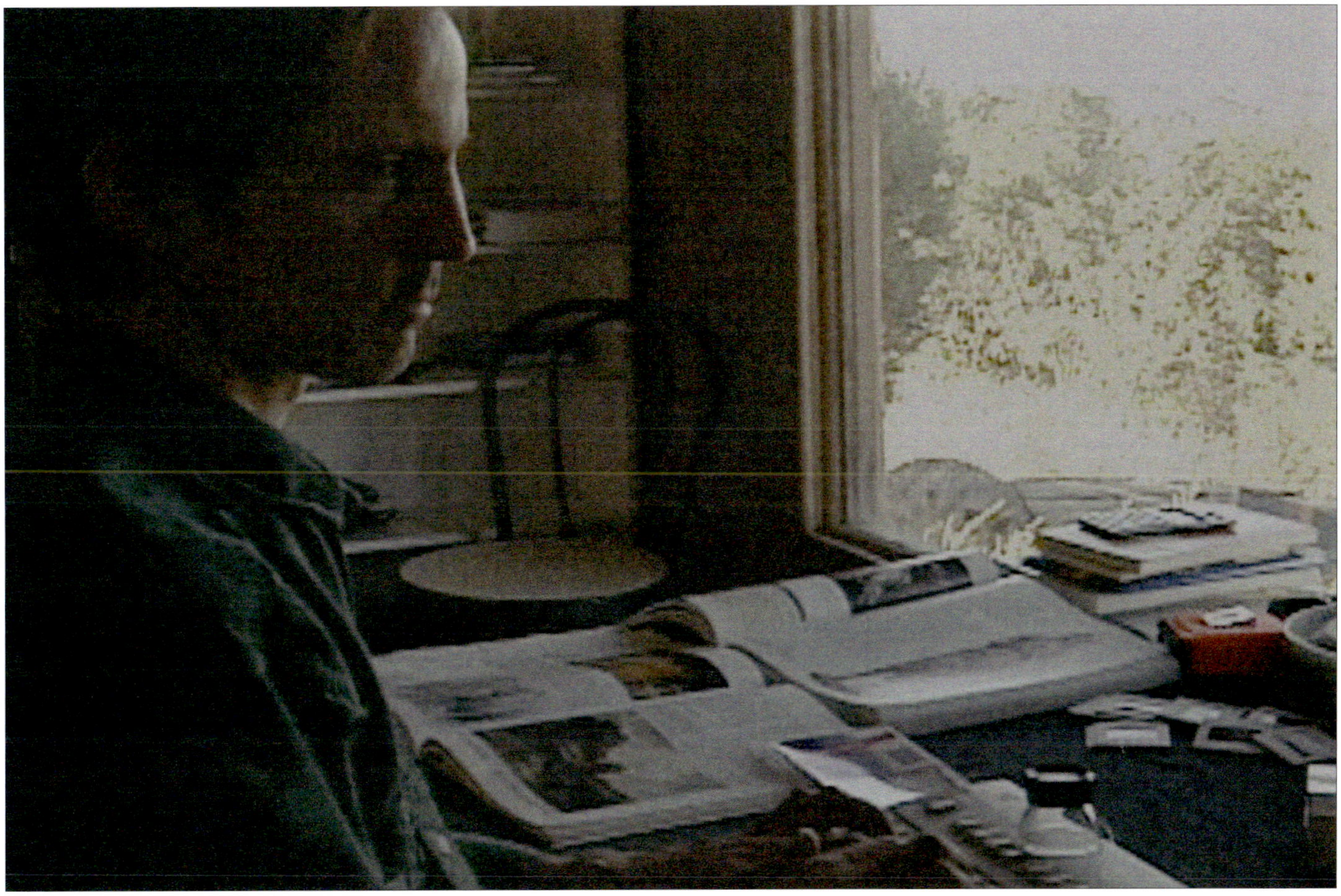

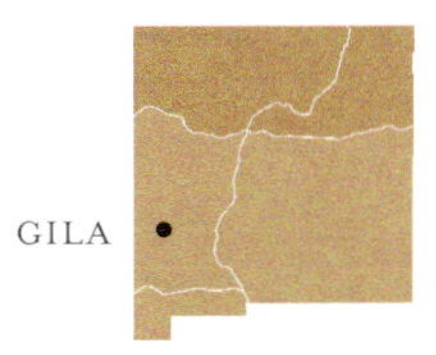

MATTHEW SOMMERVILLE
INSIDEOUT
2002
DVD

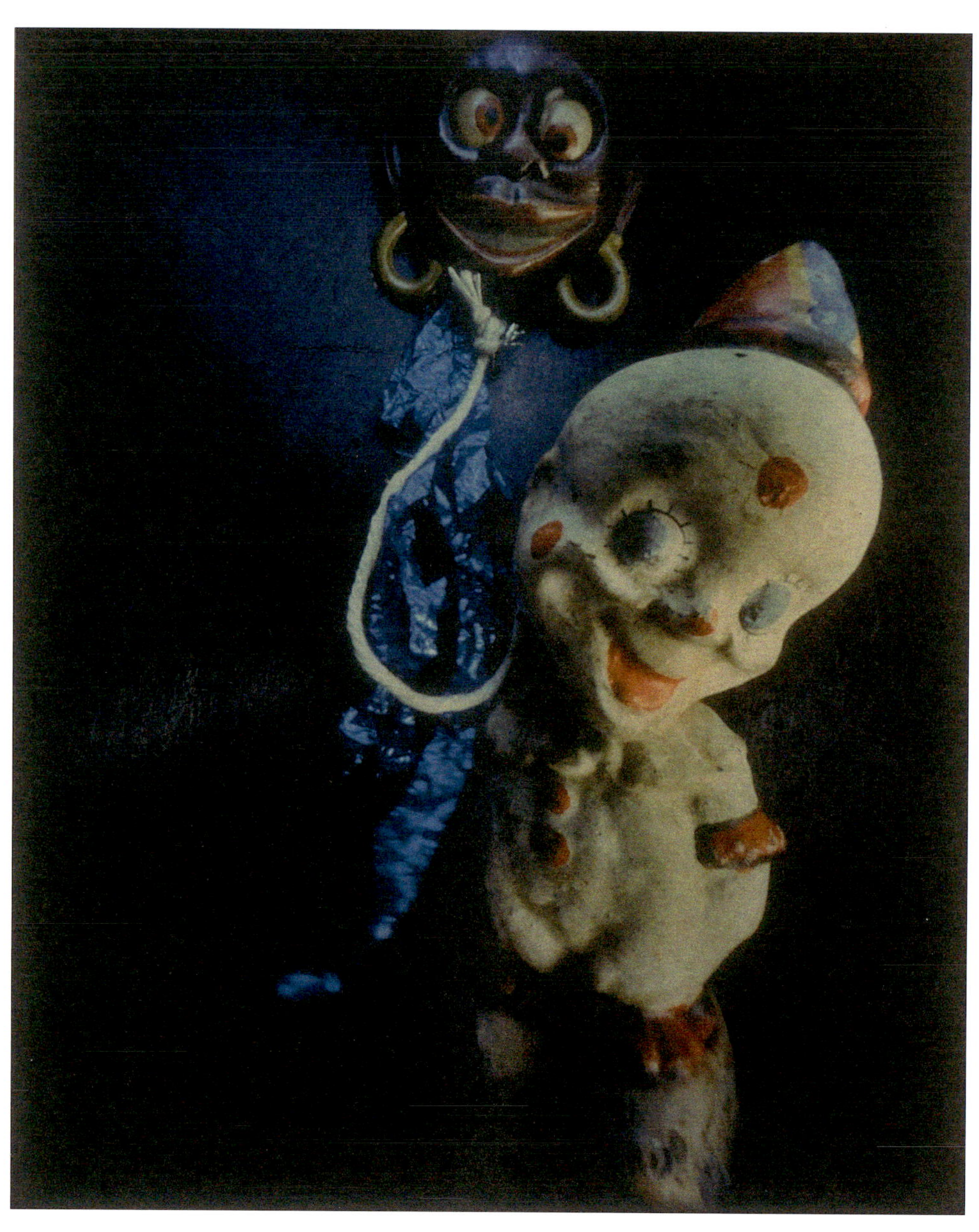

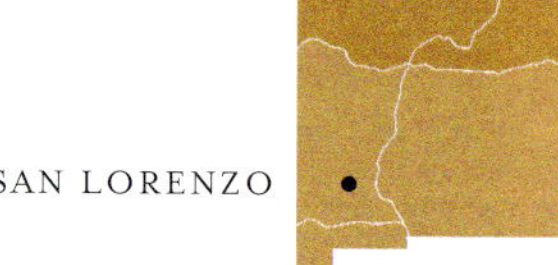

NANCY SPENCER AND ERIC RENNER
Topsy and the Ghost of Jim Crow (from the series On Deaf Ears)
2002
Type C pinhole photograph
20" x 16"

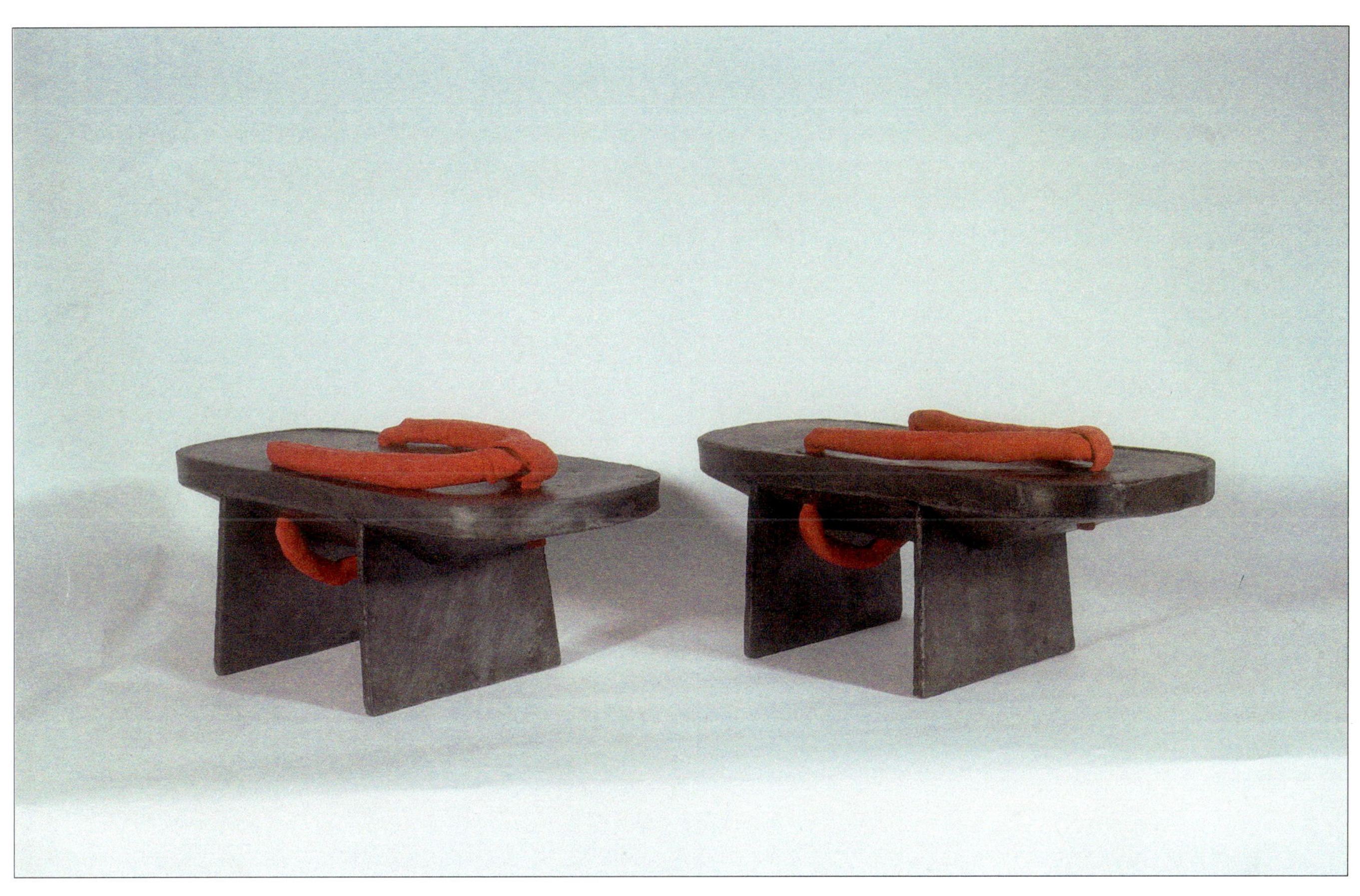

LAS CRUCES

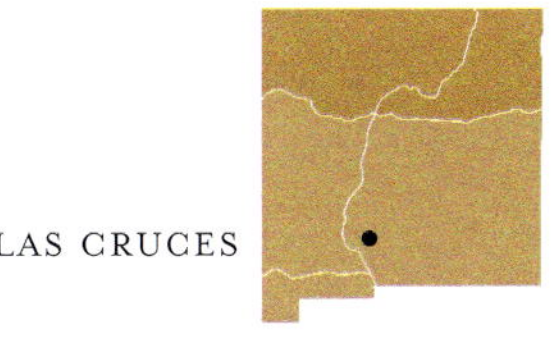

RACHEL STEVENS
Gita
2003
Steel, flock
7" x 16" x 16"

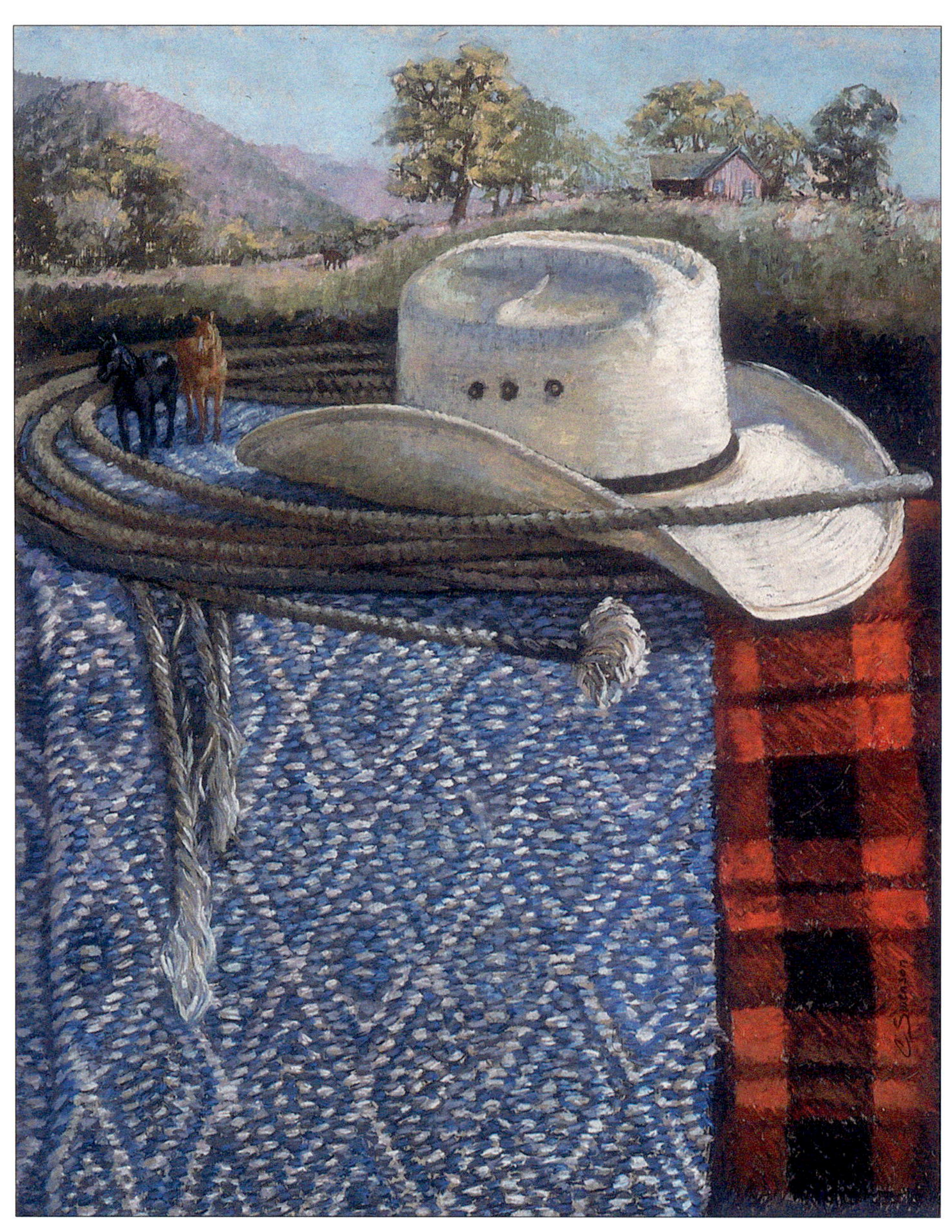

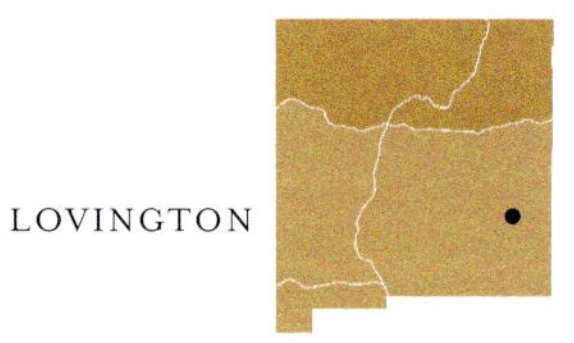

CARRIE SWENSON
Tools of the Trade
2000
Pastel on paper
27" x 21"

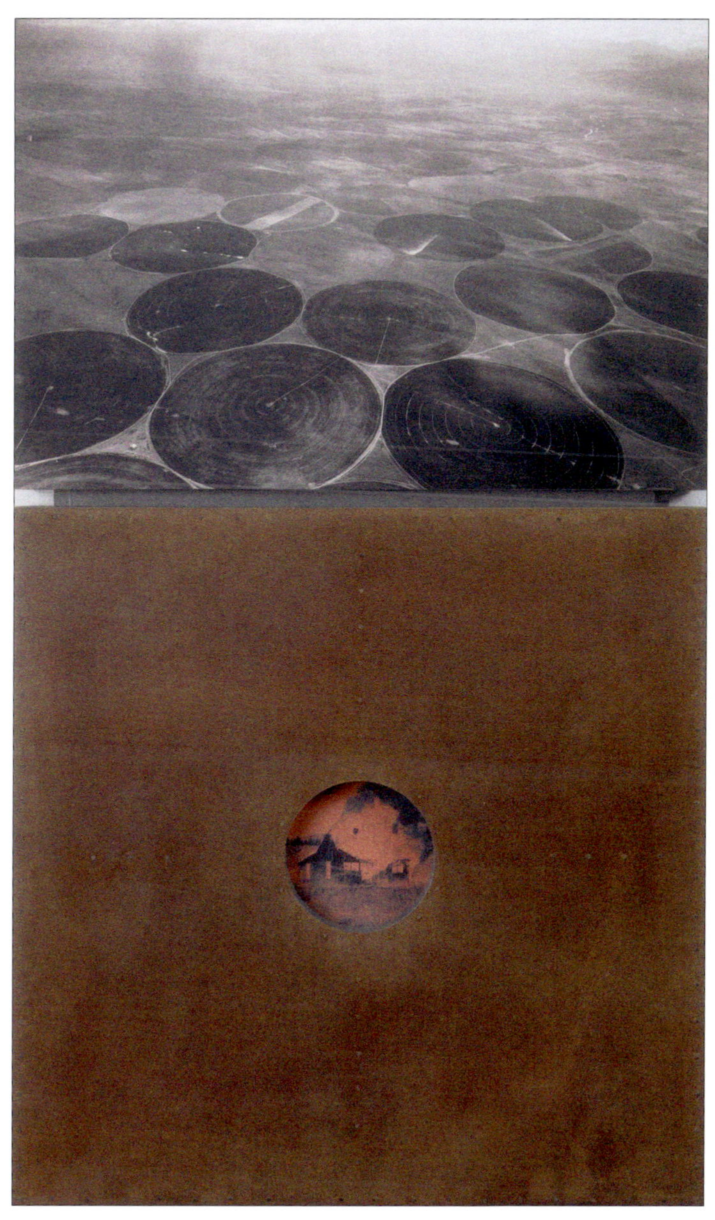

LAS CRUCES

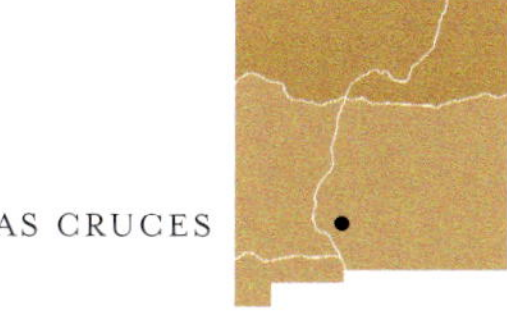

DAVID TAYLOR

Pivot Irrigation/Burning House

2000

Gelatin silver print, ink jet print, steel

33" x 19.5" x 2"

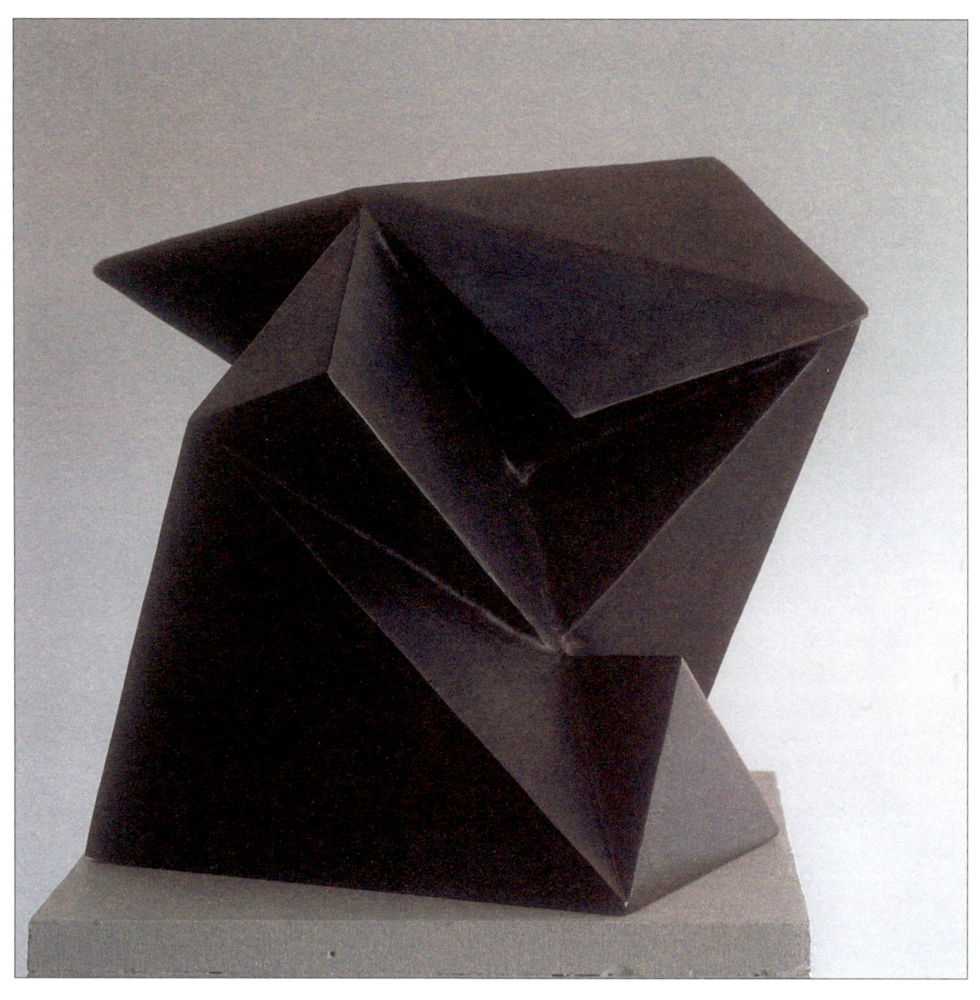

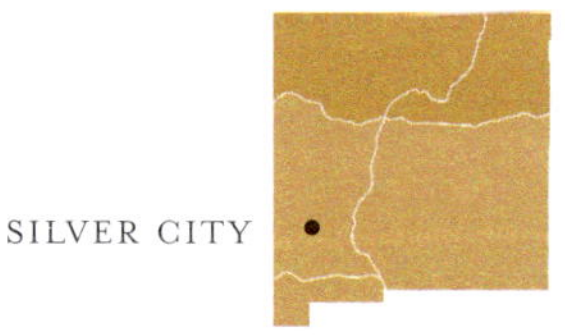

SILVER CITY

JEFF TURNER
A Day Like Any Other
2003
Steel
11.25" x 14.25" x 13"

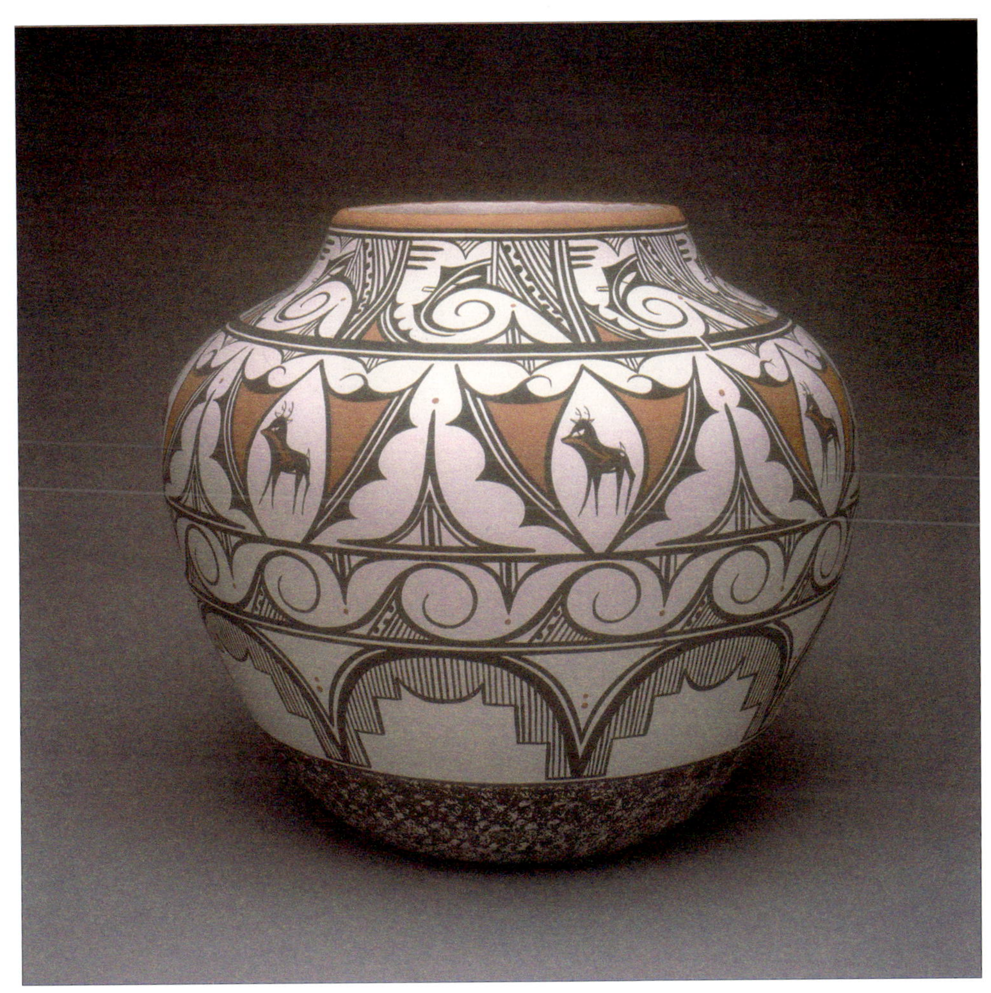

ACOMA

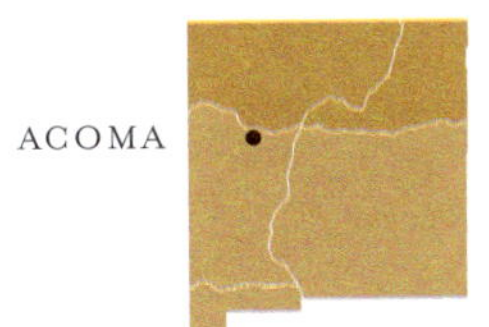

SANDRA VICTORINO
Untitled
2002
Clay
11" x 9.75" diameter
Lent by Earl and Suzanne Swenson, Franklin, TN

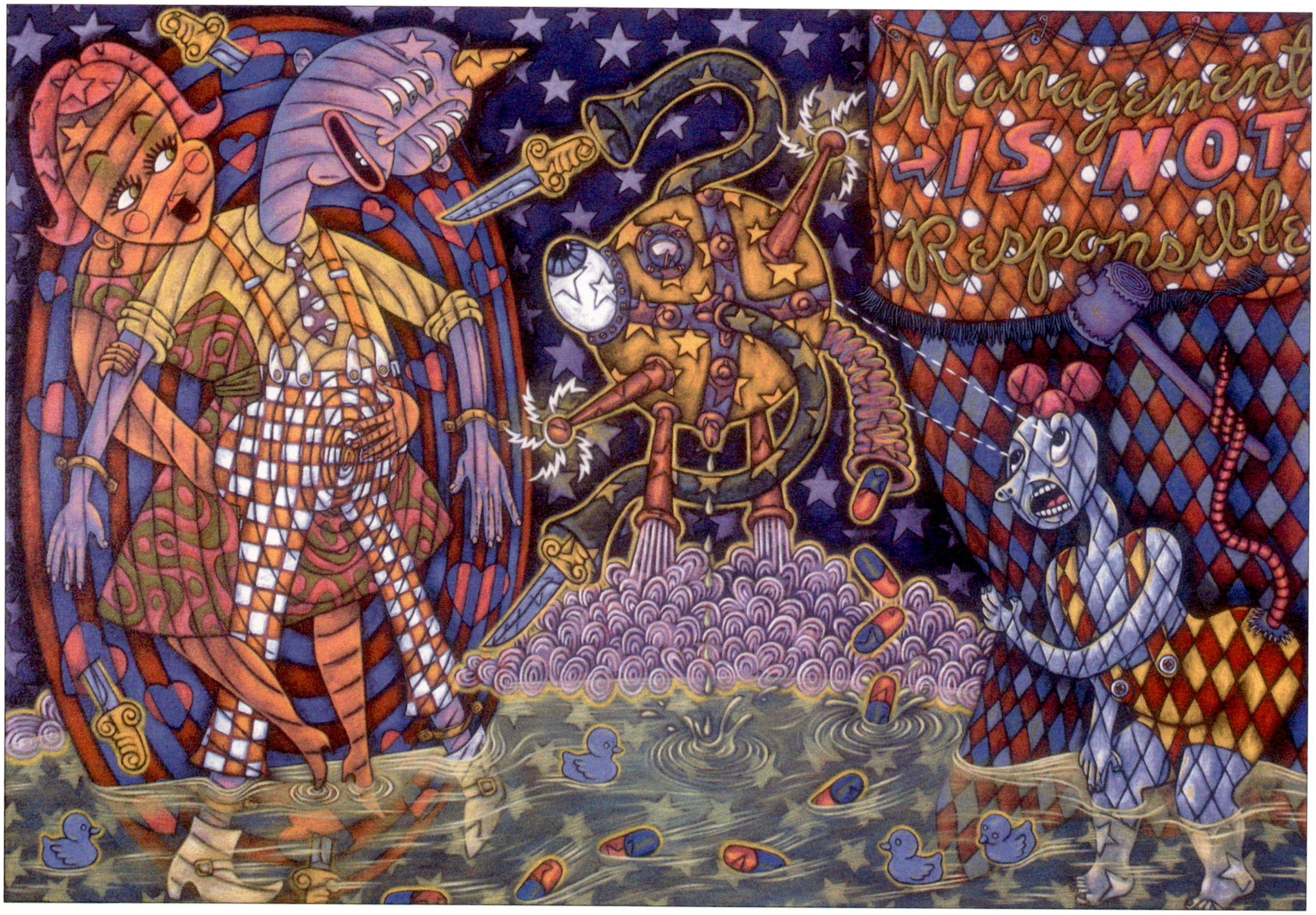

BERNARDO

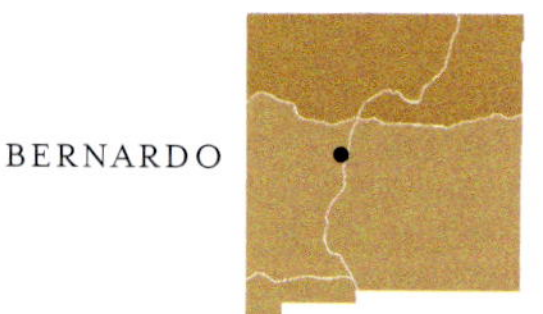

LAURA WACHA

Not Responsible

2000

Acrylic on canvas

48" x 68"

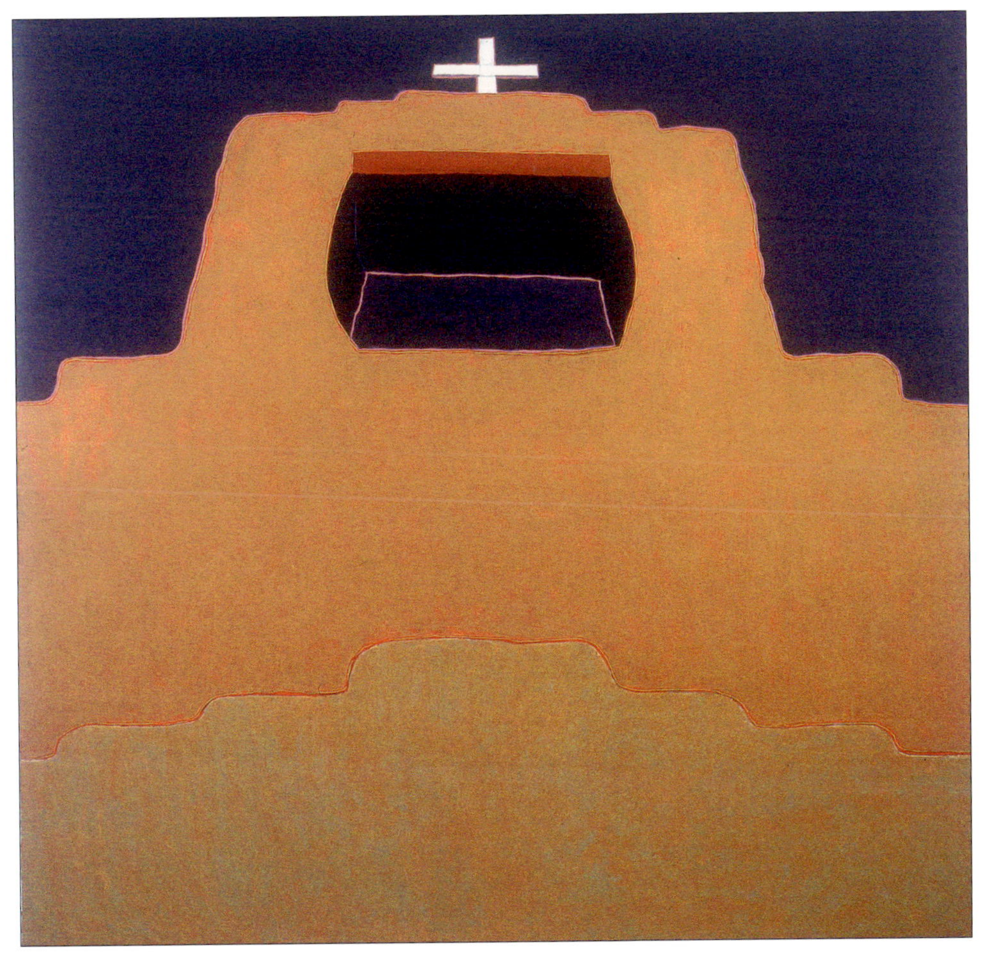

TRUTH OR CONSEQUENCES

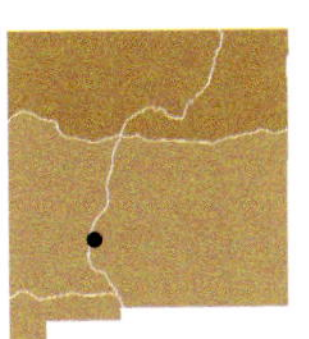

H. JOE WALDRUM

La cruz arriba de la iglesia abandonada de Hernandez

2003

Acrylic on canvas

64" x 64"

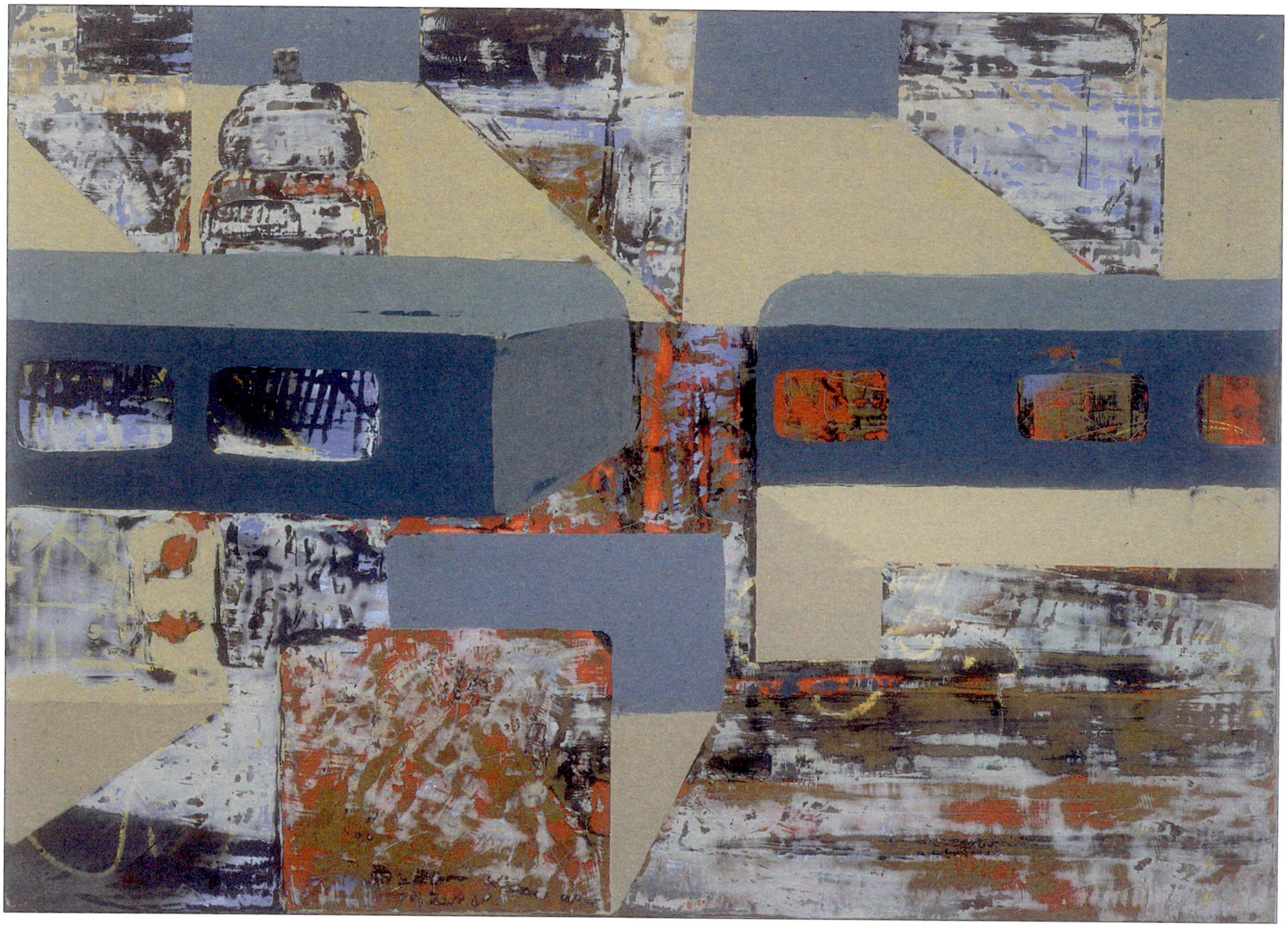

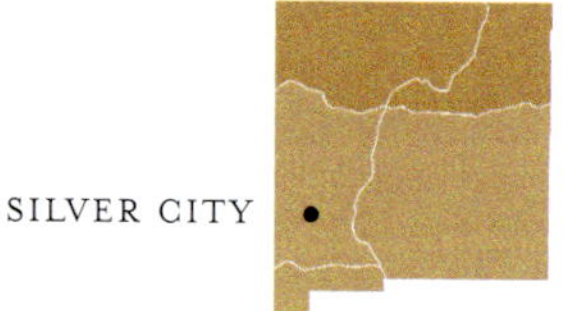

JASON S. WILLAFORD
Nash
2003
Encaustic on canvas and panel
34" x 42"

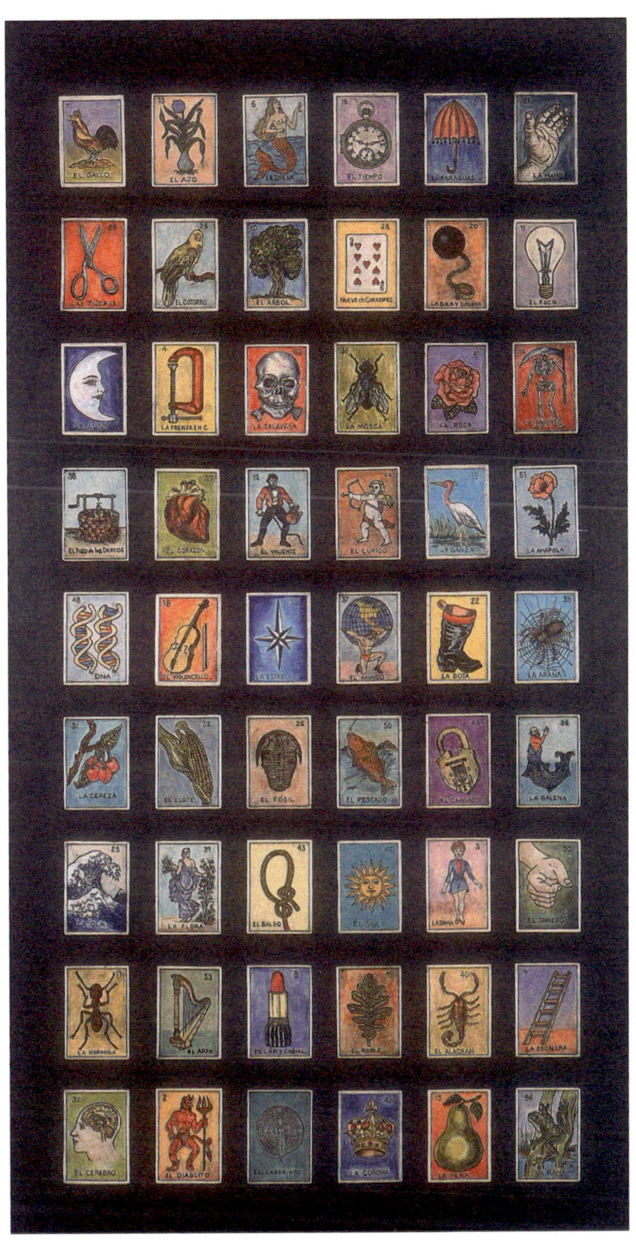

ROSWELL

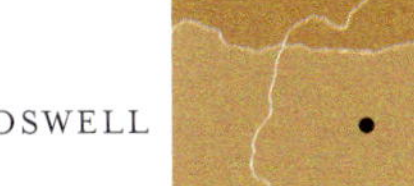

SUSAN WINK
Lotería
2002
Clay
52" x 24.25"

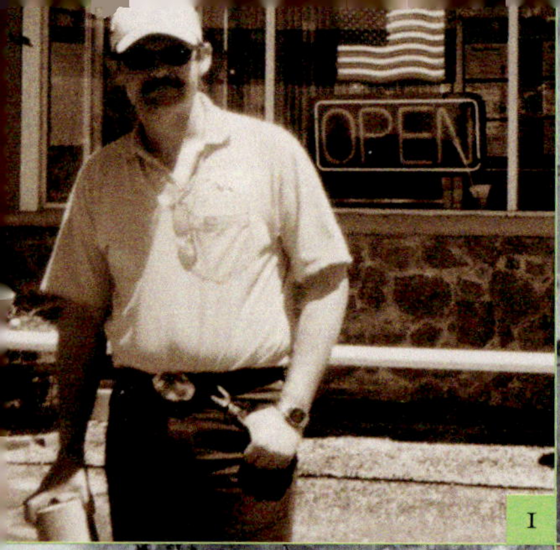

1

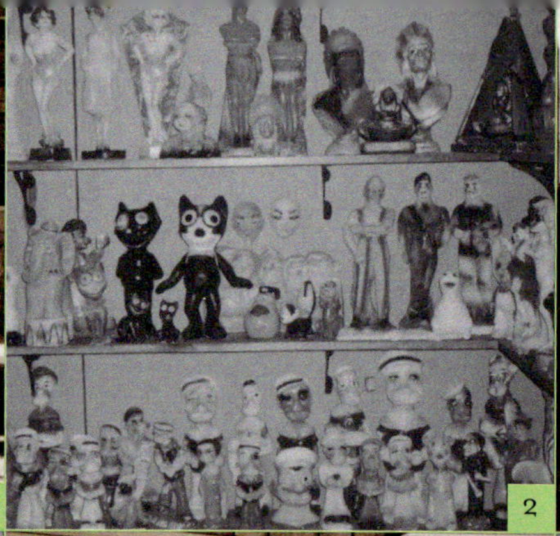

2

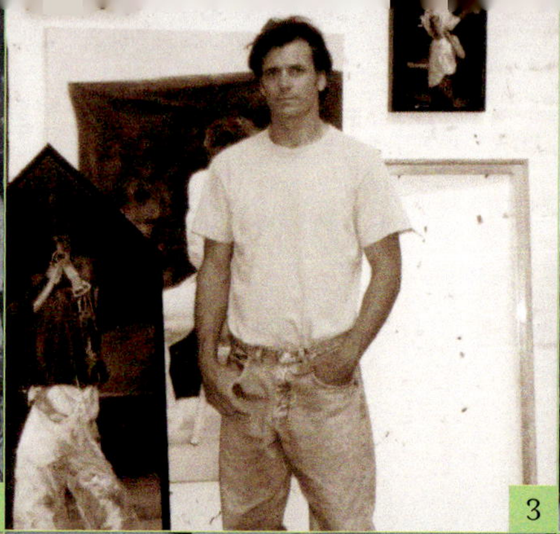

3

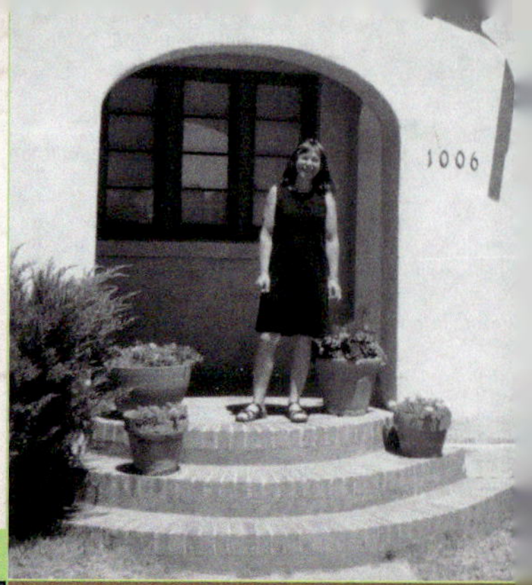

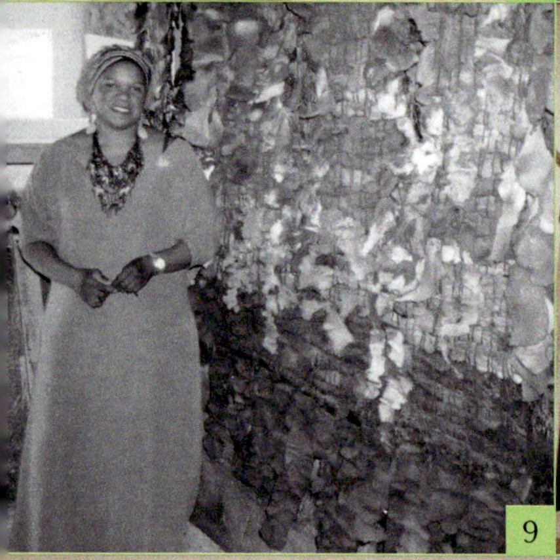

9

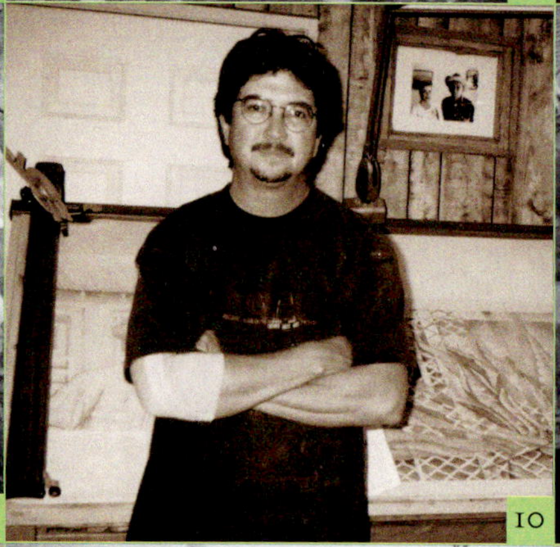

10

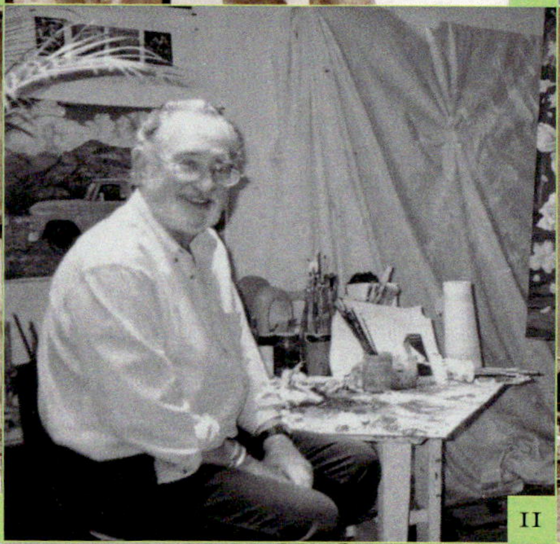

11

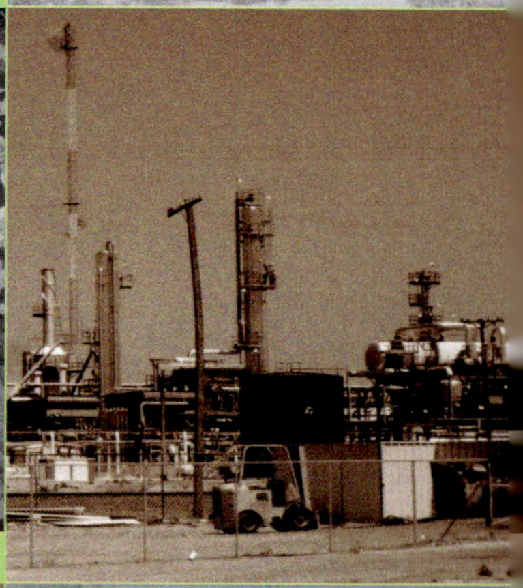

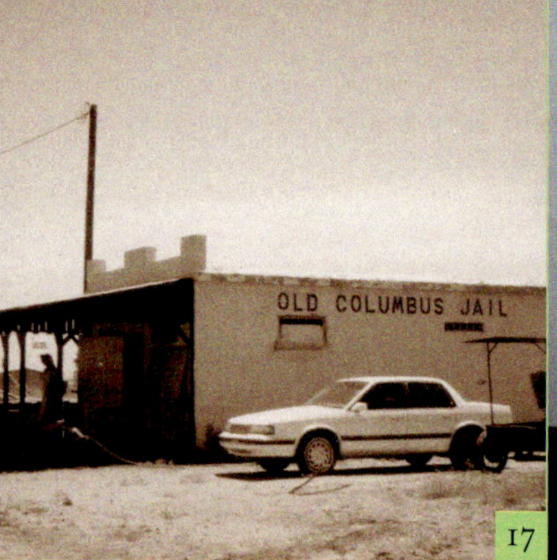

17

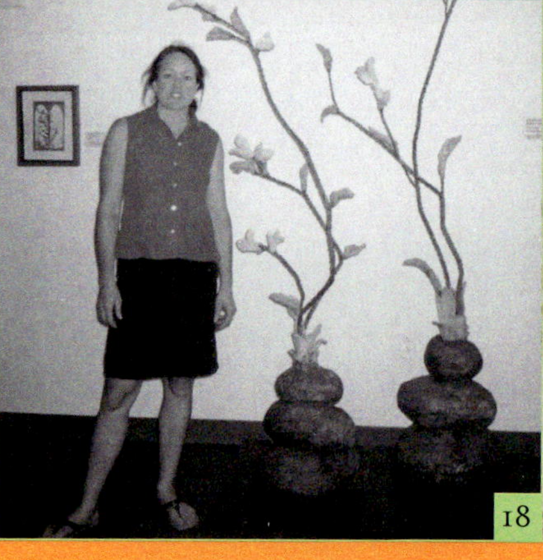

18

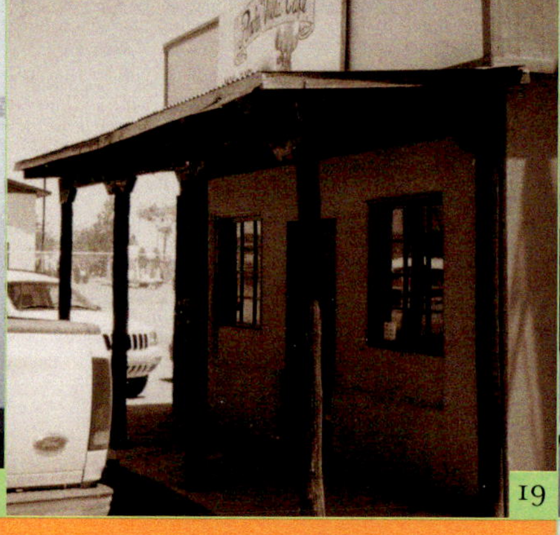

19

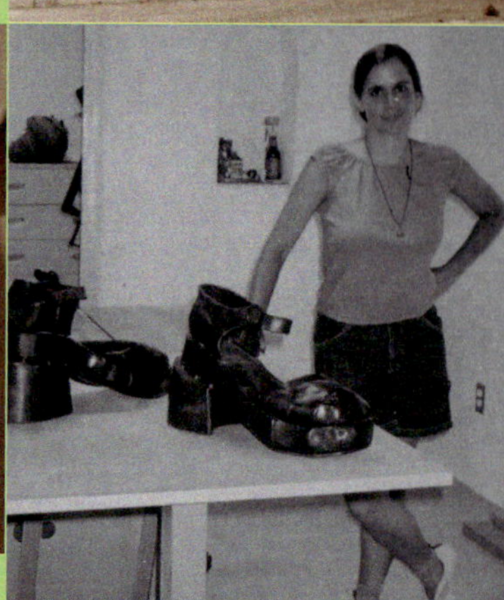

1 Brian Norwood
2 Chalkware collection, San Lorenzo
3 Brian O'Connor
4 Amanda Jaffe
5 Michael Berman
6 Tamiris Duke
7 Theater, Columbus
8 Timothy McAndrews
9 Georjeanna Feltha
10 Noel Márquez
11 Delmas Howe
12 View of refinery from Noel Márquez' studio
13 Jason S. Willaford
14 Nancy Spencer and Eric Renner
15 H. Joe Waldrum
16 Rachel Stevens' studio
17 Jail, Columbus
18 Suzanne Kane
19 Pancho Villa Cafe, Columbus
20 Rachel Stevens
21 Luis Jimenez' studio
22 Ann Lowe
23 Serge Raoul
24 Ray Parish
25 Rep. J. Paul Taylor and Marsha Bol
26 Lea County Museum, Lovington
27 Linda Brewer
28 David Taylor
29 Chip Simons
30 Bud Latven's studio
31 Lea Rano
32 General Store, Tajique
33 Iva Morris
34 Harry Benjamin
35 Laura Wacha's trailer
36 Stuart Arends
37 Bud Latven

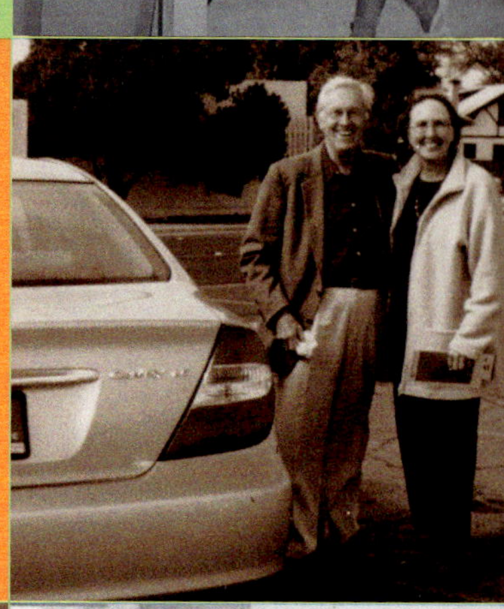

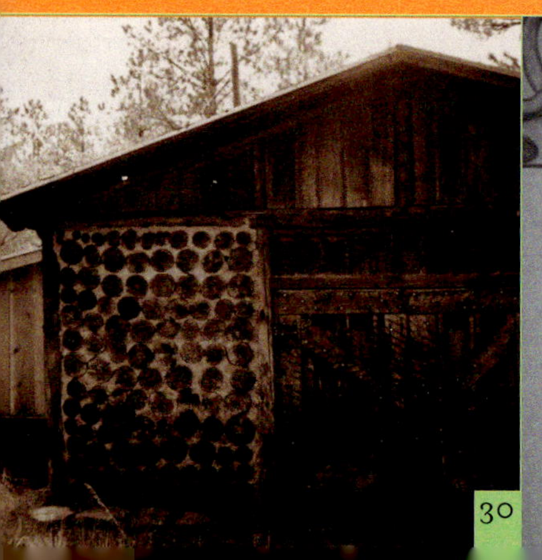

30

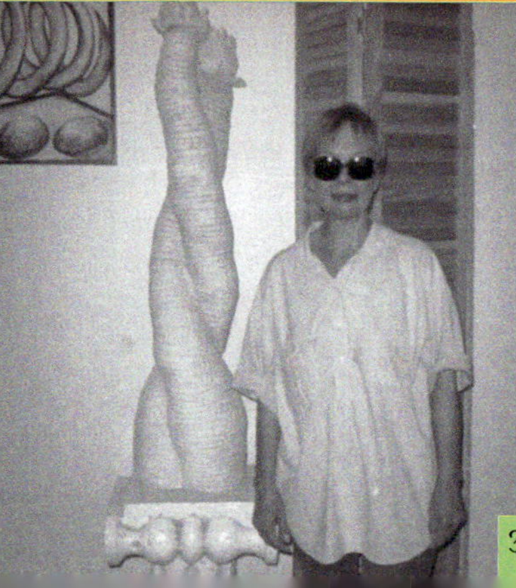

31

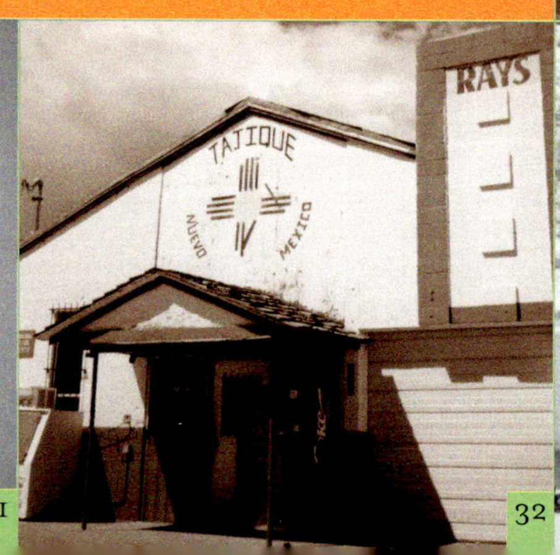

32

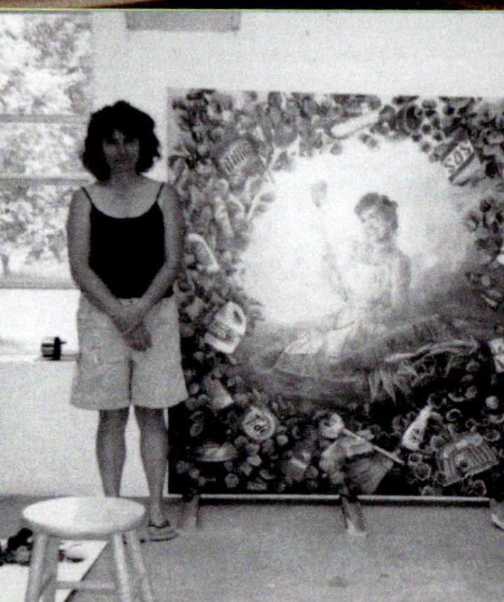

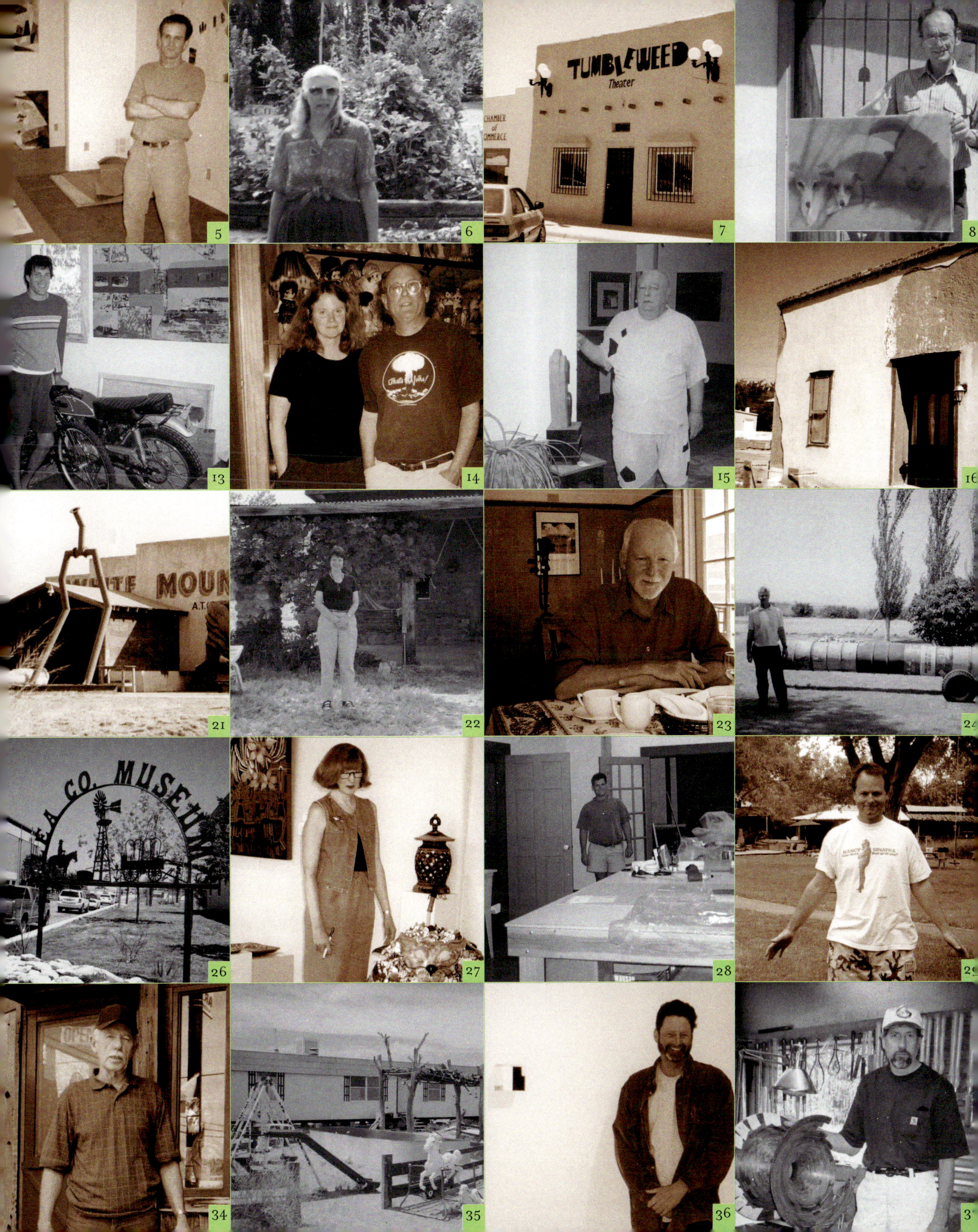
5
6
TUMBLEWEED
Theater
7
8
13
14
15
21
22
23
CO. MUSEUM
26
27
28
34
35
36

BIOGRAPHIES

DONALD B. ANDERSON

Born: Chicago, Illinois, 1919

Lives in: Roswell, New Mexico, and Cumbria, England

Selected One-Person Exhibitions

1993 *Imagined Landscapes*. Roswell Museum and Art Center, Roswell, NM

1992 *Donald Anderson*. Copeland-Rutherford Gallery, Santa Fe, NM

1991 *Donald Anderson*. Western Colorado University Art Gallery, Gunnison, CO

1989 *Donald Anderson*. Michael Walls Gallery, New York, NY

1987 *Donald Anderson*. North Dakota Museum of Art, Grand Forks, ND

1978 *Donald Anderson*. Tally Richards Gallery, Taos, NM

1977 *Visions of Lakeland: Donald Anderson*. Abbott Hall Museum of Art, Kendal, Cumbria, England

STUART ARENDS

Born: Waterloo, Iowa, 1950

Lives in: Roswell, New Mexico

Selected One-Person Exhibitions

2002 *Stuart Arends: Four Splits, One Stand*. Hosfelt Gallery, San Francisco, CA

2002 *Stuart Arends: 6 P.A.s, 1 Split, 1 Stand*. Richard Levy Gallery, Albuquerque, NM

2001 *Stuart Arends*. Studio La Citta, Verona, Italy

2000 *Stuart Arends/Sake Boxes*. Patricia Faure Gallery, Santa Monica, CA

2000 *7 Sake Boxes*. James Kelly Contemporary, Santa Fe, NM

1998 *New Vistas New Mexico: Stuarts Arends*. Akron Art Museum, Akron, OH

1995 *Stuart Arends: Recent Works*. Angles Gallery, Santa Monica, CA

Selected Group Exhibitions

2003 *Selections from the Panza Collection*. MART (Museum of Art, Rovereto, Trento), Rovereto, Italy.

2001 *Figure Astratte*. Palazzo Pallavicini Rospigliosi, Rome, Italy

1998–2003 *The Panza di Biumo Collection, Artists of the Eighties and Nineties*. Museo del Palazzo Ducale, Gubbio, Italy

1997 *The Magic of Numbers*. Staatsgalerie, Stuttgart, Germany

1996 *Small Scale*. Joseph Helman Gallery, New York, NY

1995 *Painting Outside Painting, 44th Biennial Exhibition of Contemporary American Art*. Corcoran Gallery of Art, Washington, D.C.

DANIELLE AUPRIX

Born: Bastia, Corsica, France, 1952

Lives in: Truth or Consequences, New Mexico

Selected One-Person Exhibitions

2003 *Rio Grande*. Coyote Art Gallery, Truth or Consequences, NM

2002 *Post Industrial*. Bakehouse Art Complex, Miami, FL

1989 *Going Down to the Darkness*. Gallery Imagine, Montreal, Canada

1984 *Silence Conspirators*. Complexe Desjardines, Montreal, Canada

Selected Group Exhibition

2003 Rio Bravo Fine Art, Truth or Consequences, NM

DAVE BARNETT

Born: Paris, Texas, 1941

Lives in: Elephant Butte, New Mexico

Selected One-Person Exhibitions

2003 *Dave Barnett: Recent Works*. Geronimo Springs Museum, Truth or Consequences, NM

1998 *Dave Barnett: A Rediscovery*. Carlsbad Museum and Art Center, Carlsbad, NM

Selected Group Exhibition

2000 *National Juried Landscape Exhibition*. Canyon Road Contemporary Art, Santa Fe, NM

HARRY BENJAMIN

Born: Silver City, New Mexico, 1945

Lives in: Silver City, New Mexico

Selected One-Person Exhibitions

2000 *Clay*. Gallery Zipp, Santa Fe, NM

1986 *Clay Figures*. Illinois University,Champaign-Urbana, IL

1971 *Harry Benjamin*. Hills Gallery, Santa Fe, NM

1970 *Museum of Fine Arts Biennial*. Museum of Fine Arts, Santa Fe, NM

Selected Group Exhibition

2002 *Trading Places*. Las Cruces Museum of Fine Art and Culture, Las Cruces, NM

MICHAEL P. BERMAN

Born: New York, New York, 1956

Lives in: San Lorenzo, New Mexico

Selected One-Person Exhibitions

2002 *Fragmented Images*. The Light Factory, Charlotte, NC

2001 *Crossings*. Galleri Urbane, Silver City, NM

1998 *Separate Visions*. The Harwood Art Center, Albuquerque, NM

1997 *Divided Lines*. O'Sullivan Arts Center, Regis University, Denver, CO

1994 *Adherence to Fragments*. McCray Gallery, Western New Mexico University, Silver City, NM

1992, 1989, 1987 *The Dream Line, Drawings & Photographs*. Scheinbaum & Russek, Santa Fe, NM

1990 *Continuum*. University Art Museum, University of Arizona, Tucson, AZ

1988 *Michael Berman*. Stark Gallery, New York, NY

1987 *Split Imperative*. Scottsdale Center for the Arts, Scottsdale, AZ

1986 *Trinity*. Houston Center for Photography, Houston, TX

1985 *Objects Without Rituals*. Harry Wood Fine Art Gallery, Arizona State University, Tempe, AZ

Selected Group Exhibitions

2003 *Point of Departure: Contemporary Photographic Explorations*. Magnifico, Albuquerque, NM

2001 *Shack Obscura*. Van De Griff/Marr Gallery, Santa Fe, NM

1995 *American Artist/Photographers in the Ukraine*. Soros Center for Contemporary Art, Kiev, Ukraine

1990 *1990 Phoenix Triennial*. Phoenix Art Museum, Phoenix, AZ

1986 *The Poetics of Space*. Museum of Fine Arts, Santa Fe, NM

LINDA BREWER

Born: Lebanon, Ohio, 1957

Lives in: Silver City, New Mexico

Selected Group Exhibitions

2002 *Trading Places*. Branigan Cultural Center, Las Cruces, NM

2002 *Critique Group*. La Sells Stewart Center, Oregon State University, Corvallis, OR

1999 *Women Artists in the Land of Enchantment*. LewAllen Contemporary, Santa Fe, NM

1996 *Fall Western Art Show*. Museum of the Horse, Ruidoso, NM

1995 *Los Alamos Sculpture Exhibit*. Fuller Lodge Art Center, Los Alamos, NM

1994 *Hot Pots*. Benton County Museum, Philomath, OR

1993 *Antikasian-Brewer*. Alder Gallery, Eugene, OR

SHARON BRUSH

Born: Huntington, New York, 1960

Lives in: Gila, New Mexico

Selected One-Person Exhibitions

2000 *Sharon Brush: Myhre Fellowship Exhibition*. Archie Bray Foundation, Helena, MT

1998 *Sharon Brush: Recent Works*. Sol Koffler Gallery, Providence, RI

1991 *Sharon Brush: One Woman Show*. Desurmont Ellis Gallery, Taos, NM

1989 *Sharon Brush: Works in Clay*. Lake Placid Center for the Arts, Lake Placid, NY

1987 *Sharon Brush:* The Greenhouse Gallery, Oakhurst, NJ

Selected Group Exhibitions

2001 Six *Degrees: Connections in Clay*. Trish Higgins Fine Art, Wichita, KS

2000 *Archie Bray and the Colorado Connection*. Arapaho Community College, Littleton, CO

2000 *Resident Artist Exhibition*. Archie Bray Foundation, Helena, MT

1997 *Faculty Art Exhibition*. Allan Hancock College, Santa Maria, CA

1995 *Art Walk '95*. Santa Barbara Museum of Natural History, Santa Barbara, CA

POLLY E. CHAVEZ

Born: Trujillo, New Mexico, 1940

Lives in: Carrizozo, New Mexico

Selected One-Person Exhibitions

2003 *Polly E. Chavez: Artist of the Month*. Ruidoso Valley Chamber of Commerce, Ruidoso, NM

2001 *Santos: Hispanic Art Form*. Capitan Public Library, Capitan, NM

2000 *New Mexico Santos*. Ruidoso Public Library, Ruidoso, NM

2000 *Polly E. Chavez*. Flickinger Center for the Performing Arts, Alamogordo, NM

1998 *Retablos by Polly E. Chavez*. Lincoln Heritage Trust Center, Lincoln, NM

1997 *Chavez Retablo Show*. Lincoln Heritage Trust Center, Lincoln, NM

Selected Group Exhibitions

2003 *Hispanic Art Show*. Zozo Gallery, Carrizozo, NM

2002 *Black & White Art Show*. Zozo Gallery, Carrizozo, NM

2001 *Hispanic Heritage Month*. Intel Corporation, Albuquerque, NM

2001 *Sixth Annual Santero Exhibit*. San Acacia Gallery, San Acacia, NM

2000 *Santo Exhibit*. Centennial Museum, University of Texas at El Paso, TX

2000 *Images of San Ysidro*. New Mexico Farm and Ranch Heritage Museum, Las Cruces, NM

1999 *Twenty-Fifth Anniversary Celebration*. El Paso Museum of History, El Paso, TX

1997 Carrizozo Chamber of Commerce Arts Festival. Carrizozo Recreation Center, Carrizozo, NM

DANA CHODZKO

Born: Long Beach, California, 1952
Lives in: Abiquiu, New Mexico

Selected One-Person Exhibitions

2002 *In Retrospect*. Evo Gallery, Santa Fe, NM
2001 *The Einstein Alphabet*. Chiaroscuro Gallery, Santa Fe, NM
1998 *Circle of Evolution*. Graham Gallery, Albuquerque, NM
1994 *Rocks and Shards*. Graham Gallery, Albuquerque, NM
1990 *Earth Wedges with Sound*. Braunstein Quay Gallery, San Francisco, CA
1984 *Adobe Altar Installation*. Intersection for the Arts, San Francisco, CA

Selected Group Exhibitions

2003 *The Art of Community*. Institute of American Indian Arts Museum, Santa Fe, NM
2002 *Wrapped*. Evo Gallery, Santa Fe, NM
2001 *Spatial Relations Alphabet*. Andrea Schwartz Gallery, San Francisco, CA
1998 *Sculpture Project*. College of Santa Fe, Santa Fe, NM
1989 *The New Genre*. Berkeley Art Center, Berkeley, CA
1985 *Between the Worlds: The Art of Women's Altars*. Orange County Center for Contemporary Art, Santa Ana, CA

Selected Earthwork

1998 *Sacrifice*. The Land: An Art Site, Mountainair, NM

WALTER DE MARIA

Born: Albany, California, 1935
Lives in: New York, New York

Selected One-Person Exhibitions

1999–2000 *Walter De Maria*. Kunsthaus, Zurich, Switzerland
1991 *Walter De Maria*. Museum für Moderne Kunst, Frankfurt, Germany
1987 *Walter De Maria*. Staatsgalerie, Stuttgart, Germany
1984 *Walter De Maria*. Museum Boymans-van Beuningen, Rotterdam, Holland
1981 *Sculpture*. Center Georges Pompidou, Paris, France
1977 *Walter De Maria*. Heiner Frederick Gallery, New York, NY
1972 *Skulpturen*. Kunst Museum, Basel, Switzerland
1968 *Walter De Maria*. Galerie Heiner Friedrick, Munich, Germany
1966 *Walter De Maria*. Cordier and Ekstrom, New York, NY
1963 *Sculpture*. 9 Great Jones Street Gallery, New York, NY

Selected Group Shows

1977 *Documenta VI*. Kassel, Germany
1968 *Documenta IV*. Kassel, Germany
1963 *Primary Structures*. Jewish Museum, New York, NY

Selected Earthworks

1977 *Lightning Field*. Quemado, NM

1968 *Mile Long Drawing*. Mojave Desert, CA

GORDON DIPPLE

Born: Kevin, Montana, 1928

Lives in: Deming, New Mexico

Selected One-Person Exhibitions

1992 *Gordon Dipple: Painting and Sculpture*. Deming Art Center, Deming, NM

1992 *Gordon Dipple: Jewelry*. Santa Barbara Museum of Art, Santa Barbara, CA

1960 *Gordon Dipple: Painting and Sculpture*. Santa Barbara Museum of Art, Santa Barbara, CA

1957 *Gordon Dipple: Paintings*. 6 Gallery, San Francisco, CA

Selected Group Exhibitions

1983 *Faculty Show*. Santa Barbara Community College Art Gallery, Santa Barbara, CA

1980s Friends Gallery, Minneapolis Art Institute, Minneapolis, MN

1960s Rex Evans Gallery, Los Angeles, CA

JOSEPH J. DOMINICK

Born: Chicago, Illinois, 1931

Lives in: Las Cruces, New Mexico

Selected One-Person Exhibitions

2003 *Photography by Joe Dominick*. JME Studios, Las Cruces, NM

2002 *We Were Here: The People Before Us, Petroglyphs and Cliff Dwellings*. Centennial Museum, University of Texas at El Paso, TX

2001 *Photographs by Joe Dominick*. Branigan Cultural Center, Las Cruces, NM

1999 *Petroglyphs: We Were Here*. Branigan Cultural Center, Las Cruces, NM

Selected Group Exhibitions

2002 *The Southwest from Petroglyphs to Plazas*. Governor's Gallery, Santa Fe, NM

2001 *Annual Fall American Photography Competition*. Hubbard Museum of the American West, Ruidoso, NM

2001 *Fiesta Art Exhibit*. Tom Baugh Gallery, Las Cruces, NM

2001 *Rivers, Falls and Reflections*. Glenn Cutter Gallery, Las Cruces, NM

TAMIRIS DUKE

Born: Ely, Nevada, 1938
Lives in: Tularosa, New Mexico

Selected One-Person Exhibitions

2002 *Meditation Paintings*. Zozo Gallery, Carrizozo, NM
2001 *Paintings from the Source*. Eagle Ranch Gallery, Alamogordo, NM
2001 *Retrospective and Meditation Series*. Flickinger Center for the Performing Arts, Alamogordo, NM

Selected Group Exhibition

2003 *Celebrating Community Arts*. Flickinger Center for the Performing Arts, Alamogordo, NM

JOHN DUNN

Born: Albuquerque, New Mexico, 1954
Lives in: Las Cruces, New Mexico

Selected One Person Exhibitions

2003 *Empora: New Work by John Dunn*. El Paso Museum of Art, El Paso, TX
1996 *Epet works: Recent Paintings*. Linda Durham Contemporary Art, Galisteo, NM
1993 *Emish works: Recent Paintings*. Linda Durham Gallery, Santa Fe, NM
1990 *John Dunn*. Roy Boyd Gallery, Chicago, IL
1988 *John Dunn*. Isis Gallery, University of Notre Dame, IN
1986 *John Dunn*. Wright Gallery, Dallas, TX

Selected Group Exhibitions

2003 *Faculty Exhibition*. University Art Gallery, New Mexico State University, Las Cruces, NM
1997 *Square Painting/Plane Painting: Rigorous Non-Objective Painting*. Center for Contemporary Art, Seattle, WA
1996 *Contemporary New Mexico Artists: Sketches and Schemas*. SITE Santa Fe, Santa Fe, NM
1994 *Dunn, Mers, Preis, Stockholder*. NAME Gallery, Chicago, IL
1994 *The University of New Mexico Faculty Exhibition*. Fuller Lodge Art Center, Los Alamos, NM
1993 *The Eidetic Image*. Kranert Art Museum, University of Illinois, Champaign-Urbana, IL
1990 *The University of Iowa Faculty Exhibition*. University of Iowa Museum of Art, Iowa City, IA
1989 *Surrounding Abstraction: Five Painters from Chicago*. Cornell College Art Gallery, Mount Vernon, IA
1989 *Invitational*. Artemisia Gallery, Chicago, IL

RICHARD EARNHEART

Born: Dallas, Texas, 1950
Lives in: Silver City, New Mexico

Selected One-Person Exhibitions

2003 *Rocket Science: Time & Transformation*. ArtHaus, Silver City, NM
2002 *Mixed Metals by Richard Earnheart*. ArtHaus, Silver City, NM
2001 *Weekend at the Galleries Opening Exhibition: New Work by Richard Earnheart*. ArtHaus Silver City, NM
1999 *Richard Earnheart-New Vision: Metal Paintings*. Stephenson Gallery, Santa Fe, NM
1997 *Hearts on Fire, by Richard Earnheart*. El Prado Gallery, Santa Fe, NM
1995 *Richard Earnheart: The Art of Sacred Spaces*. The Squash Blossom, Aspen, CO
1993 *Richard Earnheart: The Core of Man*. Cogswell Gallery, Vail, CO
1992 *Richard Earnheart: Ancient Images*. The Squash Blossom, Aspen, CO

Selected Group Exhibitions

2003 *Summer Regional Invitational*. University Art Gallery, New Mexico State University, Las Cruces, NM
1999 *Group Shows by Gallery Artists*. Jordan Road Gallery, Sedona, AZ
1994 *People of the Mimbres*. Museum of Indian Art and Culture, Santa Fe, NM
1993 *Group Exhibition*. Cogswell Gallery, Vail, CO
1992 *Southwest Art Exhibition: Del Rio Council for the Arts*. Firehouse Gallery, Del Rio, TX
1991 *Spring Show by Gallery Artists*. Adagio Gallery, Palm Desert, CA

JACKIE MITCHELL EDWARDS

Born: Monterey, California, 1956
Lives in: Las Cruces, New Mexico

Selected One-Person Exhibitions

2002 *The Tower Elegies*. JME Studios, Las Cruces, NM
2001 *New Horizons in the Desert*. Glenn Cutter Gallery, Las Cruces, NM
2000 *A Sense of Place*. Denise Bibro Fine Art, New York, NY
1999 *Fragments/Discontinuities*. Denise Bibro Fine Art, New York, NY
1997 *Recent Paintings and Works on Paper*. Denise Bibro Fine Art, New York, NY
1996 *Artist as Shaman*. Mattituck-Laurel Library, Mattituck, Long Island, NY
1995 *Paintings and Collages*. Burke-Lodden Gallery, New York, NY
1994 *Paintings and Collages*. Burke-Lodden Gallery, New York, NY

Selected Group Exhibitions

2003 *Crossing Borders*. International Museum of Art, El Paso, TX

2002 *2002–2003 New York Collection*. Albright-Knox Museum and Gallery, Buffalo, NY

2002 *Border Artists and Friends*. Las Cruces Museum of Fine Art and Culture, Las Cruces, NM

2001 *Cruzando Fronteras Juntos/Crossing Borders Together*. Chamizal National Memorial, Los Paisanos Gallery, El Paso, TX

2000 *Intuitive Abstract Painting*. William Patterson University, Wayne, NJ

1996 *National Juried Exhibition.* Juried by Thelma Golden, Assistant Curator, Whitney Museum. Ceres Gallery, New York, NY

GREG ERF

Born: Columbus, Ohio, 1953

Lives in: Portales, New Mexico

Selected One-Person Exhibitions

2002 *Dislocate*. Linda Durham Contemporary Art, Galisteo, NM

1999 *Dislocations*. Art Center University of Arkansas, Fayetteville, AR

1999 *Constructed Views*. Shore Art Gallery, Abilene, TX

1992 *Diptychs*. Art Gallery, University of Notre Dame, South Bend, IN

1989 *Greg Erf: Photographs*. Southern Light Gallery, Amarillo, TX

Selected Group Exhibitions

2002 *Large Format Photography of NM*. Magnifico, Albuquerque, NM

2001 *Dis/Content*. Fine Arts Gallery, College of Santa Fe, Santa Fe, NM

2001 *Portales Nine*. Peterson Gallery, St. John's College, Santa Fe, NM

2000 *Fifth Biennial Photography Show*. CEPA Gallery, Buffalo, NY

1998 *Fourth Biennial Photography Show*. CEPA Gallery, Buffalo,NY

1997 *Light Images: A Selection of New Mexico Photographers*. Sweeney Center Gallery, Santa Fe, NM

1991 *U.S. Biennial IV.* Museum of Art, University of Oklahoma, Norman, OK

1991 *Emerging New Mexico Photographers*. Governor's Gallery, Santa Fe, NM

GEORJEANNA FELTHA

Born: Cincinnati, Ohio, 1955

Lives in: Las Cruces New Mexico

Selected One-Person Exhibitions

2002 *From the Valley to the Desert*. Las Cruces Museum of Fine Art and Culture, Las Cruces, NM

1999 *One Person Exhibition*. Sand Dancer Gallery, Las Cruces, NM

Selected Group Exhibitions

2003 *Crossing Borders*. International Museum of Art, El Paso, TX

2003 *Three Women Using Paper as Paint & Paint as Paper*. International Museum of Art,El Paso, TX

2002 *Trading Places*. Las Cruces Museum of Fine Art and Culture, Las Cruces, NM and McCray Gallery, Western New Mexico University, Silver City, NM

2001 *Wearable Art Show*. JME Studios, Las Cruces, NM

2000 *Art Without End*. Stele Gallery, Las Cruces, NM

STEPHEN FLEMING

Born: Oxford, Pennsylvania, 1950

Lives in: Roswell, New Mexico

Selected One-Person Exhibitions

2002 *Other Objects*. Joseph Nease Gallery, Kansas City, MO

2002 *Stephen Fleming, Nancy Johns Fleming*. Baylor University, Waco, TX

2001 *Ether/Ore*. Joseph Nease Gallery, Kansas City, MO

1999 *Stephen Fleming*. Natsoulas Gallery, Davis, CA

1991 *Recent Works*. Nancy Margolis Gallery, New York, NY

1990 *Spinning at the Heart*. Allrich Gallery, San Francisco, CA

1989 *Stephen Fleming*. Morgan Gallery, Kansas City, MO

Selected Group Exhibitions

2003 *Clay: Making Connections*. Roswell Museum and Art Center, Roswell, NM

2003 *Is/Was*. Joseph Nease Gallery, Kansas City, MO

2002 *Contemporary Ceramics East to West*. Spencer Museum of Art, University of Kansas, Lawrence, KS

2001 *Black and White and Read All Over*. Sloan Miyasato, San Francisco, CA

2001 *Portales Nine*. St. John's College, Santa Fe, NM

1998 *LSU School of Art Faculty Show*. Louisiana State University, Baton Rouge, LA

1997 *Scene/Unseen*. Eastern New Mexico University, Portales, NM

JOSÉ ANDRÉS GIRÓN

Born: Phoenix, Arizona, 1945
Lives in: Reserve, New Mexico

Selected One-Person Exhibition

2002 El Arte de José Andrés Girón. The Madrid Family, Chandler, AZ
1996 José Andrés Girón Presents. The Flores Family, Phoenix, AZ

Selected Group Exhibitions

2003 *Contemporary Hispanic Market*. El Museo Cultural de Santa Fe, Santa Fe, NM
2003 *Pinos Altos Art Fair*. San Vicente Artists of Silver City, Silver, City, NM
2002 *Contemporary Hispanic Market*. El Museo Cultural de Santa Fe, Santa Fe, NM
2002 *Fiesta de Garibaldi*. Tucson International Mariachi Conference, Armory Park, Tucson, AZ
2001 *Contemporary Hispanic Market*. El Museo Cultural de Santa Fe, Santa Fe, NM

GEORGE GREEN

Born: Paris, Texas, 1942
Lives in: Cloudcroft, New Mexico

Selected One-Person Exhibitions

2000 *George Green: Photographs*. Flickinger Center for the Performing Arts, Alamogordo, NM
1986 *George Green: Paintings*. Moody Gallery, Houston, TX
1981 *George Green: Sculptures*. Landfall Gallery, Chicago, IL
1978 *George Green: Sculptures, Drawings*. Hansen Gallery, New York, NY
1977 *George Green: Sculptures, Drawings*. Delahunty Gallery, Dallas, TX
1974 *George Green: Sculptures, Drawings*. Henri Gallery, Washington, DC
1970 *George Green: Sculptures*. A Clean Well Lighted Place Gallery, Austin, TX

Selected Group Exhibitions

1994 *Before There Were Borders/Beyond Imaginary Lines*. The Gallery at the Rep, Santa Fe, NM
1990 *Fifteen Year Anniversary*. Moody Gallery, Houston, TX
1988 *An Awareness of Place*. Richard Green Gallery, New York, NY
1988 *Nocturne: Portraying the Night*. Charlotte Crosby Kemper Gallery, Kansas City Art Institute, Kansas City, MO
1986 *The Texas Landscape, 1900–1986*. Museum of Fine Arts, Houston, TX
1984 *Venice Biennale, 1984, Paradise Lost/Paradise Regained: American Visions of the New Decade*. United States Pavilion, organized by the New Museum, New York, NY. Traveled throughout Western Europe.
1975 *1975 Biennial Exhibition of Contemporary American Art*. Whitney Museum of American Art, New York, NY

HELEN GWINN

Born: Sanco, Texas, 1940
Lives in: Carlsbad, New Mexico

Selected One-Person Exhibitions

2000 *The Cliff Gifts*. Weems Gallery, Albuquerque, NM
1999 *Helen Gwinn/The Envelope Series*. Flickinger Center for the Performing Arts, Alamogordo, NM
1999 *Helen Gwinn/The Envelope Series*. Carlsbad Museum and Art Center, Carlsbad, NM
1989 *Reminders, Mementos, Hopes*. Carlsbad Museum and Art Center, Carlsbad, NM
1979 *Summer Expressions*. University of Texas at El Paso, El Paso, TX

Selected Group Exhibitions

2003 *International Society of Experimental Artists*. Watermedia 2003, Houston, TX
2003 *Western Federation of Watercolor Societies*. Marjorie Barrick Museum at University of Nevada, Las Vegas, Las Vegas, NV
2002 *Vecchio Mondo Visto Dal Nuovo*. Palazzo Gozzoli, Terni, Italy
2001 *175th Annual Exhibition*. National Academy of Design, New York, NY
2000 *Arizona Aqueous National Exhibition*. Tubac Center for the Arts, Tubac, AZ
1999 *Art in the Woods*. Overland Park Arts Commission, Overland Park, KS

BECKY HENDRICK

Born: Memphis, Tennessee, 1947
Lives in: La Union, New Mexico

Selected One-Person Exhibitions

2001 *Reflections*. Pennebaker Gallery, Jackson, MS
1999 *Black/White/Other*. Adair Margo Gallery, El Paso, TX
1995 *Becky Hendrick: Recent Work*. Craighead-Green Gallery, Dallas, TX
1994 *Becky Hendrick: Paintings*. Gaier Contemporary Gallery, Orlando, FL
1991 *Vision/Revision*. Bridge Center for Contemporary Art, El Paso, TX
1987 *One World: A Series of Meditations*. University of Texas at El Paso, El Paso, TX

Selected Group Exhibitions

2003 *Summer Art Invitational*. New Mexico State University, Las Cruces, NM
2003 *Monumental Works*. El Paso Museum of Art, El Paso, TX
2002 *Snapshots*. Contemporary Museum, Baltimore, MD
1999 *Binacional Exposición del Arte*. Chihuahua Museum of Art, Chihuahua, Mexico
1994 *Texas International*. University of Texas at El Paso, El Paso, TX
1993 *Texas Biennial*. Fair Park, Dallas, TX
1992 *Primarily Paint*. Laguna Gloria Museum, Austin, TX
1991 *Capirotado: 8 El Paso Artists*. El Paso Museum of Art, El Paso, TX

DELMAS HOWE

Born: El Paso, Texas, 1935
Lives in: Truth or Consequences, New Mexico

Selected One-Person Exhibitions

2002 *Drawings & Paintings*. 6th St. Gallery, Albuquerque, NM
2001 *Stations, A Gay Passion*. Rio Bravo Fine Art, Truth or Consequences, NM
2000 *Flowers with Attitude*. Peter Eller Gallery, Albuquerque, NM
1998 *Gestures & Texture*. Leslie-Lohman, New York, NY
1993 *Delmas Howe*. Bridge Center Contemporary Art, El Paso, TX
1991–95 *Delmas Howe*. Copeland-Rutherford, Santa Fe, NM
1990 *Delmas Howe*. Umbrello, Los Angeles, CA

Selected Group Exhibitions

2002 *Artists of the Ideal*. Galleria d'Arte Moderna e Contemporanea, Palazzo Forti, Verona, Italy
2001 *From Earth to Heaven*. Museum of Modern Art, Ostunde, Belgium
1999 *The New Classicism*. Museum of New Art, Parnu, Estonia
1996 *Contemporary Art in New Mexico*. SITE Santa Fe, Santa Fe, NM
1995 *Contemporary Art in New Mexico*. University of California, Irvine, CA
1993 *Phoenix Triennial*. Phoenix Art Museum, Phoenix, AZ
1983 The *Male Nude, A Modern View*. Homeworks Gallery, London, England
1982 *Rodeo Pantheon*. Leslie-Lohman, New York, NY

MICHAEL HURD

Born: Roswell, New Mexico, 1946
Lives in: San Patricio, New Mexico

Selected One-Person Exhibitions

2003 *Straw Bale Forum*. Hat Ranch, Williams, AZ
2001 *Flickinger Center Presents - Michael Hurd*. Flickinger Center for the Performing Arts, Alamogordo, NM
1993 *La Nieta "Chiste": A Celebration*. Bank of the Southwest, Roswell, NM
1993 *Michael Hurd Paints the West*. Lakes Art Center, Oko Boji, IA

Selected Group Exhibitions

2003 *Master Works of NM Spring Art Show*. State Fair Grounds, Albuquerque, NM
2001 *Grand Opening of Museum Wing*. Texas Tech University Museum, Lubbock, TX
1991 *Hubbard Art Award: Traveling Exhibit*. Museum of USSR, Moscow, Russia
1990–91 *Hubbard Art Award Participant*. Museum of the Horse, Ruidoso Downs, NM
1985 *Ruidoso Summer Festival*. Ruidoso Convention Center, Ruidoso, NM

AMANDA JAFFE

Born: Pasadena, California, 1953

Lives in: Las Cruces, New Mexico

Selected One-Person Exhibitions

2002 *Garden of Pools*. Holter Museum of Art, Helena, MT

1997 *Soothing Water: A Garden of Pools*. St. Xavier University Gallery, Chicago, IL

1983 *Amanda Jaffe: New Work*. Garth Clark Gallery, Los Angeles, CA

1981 *Tables & Chairs*. Wooster College Gallery, Wooster, OH

Selected Group Exhibitions

2003 *2003 Scripps Ceramics Annual*. Scripps College, Claremont, CA

2003 *Clay: Making Connections*. Roswell Museum and Art Center, Roswell, NM

2002–04 *Contemporary American Ceramics 1950–1990; A Survey of American Objects and Vessels*. Traveling: Aichi, Kyoto, Ibaraki, Nigata, Setagaya, Fukuoka, Japan

2002 *Gold Coast Ceramic Art Award*. Gold Coast City Gallery, Surfers Paradise, Australia

2002 *Sidney Myer Fund International Ceramics Award*. Shepparton Art Gallery, Shepparton, Australia

LUIS JIMENEZ

Born: El Paso, Texas, 1940

Lives in: Hondo, New Mexico

Selected One-Person Exhibitions

2003 *Luis Jimenez*. UVSC Woodbury Gallery, Utah Valley State College, Orem, UT

2001 *Luis Jimenez*. Mexic-Arte Museum, Austin, TX

1999 *Luis Jimenez*. Betty Moody Gallery, Houston, TX

1997 *Steelworker*. University of Massachusetts, Boston, MA

1994 *Man on Fire (retrospective)*. The Albuquerque Museum, Albuquerque, NM; The National Museum of American Art, Washington, DC

1992 *Luis Jimenez*. Wichita Museum of Art, Wichita, KS

1991 *Luis Jimenez*. Scottsdale Center for the Arts, Scottsdale, AZ

1990 *Luis Jimenez*. Moody Gallery, Houston, TX

1988 *Luis Jimenez*. Adair Margo Gallery, El Paso, TX

1986 *Luis Jimenez, Recent Work*. University of Texas at El Paso Art Museum, El Paso, TX

1981 *Luis Jimenez, Jr.: Sculpture, Prints, Drawings*. Pepperdine Gallery, U

niversity of Southern California, Los Angeles, CA

1979 *Luis Jimenez: Sculpture, Drawings and Prints*. Museum of Fine Arts, Santa Fe, NM

1977 *Luis Jimenez: Sculpture, Drawings, Graphics*. De Saisset Gallery, University of Santa Clara, CA

1972–79 O.K. Harris Works of Art, New York, NY

1969–70 Graham Gallery, New York, NY

Selected Group Exhibitions

2003 *Sodbuster*. New Mexico Farm and Ranch Heritage Museum, Las Cruces, NM

2002–03 *Rhythms and Rituals That Feed My Spirit: A Project by Blondell Cumings*. The Bronx Museum of the Arts, Bronx, NY

2001 *Editions and Artist Book Fair*. Brooke Alexander Gallery, New York, NY

2000 *La Luz*. National Hispanic Cultural Center of New Mexico, Albuquerque, NM

1997 *A Singular Vision, Prints from Landfall Press*. Museum of Modern Art, New York, NY

1994 *Altering Boundaries*. Jonson Gallery, The University of New Mexico, Albuquerque, NM

1992 *Figures of Contemporary Sculpture*. (Traveling Exhibit) Tokyo, Osaka, Hiroshima, Japan

1991 *1991 Biennial Exhibition of Contemporary Art*. Whitney Museum of American Art, NY

1988 *Committed To Print*. The Museum of Modern Art, New York, NY

1984 *Automobile and Culture*. The Museum of Contemporary Art, Los Angeles, CA

1982 *Early Work*. The New Museum of Contemporary Art, New York, NY

1980 *New Mexico Contemporary Art from New Mexico*. Fruit Market Gallery, Edinburgh, Scotland

1976 *A Survey of Contemporary New Mexico Sculpture*. Museum of Fine Arts, Santa Fe, NM

1975 *Richard Brown Collects!* Yale University Art Gallery, New Haven, CT

1972 *Recent Figure Sculpture*. Fogg Art Museum, Harvard University, Cambridge, MA

1968 *Group Show*. Allan Stone Gallery, New York, NY

1967 Group Show. Stanford Museum, Stanford, CT

SUZANNE KANE

Born: Detroit, Michigan, 1957

Lives in: Las Cruces, New Mexico

Selected One-Person Exhibitions

1999 *Subject/Object*. Macomb Center for the Arts, Clinton Township, MI

1998 *Talking Objects*. Corbett Center Gallery, Las Cruces, NM

Selected Group Exhibitions

2003 *Between the Spaces*. Las Cruces Museum of Fine Arts, Las Cruces, NM

2003 *Clay: Making Connections*. Roswell Museum and Art Center, Roswell, NM

2003 *Prix de la Ville de Carouge 2003, Photos*. Musee de Carouge, Carouge, Switzerland

2002 *Hot Tea*. Del Mano Gallery, Los Angeles, CA

2002 *La Petite X*. Alder Gallery, Coburg, OR

2001 *The Wichita National 2001*. Wichita Center for the Arts, Wichita, KS

2001 *AI2035i, Governor's Invitational*. Governor's Gallery, Santa Fe, NM

2001 *Made of Clay*. Patina Gallery, Santa Fe, NM

2000 *The House Form: A Universal Symbol*. Torpedo Factory Art Center, Alexandria, VA

JOHN LATHROP

Born: Hagerman, New Mexico, 1934

Lives in: Hobbs, New Mexico

Selected One-Person Exhibitions

2003 *A Pot of Gold*. Lea County Museum, Lovington, NM

1989 *John Lathrop*. Golden Library, Eastern New Mexico University, Portales, NM

Selected Group Exhibition

1987 *Arts Week*. Clovis Community College, Clovis, NM

BUD LATVEN

Born: Philidelphia, Pennsylvania, 1949

Lives in: Tajique, New Mexico

Selected One-Person Exhibitions

1998 *Bud Latven: New Work*. Susan Conway Gallery, Washington, DC

1992 *Bud Latven: New Work*. Worth Gallery, Taos, NM

1991 *Bud Latven: New Work*. Sansar Gallery, Washington, DC

1993 *1993: Year of American Craft*. Albuquerque Museum, Albuquerque, NM

Selected Group Exhibitions

2003 *SOFA*. New York, NY

2003 *Turned and Sculptured Wood*. Del Mano Gallery, Los Angeles, CA

2003 *One Step Back - Two Steps Forward*. Patina Gallery, Santa Fe, NM

2001–02 *Wood Turning in North America Since 1930*. Minneapolis Institute of Arts, Smithsonian Institution and Yale University Art Gallery.

2000 *Turning Wood Into Art*: *The Jane and Arthur Mason Collection*. Mint Museum of Craft & Design, Charlotte, NC

2000 *Living with Form*. Arkansas Decorative Arts Center, Little Rock, AR

1999 *The Art of Turned Wood: Selections from the Lipton Collection*. The World Forestry Center, Portland, OR

1997 *The Renwick at 25*. The Renwick Gallery of the National Museum of American Art,Smithsonian Institution, Washington, DC

1993 *Contemporary Crafts from the Horn Collection*. Decorative Arts Museum, The Arkansas Arts Center, Little Rock, AR

1993 *Hand of a Craftsman/Eye of an Artist: A New Generation of Woodturners*. Hunter Museum, Chattanooga, TN

1993 *The Art of the Wood Turner*. High Museum of Art, Atlanta, GA

ANN LOWE

Born: Fayetteville, Arkansas, 1951

Lives in: Sherman, New Mexico

Selected One-Person Exhibitions

1998 *I Found My Dreams in Wal-Mart*. Super Wal-Mart, Silver City, NM

1996 *Between Dimensions*. Weekend Gallery, Houston, TX

1994 *Grand Opening*. Mimbres Region Art Council Gallery, Silver City, NM

1993 *Ann Lowe: New Work*. Gallery 400, Silver City, NM

Selected Group Exhibitions

2001 *Originals: New Mexico Women Artists*. Harwood Museum, Taos, NM

2001 *21st Suffragettes*. Sideshow Gallery, Williamsburg, Brooklyn, NY

2000 *Group Show*. McCray Gallery, Western New Mexico University, Silver City, NM

1999 *Contemporaries of the Great Southwest*. El Paso Museum of Art, El Paso, TX

1997 *New American Talent 13*. Jones Center for Contemporary Art, Austin, TX

1995 *Art in the Wild*. Bridge Center for Contemporary Art, El Paso, TX

1994 *Close to the Border*. University Art Gallery, New Mexico State University, Las Cruces, NM

1992 *Close to the Border*. University Art Gallery, New Mexico State University, Las Cruces, NM

LORETTA LOWMAN

Born: Havre De Grace, Maryland, 1969

Lives in: Socorro, New Mexico

Selected One-Person Exhibitions

2003 *Confluence*. Las Cruces Museum of Fine Art, Las Cruces, NM

2000 *Cultivating Place*. University Art Gallery, New Mexico State University, Las Cruces, NM

Selected Group Exhibitions

2003 *Pleasurework*. Fort 508, Albuquerque, NM

2002 *Huldufolk: Hidden Places*. Pilchuck Glass School, Stanwood, WA

2001 *Synesthesia*. Harwood Art Center, Albuquerque, NM

2001 *Objects and Space: A National Exhibition*. McCray Gallery, Western New Mexico University, Silver City, NM

2000 *The Land and Sky through Others' Eyes*. Stele Gallery, Las Cruces, NM

1999 *Maryland Artists Equity Foundation Alumni Exhibition*. Decker Gallery, Maryland Institute College of Art, Baltimore, MD

BRUCE LOWNEY

Born: Los Angeles, California, 1937
Lives in: El Morro, New Mexico

Selected One-Person Exhibitions

2002 *One-Man Exhibition*. Eldridge McCarthy Gallery, Santa Fe, NM
2001 *One-Man Exhibition*. Exhibit/208 Gallery, Albuquerque, NM
1999 *One-Man Exhibition*. Parks Gallery, Taos, NM
1998 *One-Man Exhibition*. Rolling Thunder Gallery, Gallup, NM

Selected Group Exhibitions

2003 *Invitational Print Exhibition*. Santa Fe Art Institute, Santa Fe, NM
2002 *Invitational Exhibition*. Governor's Gallery, Santa Fe, NM
1996 *Southwest '96*. Museum of Fine Arts, Santa Fe, NM

JOYCE T. MACRORIE

Born: Vicksburg, Michigan, 1931
Lives in: Las Cruces, New Mexico

Selected One-Person Exhibitions

2002 *Rio*. Running Ridge Gallery, Santa Fe, NM
2001 *Walking Oaxaca*. Running Ridge Gallery, Santa Fe, NM
1999 *New Work*. Waxlander Gallery, Santa Fe, NM
1998 *New Work*. Waxlander Gallery, Santa Fe, NM
1995–2000 *New Work*. Joyce Petter Gallery, Douglas/Saugatuck, MI
1989–94 *New Work: Old Mexico/New Mexico*. Munson Gallery, Santa Fe, NM

Selected Group Exhibitions

2003 *Crossing Borders*. International Museum of Art, El Paso, TX
2003 *The Mesilla Valley 8th Regional Exhibition*. Court Youth Center, Las Cruces, NM

BEVERLY MAGENNIS

Born: Toronto, Ontario, Canada, 1942
Lives in: Apache Creek, New Mexico

Selected One-Person Exhibitions

2001 *Good Fortune Dolls*. Munson Gallery, Santa Fe, NM
1999 *Garden Art*. Munson Gallery, Santa Fe, NM
1990 *Pots of the Day*. Graham Gallery, Albuquerque, NM
1984 *Ceramic Sculpture*. Robischon Gallery, Denver, CO
1982 *Ceramic Sculpture*. Governor's Gallery, Santa Fe, NM
1981 *Ceramic Sculpture*. BFM Gallery, New York, NY
1976 *Ceramic Sculpture*. Roswell Museum, Roswell, NM

Selected Group Exhibitions

1995 *Roswell Invitational Exhibition*. Roswell Museum and Art Center, Roswell, NM
1991 *Miniatures*. Albuquerque Museum, Albuquerque, NM
1990 *Art from the American Southwest*. Society for Art in Crafts, Pittsburgh, PA
1989 *45th Scripps Invitational*. Lang Art Gallery, Scripps College, Claremont, CA
1980 *New Mexico: Space & Images*. Los Angeles Craft & Folk Art Museum, Los Angeles, CA
1979 *Clay Now*. Pratt Institute, New York, NY
1976 *20th Birthday Celebration Exhibition*. Museum of Contemporary Crafts, New York, NY

NOEL MÁRQUEZ

Born: Artesia, New Mexico, 1953
Lives in: Artesia, New Mexico

Selected One-Person Exhibitions

2001 *Affecting the Domain*. Carlsbad Museum & Art Center, Carlsbad, NM
1999 *Cosmovision*. Centro Cultural de La Raza, San Diego, CA
1998 *Tlal Tic Pac*. University of California at San Diego, Cross Cultural Center Gallery, La Jolla, CA
1997 *Noel Marquez*. Artesia Arts Council Gallery, Artesia, NM

Selected Group Exhibitions

2003 *Ahora: New Mexican Hispanic Art*. National Hispanic Cultural Center of New Mexico, Albuquerque, NM
2002 *The Trail of the Painted Ponies*. El Paso International Airport, El Paso, TX
2000 *Dia de los Muertos*. Kimo Theatre, Albuquerque, NM
1998 *New Work*. University of California at San Diego, Visual Arts Facility Gallery, La Jolla, CA
1992 *Spring Exhibition*. Artesia Arts Council Gallery, Artesia, NM
1989 *Visiones Nuevo Mexicanos*. Centennial Gallery, University of New Mexico, Albuquerque, NM
1989 *New Mexico Print Makers*. Pennsylvania St. University Art Gallery, University Park, PA
1989 *February Exhibition*. Gallery of the Reptoire, Santa Fe, NM

TIMOTHY McANDREWS

Born: New York, NY, 1944
Lives in: Columbus, New Mexico

Selected One-Person Exhibition

2002 *Tim McAndrews-Paintings*. Patio Cafe, Columbus, NM

Selected Group Exhibition

2002 *Sunbowl 2002*. International Museum of Art, El Paso, TX

ROSEMARY McLOUGHLIN

Born: Brooklyn, New York, 1936
Lives in: Mesilla, New Mexico

Selected One-Person Exhibitions

2003 *Border Folk Festival Exhibition*. Los Paisanos Gallery, Chamizal National Memorial, El Paso, TX

2003 *Sentimental Journeys*. Glenn Cutter Gallery, Las Cruces, NM

2001 *Flights of Fancy: Memories Real and Imagined*. Glenn Cutter Gallery, Las Cruces, NM

1999 *Vibrant and Colorful: New Paintings by Rosemary McLoughlin*. Glenn Cutter Gallery, Las Cruces, NM

1998 *Dreams, Wishes and Memories: A Retrospective, 1977–1997*. Las Cruces Museum of Fine Art, Las Cruces, NM

1996 *Rosemary McLoughlin: New Works*. Galeri Azul, Mesilla, NM

1993 *Rosemary McLoughlin: New Works*. Las Cruces City Hall, Las Cruces, NM

1990 *Rosemary McLoughlin: New Works*. Branigan Cultural Center, Las Cruces, NM

1987 *Rosemary McLoughlin: New Works*. Adobe Patio Gallery, Mesilla, NM

Selected Group Exhibitions

2003 *Crossing Borders: The Border Artists*. International Museum of Art, El Paso, TX

2001 *Cruzando Fronteras Juntos*. Los Paisanos Gallery, Chamizal National Memorial, El Paso, TX

1998 *Delicious! Three Women*. University Art Gallery, New Mexico State University, Las Cruces, NM

1994 *The Mesilla Valley: A Curator's Selection*. Governor's Gallery, Santa Fe, NM

1993 *Women's Work V Invitational.* El Paso Community College, El Paso, TX

1992 *The Mystique of Frida Kahlo*. Albuquerque Public Library, Albuquerque, NM

FERNANDO MERCADO

Born: El Paso, Texas, 1936
Lives in: San Acacia, New Mexico

Selected One-Person Exhibitions

2003 *Mercado: New Work*. Macey Center, New Mexico Tech, Socorro, NM

2001 *Fernando Mercado: New Landscapes*. San Acacia Gallery, San Acacia, NM

1998 *Mercado: Current Landscapes*. San Acacia Gallery, San Acacia, NM

1996 *The New Mexico Light*. San Acacia Gallery, San Acacia, NM

1994 *Introduction: Paintings by Mercado*. San Acacia Gallery, San Acacia, NM

1979 *Paintings: F. Mercado*. Rakestraw Gallery, Danville, CA

1974 *Origins: Paintings & Drawings*. Alamo Gallery, Alamo, CA

1970 *Current Works: F. Mercado*. Edward Cory Gallery, San Francisco, CA

Selected Group Exhibitions

2000 *Opening Show, Mercado: Quemada*. La Paloma Gallery, Lincoln, NM

1999 *New Beginnings: Group Show*. Rivera-Peterson Gallery, Albuquerque, NM

1998 *Summer Group Show*. Dartmouth Street Gallery, Albuquerque, NM

1980 *5 Artists: Group Show*. Continental Gallery, San Francisco, CA

1978 *F. Mercado: Richard Gunn*. Holy Names College, Oakland, CA

1971 *International Festival of Culture*. National Gallery, Santo Domingo, Dominican Republic

1969 *University Gallery, New Faces: Group Show*. University of Seattle, Seattle, WA

JACKIE MITCHELL

Born: Washington, DC, 1955

Lives in: Las Cruces, New Mexico

Selected One-Person Exhibitions

1996 *Jackie Mitchell*. Imogen Cunningham Gallery, University of Washington Women's Center, Seattle, WA

1995 *Jackie Mitchell: New Work*. Highline Community College, Seattle, WA

1994 *Exiltant: Paintings and Drawings*. King County Arts Commission Gallery, Seattle, WA

1991 *Jackie Mitchell*. Waterfront Books Gallery, Bremerton, WA

1989 *Jackie Mitchell: U Gardens*. Teaching Gallery, University of New Mexico, Albuquerque, NM

Selected Group Exhibitions

2003 *The Show*. Museum of Fine Arts, Santa Fe, NM

2003 *Faculty Exhibition 2003*. University Art Gallery, New Mexico State University, Las Cruces, NM

2001 *Art Forms Annual Exhibition*. Las Cruces Museum of Fine Art and Culture, Las Cruces, NM

2000 *Art Forms Annual Exhibition*. New Mexico Farm and Ranch Heritage Museum, Las Cruces, NM

1999 *El Paso Community College Faculty Exhibition 1999*. People's Gallery, El Paso City Hall, El Paso TX

1996 S*ixteenth Annual Northwest International Art Competition*. Whatcom Museum of History and Art, Bellingham, WA

1991 *1991 University of Washington, MFA Exhibition*. Henry Art Gallery, Seattle, WA

1985 *El Paso Scholastic Invitational*. El Paso Community College Valle Verde, El Paso, TX

1979 *Third Annual Exhibition of Fine Arts - Manassas*. Northern Virginia Community College, Manassas, VA

1975 *Virginia Museum: Juried Exhibition*. Lawrence Alloway, Juror. Dillard Gallery, Virginia Fine Art Center, Richmond, VA

IVA MORRIS

Born: Kitzmiller, Maryland, 1959

Lives in: Veguita, New Mexico

Selected One-Person Exhibitions

2002 *Iva Morris: Recent Works*. Diane Nelson Fine Art, Laguna Beach, CA

1999 *One-Person Show*. Harwood Art Center, Albuquerque, NM

1997 *One-Person Show*. Cafe Gallery, Albuquerque, NM

1996 *One-Person Show*. L. A. Nicola Fine Art, Los Angeles, CA

1988 *Going Home*. Kron/Reck Gallery, Albuquerque, NM

1986 *One-Person Show*. Kron/Reeves Gallery, Albuquerque, NM

Selected Group Exhibitions

2003 *Magnifico*. Albuquerque Museum of Art, Albuquerque, NM

2002 *Fin, Fur, and Feathers*. Diane Nelson Fine Art, Laguna Beach, CA

2002 *Commercial Art by Now Commercial Artists*. La Luz de Jesus Gallery, Los Angeles, CA

2000 *Go Figure*. LewAllen Contemporary, Santa Fe, NM

1999 *Celebration of the Nude*. Van de Griff Gallery, Santa Fe, NM

1995 *SEXSW*. Museum of Art, Alfred University, Alfred, NY

1994 *Reproduction in the Age of Multiples*. Pyramid Center of Fine Art, Rochester, NY

1994 *Southwest '94*. Museum of Fine Arts, Santa Fe, NM

BRIAN NORWOOD

Born: Big Lake, Texas, 1957

Lives in: Jal, New Mexico

Selected One-Person Exhibitions

2003 *Unframed: New Works by Brian Norwood*. Woolworth Community Library, Jal, NM

2003 *Along Many Trails: Art of Brian Norwood*. Lea County Museum, Lovington, NM

1996 *Paintings and Other Works*. Woolworth Community Library, Jal, NM

1995 *Paintings by Brian Norwood*. Woolworth Community Library, Jal, NM

1992 *Paintings by Brian Norwood*. New Mexico Junior College, Pannell Library, Hobbs, NM

1989 *Paintings and Drawings by Brian Norwood*. The Art Palette, Hobbs, NM

1987 *Mountain Men and Native Americans*. College of the Southwest, Hobbs, NM

Selected Group Exhibitions

1995 *Llano Estacado Art Association Fall Show*. New Mexico Junior College, Hobbs, NM

1992 *Llano Estacado Art Association Christmas Gallery*. Broadmoor Mall, Hobbs, NM

1991 *Llano Estacado Art Association Christmas Gallery*. Broadmoor Mall, Hobbs, NM

1982 *October Affair*. Winkler County Recreational Building, Kermit, TX

Selected Public Commission

2003 *The Trail Ahead*. Jal, NM

BRIAN O'CONNOR

Born: Hartford, Connecticut, 1958
Lives in: Veguita, New Mexico

Selected One-Person Exhibitions

2003 *A Thousand Lies*. La Luz de Jesus, Los Angeles, CA
2002 *Idiot's Prayer*. Klaudia Marr Gallery, Santa Fe, NM
2000 *Sugarland*. La Luz de Jesus, Los Angeles, CA
1999 *Brian O'Connor: New Work*. LewAllen Contemporary, Santa Fe, NM
1998 *Brian O'Connor: Recent Paintings*. J. Cacciola Gallery, New York, NY
1997 *Brian O'Connor: New Work*. LewAllen Contemporary, Santa Fe, NM
1994 *Brian O'Connor: Visiting Artist*. Southwest Texas State University, San Marcos, TX
1990 *King of Hearts*. Andrea Ross Gallery, Santa Monica, CA

Selected Group Exhibitions

2003 *A New Generation of Magic Realists*. Sangre de Cristo Center for the Arts, Pueblo, CO
2003 *The Show*. Museum of Fine Arts, Santa Fe, NM
2002 *Harboring Beauty*. Lyons Wier Gallery, Chicago, IL
2001 *Figure Eight*. Diane Nelson Fine Art, Laguna Beach, CA
1996 *The Mythic Narrative*. Palo Alto Cultural Center, Palo Alto, CA
1989 *Contemporary Narrative Painters of the Southwest*. San Antonio Museum of Fine Art, San Antonio, TX
1988 *New Mexico '88*. Museum of Fine Arts, Santa Fe, NM

WILLIE RAY PARISH

Born: Tupelo, Mississippi, 1947
Lives in: La Union, New Mexico

Selected One-Person Exhibitions

1998 *Sculpture*. Louisiana State University, Baton Rouge, LA
1995 *New Work*. Marilyn Wilson Gallery, Birmingham, AL
1994 *No Justice*. Weber State Art Gallery, Weber State University, Ogden, UT
1992 & 1990 & 1989 *New Work*. Shidoni Contemporary Gallery, Santa Fe, NM
1988 *Memorials*. University Art Gallery, New Mexico State University, Las Cruces, NM
1989 *New Work*. Art Institute of the Permian Basin, Odessa, TX
1986 *New Work*. Main Gallery, University of Texas at El Paso, TX

Selected Group Exhibitions

2003 *Summer Regional Invitational*. University Art Gallery, New Mexico State University, Las Cruces, NM

2002 *15th Annual*. Outdoor Sculpture Exhibition, City of Lawrence, KS

2003 *Sculpture Garden Exhibition*. Louisiana State University, Batan Rouge, LA

2001 *War Stories*. The Newseum, Arlington, VA

1999 *Refocus*. El Paso Museum of Art, El Paso, TX

1996 *Transpositionen*. Gallery M, Berlin, Germany

1993 *Reminiscing; A Show of Sculpture*. Charlotte Jackson Gallery, Santa Fe, NM

1991 *Singular Vision*. Museum of Fine Arts, Santa Fe, NM

PRISCILLA PEYNETSA

Born: Zuni, New Mexico, 1961

Lives in: Zuni, New Mexico

Selected Group Exhibitions

1994 to Present *Eight Northern Indian Pueblos Arts & Crafts Fair*. San Juan Pueblo, NM

1998 to Present *Indian Market*. Santa Fe, NM

1988 *Zuni Show*. Museum of Northern Arizona, Flagstaff, AZ

Selected Awards

1988 Heard Museum, Phoenix, AZ

1988 Museum of Northern Arizona, Flagstaff, AZ

KAREN PRITCHETT

Born: Charlottesville, Virginia, 1964

Lives in: Capitan, New Mexico

Selected One-Person Exhibition

1987 *Uncaged*. Berea College Art Gallery, Berea, KY

Selected Group Exhibitions

2001 *Fabulous Mammals*. Blue Dome Gallery, Silver City, NM

1994 *Big Heads*. Bisbee's Finest Gallery, Bisbee, AZ

1990 *Spirals, Spots & Spouts*. Design Arts Gallery, Cincinnati, OH

LEA RANO

Born: Abilene, Kansas, 1946
Lives in: Alamogordo, New Mexico

Selected One-Person Exhibitions

2003 *Mostly Not-So-Serious Art*. Townsend Library, New Mexico State University–Alamogordo, Alamogordo, NM

2002 *Lea Rano Sabatical Exhibition*. Townsend Library, New Mexico State University–Alamogordo, Alamogordo, NM

1998 *Lea Rano Current Work*. Flickinger Center for the Performing Arts, Alamogordo, NM

1995 *Lea Rano: New Work*. Townsend Library, New Mexico State University–Alamogordo, Alamogordo, NM

1992 *Lea Rano: Reliquaries*. California Museum of Art, Santa Rosa, CA

Selected Group Exhibitions

2001 *Alamogordo Arts Alliance Member Exhibition*. Eagle Ranch Art Gallery, Alamogordo, NM

1998 *New Mexico State University–Alamogordo Art Faculty Exhibition*. Alamogordo Public Library, Alamogordo, NM

1995 *Arts Night*. Nicolosen Art Museum, Casper, WY

1993 *Points of View*. Branigan Cultural Center, Las Cruces, NM

1992 *Scene and Unseen*. Eastern New Mexico State University, Portales, NM

1991 *Women Artists 91*. Matrix Gallery, Sacramento, CA

1990 & 1994 *Close to the Border*. University Art Gallery, New Mexico State University, Las Cruces, NM

ERIC RENNER

Born: Philadelphia, Pennsylvania, 1941
Lives in: San Lorenzo, New Mexico

Selected One-Person Exhibitions

2003 *On Deaf Ears*. Harwood Art Center, Albuquerque, NM

2001 *Eric Renner/Nancy Spencer: Pinhole Photography & Assemblage*. McCray Gallery,Western New Mexico University, Silver City, NM

2001 *Eric Renner/Nancy Spencer: Pinhole Photographs*. Escuela Nacional de Fotografía, Buenos Aires, Argentina

2001 *Eric Renner*. Soho Photo, New York City, NY

1985 *Eric Renner*. Rhode Island School of Design, Providence, RI

1980 *Eric Renner*. Museo de Arte de Sao Paulo Brazil, Sao Paulo, Brazil

1971 *Eric Renner*. Museo de Arte Moderno, Mexico City, Mexico

Selected Group Exhibitions

2003 *Pure Light: Southern Pinhole Photography*. Southeast Center for Contemporary Art, Winston-Salem, NC

2003 *Fresh*. Galleri Urbane, Silver City, NM

2002 *Senza Obiettivo*. Festival Visionaria, Siena, Italy

2001 *Sun Works: Contemporary Alternative Photography*. Institute of Contemporary Art, Boston, MA

2000 *Sténopé Photographie*. Bibliothèque Municipal, Lille, France

2000 *Pinhole Photography*. David Scott Gallery, Toronto,Canada

1998 *The World Through a Pinhole*. Michael Fowler Centre, Wellington, New Zealand

JOSHUA ROSE

Born: New York, New York, 1948

Lives in: Las Cruces, New Mexico

Selected One-Person Exhibitions

1997 *Josh Rose*. El Paso Museum of Art, El Paso, TX

1988 *Paintings from the Roswell Grant*. University Art Gallery, New Mexico State University, Las Cruces, NM

1988 *Recent Paintings*. Roswell Museum and Art Center, Roswell, NM

Selected Group Exhibitions

2003 *The Show*. Museum of Fine Arts, Santa Fe, NM

2002 *Lost and Found*. Savage Gallery, Portland, OR

2001 *Group Show*. Adair Margo Gallery, El Paso, TX

2001 *Digital Salon*. Stele Gallery, Las Cruces, NM

2000 *Print 2000*. Las Cruces Museum of Fine Art and Culture, Las Cruces, NM

1997 *Arte Sin Límites*. Museo de Arte del INBA, Juarez, Mexico

1995 *The Idea of the Icon*. University Art Gallery, New Mexico State University, Las Cruces, NM

CARLENE ROTERS

Born: Hagerstown, Maryland, 1945

Lives in: Silver City, New Mexico

Selected One-Person Exhibitions

1999 *Carlene Roters: Personal Myths*. Tointon Gallery for the Visual Arts, Greeley, CO

1997 *Carlene Roters: Personal Myths*. Civic Fine Arts Center, Sioux Falls, SD

1997 *Carlene Roters*. The Great Provincial Hall of Social Education, Shin-Chu, Taiwan, Republic of China

1994 *Carlene Roters: Soul Paintings*. Isaac Lincoln Gallery, Northern State University, Aberdeen, SD

1991 *Carlene Roters: Oil Paintings*. Isaac Lincoln Gallery, Northern State University, Aberdeen, SD

Selected Group Exhibitions

2002 *Transparencies*. Blue Dome Gallery, Silver City, NM

2000 *Eros/Thanatos*. McCray Gallery, Western New Mexico University, Silver City, NM

1999 *Western New Mexico University Art Faculty Exhibition*. Western Montana College Gallery, Dillion, MT

1995 *Spirit Flags*. Beijing Women's Conference, Beijing, China

1995 *Spirit Flags*. Library of Celsus, Ephesus, Turkey

ELMER SCHOOLEY

Born: Lawrence, Kansas, 1916

Lives in: Roswell, New Mexico

Selected One-Person Exhibitions

2000 *The Rapture of High Altitude.* Munson Gallery, Santa Fe, NM

1999 *Recent Schooley Landscapes: Transport to Nature and Solitude.* Munson Gallery, Santa Fe, NM

1992 *Elmer Schooley: Wilderness Series*. Museum of Fine Arts, Santa Fe, NM

Selected Group Exhibitions

1987 *The Abstracted Landscape.* Jonson Gallery, University of New Mexico, Albuquerque, NM

1987 *Common Ground: Art in New Mexico*. Albuquerque Museum, Albuquerque, NM

1979 Roswell Museum and Art Center

1970, 72, 74 *Southwest Biennials*. Museum of Fine Arts, Santa Fe, NM

1965 *15th Exhibition of Southwestern Prints and Drawings*. Dallas Museum of Art, Dallas, TX

1965 *46th Annual Print Exhibit of The Society of American Graphic Artists*. Associated American Artists Gallery, New York, NY

1964 *14th Mid-America Annual Art Show*. Atkins Museum of Fine Arts, Kansas City, MO

1963 P*urchase Prize, Ford Foundation. Southwestern Show.* Houston Museum of Fine Arts, Houston, TX

1961 *Santa Fe Fiesta Show*. Santa Fe, NM

1953 Roswell Museum and Art Center

1952 *Library of Congress Print Show*

1949 *Philadelphia Print Club Lithography Show*

Selected Award

1986 *New Mexico Governor,s Award for Excellence in the Arts*

MARY SILVERWOOD

Born: Bryan, Texas, 1932
Lives in: Belen, New Mexico

Selected One-Person Exhibitions

2003 *Land-Marks*. Joyce Robins Gallery, Santa Fe, NM
2002 *Vibrant & Vital*. Joyce Robins Gallery, Santa Fe, NM
2001 *Palette of an Enchanted Land*. Joyce Robins Gallery, Santa Fe, NM
2000 *Celebrating the Landscape*. Joyce Robins Gallery, Santa Fe, NM
1998 *Passion for Color*. Joyce Robins Gallery, Santa Fe, NM
1996 *Autumn Pastels*. Joyce Robins Gallery, Santa Fe, NM

Selected Group Exhibitions

2003 *Originals 2003: Traces of the Journey*. Albuquerque Museum, Albuquerque, NM
2003 *Miniatures 2003*. Albuquerque Museum, Albuquerque, NM
2002 *Miniatures 2002*. Albuquerque Museum, Albuquerque, NM
2001 *Small Works 2001*. Joyce Robins Gallery, Santa Fe, NM
2000 *A Show with Heart*. Joyce Robins Gallery, Santa Fe, NM

CHIP SIMONS

Born: Lakewood, Ohio, 1958
Lives in: Bosque Farms, New Mexico

Selected One-Person Exhibitions.

2003 *20 Years of Photography*. Fort 105, Albuquerque, NM
2000 *Chip Simons/Photographs*. OK Harris Gallery, Albuquerque, NM
1992 *Photography by Chip Simons*. Fred-Alan Agency, New York, NY

Selected Group Exhibitions

2003 *Image 03*. Jay Hawkins Gallery, New York, NY
2001 *Photo District News; 15th Self-Promotion Awards*. Photo Plus Expo, Jacob Javits Center, New York, NY
1998 *Beyond Words*. Photokina '98, Cologne, Germany
1996 *Aqua*. Photokina '96, Göteborg, Sweden

MATTHEW SOMMERVILLE

Born: Providence, Rhode Island, 1955
Lives in: Gila, New Mexico

Selected One-Person Exhibitions

2003 *Dreaming of Heaven*. McCray Gallery, Western New Mexico University, Silver City, NM
2000 *Emergence*. McCray Gallery, Western New Mexico University, Silver City, NM
1995 *An-arch(y)ology*. ATA Gallery, San Francisco, CA
1990 *Axis Mundi*. Graham Gallery, Albuquerque, NM
1990 *Foreign Relations*. Center Gallery, University of New Mexico, Albuquerque, NM

Selected Group Exhibitions

2001 *Faculty Show*. McCray Gallery, Western New Mexico University, Silver City, NM
1999 *Faculty Show: Art Endurance Test #46*. McCray Gallery, Western New Mexico University, Silver City, NM
1998 *Group Show*. Eastern Oregon State University, La Grande, OR
1996 *Exit/x-it*. College of Marin Gallery, Kentfield, CA
1994 *Auto-Interview Group Show*. Artspace, San Francisco, CA
1989 *Bell Transfer (in collaboration with Nigel Heler)*. Ars Electronica, Linz, Austria

NANCY SPENCER

Born: Winston-Salem, North Carolina, 1947
Lives in: San Lorenzo, New Mexico

Selected One-Person Exhibitions

2003 *On Deaf Ears*. Harwood Art Center, Albuquerque, NM
2001 *Eric Renner/Nancy Spencer: Pinhole Photography & Assemblage*. McCray Gallery, Western New Mexico University, Silver City, NM
2001 *Eric Renner/Nancy Spencer: Pinhole Photographs*. Escuela Nacional de Fotografía, Buenos Aires, Argentina
1988 *Flight*. Southeast Center for Contemporary Art, Winston-Salem, NC

Selected Group Exhibitions

2002 *Senza Obiettivo*. Festival Visionaria, Siena, Italy
2001 *Sun Works: Contemporary Alternative Photography*. Institute of Contemporary Art, Boston, MA
2000 *Sténopé Photographie*. Bibliothèque Municipal, Lille, France
1999 *Magiae Naturalis*. Lonsdale Gallery, Toronto, Canada
1998 *The World Through a Pinhole*. Michael Fowler Centre, Wellington, New Zealand

RACHEL STEVENS

Born: Torrington, Connecticut, 1963

Lives in: Las Cruces, New Mexico

Selected One-Person Exhibitions

2001 *No Laughing Matter*. Las Cruces Museum of Fine Art and Culture, Las Cruces, NM

1997 *Canine Paradigm*. McCray Gallery, Western New Mexico University, Silver City, NM

1997 *Metapop*. Bridge Center of Contemporary Art, El Paso, TX

1996 *Artists on Art*. El Paso Museum of Art, El Paso, TX

Selected Group Exhibition

2003 *Heaven on Earth*. JME Studios, Las Cruces, NM

2003 *Sky, blue, heavens*. Stewart Center Gallery, Purdue University, West Lafayette, IN

2002 *Steel Grrris*. Jonson Gallery, University of New Mexico, Albuquerque, NM

2002 *Reactions*. Exit Art/The First World, New York, NY

2001 *Steel Grrris*. Houston Art League, Houston, TX

1998 *20/xx*. Maryland Institute, College of Art, Baltimore, MD

1996 *Imaginary Beings*. Exit Art/The First World, New York, NY

1994 *Garden of Sculptural Delights*. Exit Art/The First World, New York, NY

CARRIE SWENSON

Born: Ringwood, Oklahoma, 1935

Lives in: Lovington, New Mexico

Selected One-Person Exhibitions

2003 *Places of the Heart*. Lea County Museum, Lovington, NM

2002 *Pastel Paintings by Carrie Swenson*. New Mexico Junior College, Pannell Library, Hobbs, NM

2000 *Chamber of Commerce Art Exhibit*. Chamber Building, Hobbs, NM

1974 *Carrie Swenson*. Watson Hall, New Mexico Junior College, Hobbs, NM

Selected Group Exhibitions

2003 *Odessa Art Association: Juried Exhibition*. Ellen Noel Art Museum, Odessa, TX

2002 *Odessa Art Association: Juried Exhibition*. Ellen Noel Art Museum, Odessa, TX

2001 *Vibrant Elders: A Community of NM Artists*. Governor's Gallery, Santa Fe, NM

2000 *Southwest Cowboy Celebration Art Show*. Cowboy Hall of Fame, New Mexico Junior College, Hobbs, NM

1997 *Llano Estacado Fall Open Show*. Watson Hall, New Mexico Junior College, Hobbs, NM

1981 *Llano Estacado Art Association Juried Regional Show*. Watson Hall, New Mexico Junior College, Hobbs, NM

1976 *Llano Estacado Art Association Juried Regional Show*. Watson Hall, New Mexico Junior College, Hobbs, NM

DAVID TAYLOR

Born: Beaufort, South Carolina, 1965
Lives in: Las Cruces, New Mexico

Selected One-Person Exhibitions

2000–2002 *High Water*. El Paso Museum of Art, El Paso, TX; Savage Gallery, Portland, OR; University of Notre Dame, Notre Dame, IN; Texas Woman's University,Denton, TX

1997 *Artifacts of Western Settlement*. Stephen F. Austin State University, Nacogdoches, TX

1994 *Irresistible Forces*. Obscura Gallery, Portland, OR

Selected Group Exhibitions

2001 *The History of Landscape/The Myth of Wildness*. Ironton Studios and Gallery, Denver, CO

2001 *Re-Imaging the West: A New History*. Camerawork, San Francisco, CA

2001 *Focus on the Future: Digital Photography*. Visual Arts Gallery, University of Alabama at Birmingham, Birmingham, AL

2001 *Add:Delete*. Society for Contemporary Photography, Kansas City, MO

2001 *Beyond Novelty*. Henry Art Gallery, Seattle, WA

1999 *From Tractors to Tornadoes : Photographers of the Rural Landscape*. Whatcom Museum, Bellingham, WA

1998 *Current Works*. Society for Contemporary Photography, Kansas City, MO

JEFF TURNER

Born: Brooklyn, New York, 1946
Lives in: Silver City, New Mexico

Selected One-Person Exhibitions

1997 *New Paintings*. Higher Grounds, Silver City, NM

1994 *Only Steel*. Lehrman Art Gallery, Harrisburg Area Community College, Harrisburg, PA

1986 *Jeff Turner: New Directions in Welded Steel Sculpture*. Northport Gallieries, Northport, NY

Selected Group Exhibition

2002 *Trading Places*. Las Cruces Museum of Fine Arts and Culture, Las Cruces, NM

2001 *Chad Colby/Jeff Turner: New Paintings/Sculpture*. Galleri Urbane,
Silver City, NM

1999 *What If?* Soho West Art Gallery, Silver City, NM

1992 *Four-Person Show*. The Red Store Gallery, South Kingston, RI

1991 *Four-Person Show*. Ariel Gallery, Soho, New York, NY

1989 *Outdoor Sculpture Now*. Islip Art Museum, East Islip, NY

SANDRA VICTORINO

Born: Acoma, New Mexico, 1958
Lives in: Acoma, New Mexico

Selected Group Exhibitions:

1999, 1995, 1994, 1993, 1987 *Inter-tribal Indian Ceremonial*, Gallup, NM

1997, 1991, 1990 *Eight Northern Indian Pueblos Arts & Crafts Show*, San Juan Pueblo, NM

1994 *New Mexico State Fair*, Albuquerque, NM

1991 *Indian Market*, Santa Fe, NM

1986 *Colorado Art Show*, Boulder, CO

Selected Awards:

1999, 1991 *Indian Market*, Santa Fe, NM

1990 *Eight Northern Indian Pueblos Arts & Crafts Show*, San Juan Pueblo, NM

1987 *Inter-tribal Indian Ceremonial*, Gallup, NM

1986 *Colorado Art Show*, Boulder, CO

LAURA WACHA

Born: Sarasota, Florida, 1961
Lives in: Bernardo, New Mexico

Selected One-Person Exhibitions

2000 *More Confessions of a Compulsive Painter*. Coleman Gallery Contemporary Art, Albuquerque, NM

1999 *Confession of a Compulsive Painter*. Coleman Gallery Contemporary Art, Albuquerque, NM

1993 *Recent Paintings by Laura Wacha*. Java Joe's, Albuquerque, NM

Selected Group Exhibitions

2002 *Magnifico! Art of Albuquerque*. Albuquerque Museum, Albuquerque, NM

2001 *Uncommercial Art by Commercial Artists*. La Luz de Jesus Gallery, Los Angeles, CA

2000 *Texas National 2000*. Stephen F. Austin State University, Nacogdoches, TX

1999 *Magnifico! Why Albuquerque?* Albuquerque Museum, Albuquerque, NM

1998 *Texas National 98*. Stephen F. Austin State University, Nacogdoches, TX

1996 *Southwest '96*. Museum of Fine Arts, Santa Fe, NM

1995 *Recent Paintings by Laura Wacha*. Harwood Center Gallery and Roll Borneman, Albuquerque, NM

1993 *Women Artists '93*. Matrix Gallery, Sacramento, CA

1992 *What's It To Ya?* SaFra Gallery, San Francisco, CA

1990 *Women Artists 90*. Bristol City Museum, Bristol, England

1986 *Group Exhibit*. Brighton Gallery of Fine Arts, Brighton, England

H. JOE WALDRUM

Born: Savoy, Texas, 1934. Died December 13, 2003.
Lives in: Truth or Consequences, New Mexico

Selected One-Person Exhibitions

2003 *H. Joe Waldrum*. Wiford & Vogt, Santa Fe, NM
2001 *Ventanas e Iglesias*. Rio Bravo Fine Art, Truth or Consequences, NM
1997 *Prints of Albuquerque*. University of New Mexico Art Museum, Albuquerque, NM
1996 *H. Joe Waldrum: New Work*. Joy Tash Gallery, Scottsdale, AZ
1993 *Aquatints and Linocuts*. Munson Gallery, Santa Fe, NM
1991 *Joe Waldrum: Recent Works*. Throckmorton Fine Art, Santa Fe, NM
1990 *Joe Waldrum: New Paintings*. Gerald Peters Gallery, Santa Fe, NM
1986 *Ranchos, Ranchos*. Palm Sprinsg Desert Museum, Palm Springs, CA
1984 *The Etchings and Concomitant Pieces*. Tally Richards Gallery, Taos, NM
1981 *Windows and Landscapes*. Ellen Sragon Gallery, New York, NY

Selected Group Exhibitions

1985 *Masterpieces of the American West*. American Museum of Natural History, New York, NY
1983 *Ranchos de Taos: A Photographic History*. Amon Carter Museum, Fort Worth, TX
1981 *One of a Kind: Prints and Paper*. Bennington College, Bennington, VT
1979 *Gold Show*. Museum of Modern Art, New York, NY

JASON S. WILLAFORD

Born: Tampa, Florida, 1969
Lives in: Silver City, New Mexico

Selected One-Person Exhibitions

2003 *Public Restroom Walls*. Galleri Urbane, Silver City, NM
2002 *Public Restroom Walls*. Nash Gallery, Marfa, TX
2000 *Measure of Weight*. Harwood Art Center, Albuquerque, NM
2000 *Belly of the Cowgirl*. Bean Gallery, Durango, CO
1999 *Spatial Integrity*. Eklektikas, Silver City, NM
1994 *Cows & Gals*. Contradiction, Tampa, FL
1993 *Biomorphic Androgeny*. Grassy Knoll, Los Angeles, CA
1992 *Reclined Revolution*. 621 Gallery, Tallahassee, FL

Selected Group Exhibitions

2003 *Summer Regional Biennial*. New Mexico State University, Las Cruces, NM

2002 *Encaustic Invitational*. Countes Point Gallery, El Paso, TX

2001 *X-plicit Installation*. McCray Gallery, Western New Mexico University, Silver City, NM

2000 *Juried Show*. Governor's Gallery, Santa Fe, NM

1999 *Juried Show, Guy Coss*. McCray Gallery, Western New Mexico University, Silver City, NM

1995 *BACA Biennial*. Berkeley CA

1993 *Directions*. VSVQ Gallery, Pasadena, CA

SUSAN WINK

Born: Detroit, Michigan, 1957

Lives in: Roswell, New Mexico

Selected One-Person Exhibitions

1995 *Seed of Rememory: Site-Specific Sculpture*. Herron School of Art, Indianapolis, IN

1993 *Ecliptic Sanctuary: Site-Specific Sculpture*. Grand Valley State University, Allendale, MI

1992 *Patterns Repeated*. Kendall College of Art and Design, Grand Rapids, MI

1991 *Fractal Growth: Site-Specific Sculpture*. Carrington Polytechnic, Auckland, New Zealand.

1988 *Remembrance and Renewal*. Chicago Center for Ceramic Arts, Chicago, IL

1987 *Celtic Circle: Site-Specific Sculpture*. Culzean Castle, Culzean, Scotland

Selected Group Exhibitions

2003 *Clay: Making Connections*. Roswell Museum and Art Center, Roswell, NM

1998 *Sculpture Project*. College of Santa Fe, Santa Fe, NM

1996 *From the Earth: Clay, Water, Fire.* Stone Quarry Hill Art Park, Cazenovia, NY

1996 *Flora* 96. Chicago Botanic Gardens, Glencoe, IL

1994 *Uncommon Clay, National Ceramic Invitational*. Muskegan Museum of Art, Muskegan, MI

1992 *Around the Coyote*. Ludwig Drum Factory Building, Chicago, IL

CATALOGUE OF THE EXHIBITION

DONALD B. ANDERSON
Roswell
Black Canyon
2002
Acrylic on canvas
72.5" x 100.5"

STUART ARENDS
Roswell
Unfolded A-11
2002
Oil on aluminum
4.5" x 7.5"
Lent by James Kelly Contemporary, Santa Fe, NM

DANIELLE AUPRIX
Truth or Consequences
Fiesta
2001
Acrylic on paper
72" x 72"
Lent by Rio Bravo Fine Art, Truth or Consequences, NM

DAVE BARNETT
Elephant Butte
Turtleback Mountain
2002
Acrylic on canvas
44" x 48"
Lent by David G. Bullard, San Francisco, CA

HARRY BENJAMIN
Silver City
Love in America
2001
Acrylic on canvas
48" x 72"
Lent by Scott Nichols, Silver City, NM

HARRY BENJAMIN
Silver City
The Marriage of Mr. and Mrs. Potato Head
2002
Acrylic on canvas
48" x 72"

MICHAEL P. BERMAN
San Lorenzo
Dune, San Rosario 2001
Gelatin silver print
19" x 19"
Lent by Galleri Urbane, Silver City, NM, and Scheinbaum & Russek, Santa Fe, NM

MICHAEL P. BERMAN
San Lorenzo
Saguaro Cut, Crater Mountains
2001
Gelatin silver print
19" x 19"
Lent by Galleri Urbane, Silver City, NM, and Scheinbaum & Russek, Santa Fe, NM

LINDA BREWER
Silver City
The Lion Knew It Was The Tequila That Made Him Disappear
2001
Clay, bottle caps, tape, beads
33.5" x 33.5" x 18"
Lent by Blue Dome Gallery, Silver City, NM

SHARON BRUSH
Gila
Leaf Spring
2001
Clay
13" x 23" x 10"

POLLY E. CHAVEZ
Carrizozo
San Ysidro, Patron Saint of Farmers
2002
Acrylic on wood
11" x 14"
Lent by Joseph and Doris Rini, Copley, OH

DANA CHODZKO
Abiquiu
Photo documentation *Sacrifice*
Mountainair, NM
1999
Earth, stone
40" x 68" x 30"

All work lent by the artist unless stated otherwise. Height precedes width, precedes depth.

WALTER DE MARIA
New York
Text documentation
The Lightning Field
1977
Earthwork located in
Quemado, NM
Photo: John Cliett
© Dia Art Foundation

GORDON DIPPLE
Deming
Pomegranates
1999
Oil on canvas
10" x 14"

GORDON DIPPLE
Deming
Roses in a Jar
1997
Oil on canvas
14" x 11"

GORDON DIPPLE
Deming
Summer Garden
2001
Oil on canvas
36" x 48"

JOSEPH DOMINICK
Las Cruces
Dunes and Grass, White Sands, NM
1995
Gelatin silver print
19" x 15"

JOSEPH DOMINICK
Las Cruces
Sand Dune, White Sands, NM
1995
Gelatin silver print
19" x 15"

TAMIRIS DUKE
Tularosa
Dissolution or Approaching Dharma Kaya
2000
Acrylic on canvas
28" x 22"

JOHN DUNN
Las Cruces
easure 1
2003
Paper, ink, encaustic on panel
8" x 8"

JOHN DUNN
Las Cruces
easure 2
2003
Paper, ink, encaustic on panel
8" x 8"

JOHN DUNN
Las Cruces
easure 3
2003
Paper, ink, encaustic on panel
8" x 8"

RICHARD EARNHEART
Silver City
Tempux Rex
2003
Steel, plaster
66" x 48"

JACKIE MITCHELL EDWARDS
Las Cruces
Prickly Pear #1
2000 - 2001
Oil on linen
49" x 75"

GREG ERF
Portales
I Play Well with Others
2002
Resin coated silver print
72" x 96"

GEORJEANNA FELTHA
Las Cruces
Passages
1999 - 2003
Woven dyed paper
54" x 60" x 12"

STEPHEN FLEMING
Roswell
Untitled
2002
Clay
12" x 11" x 10"
Lent by Joseph Nease Gallery,
Kansas City, MO

STEPHEN FLEMING
Roswell
Untitled
2002
Clay
12" x 11" x 9"
Lent by Joseph Nease Gallery,
Kansas City, MO

STEPHEN FLEMING
Roswell
Untitled
2000
Clay
12" x 11" x 9"
Lent by Joseph Nease Gallery,
Kansas City, MO

JOSÉ ANDRÉS GIRÓN
Reserve
Mantel de Colores
2003
Watercolor
24" x 34"

GEORGE GREEN
Cloudcroft
Divorce
2001
Ceramic, acrylic
6" x 9.5" x 12"

HELEN GWINN
Carlsbad
Balanced Rock Canyon (Cliff Gifts Series)
2003
Watercolor, collage, assemblage
14" x 18"

BECKY HENDRICK
La Union
Foment Peace
2003
Gold and metal leaf, enamel, beads, wood
60" x 42"

DELMAS HOWE
Truth or Consequences
The Miracle (Genet's Dream)
2003
Oil on canvas
48" x 72"

MICHAEL HURD
San Patricio
Loveseat
2002
Oil on canvas
24" x 28"

AMANDA JAFFE
Las Cruces
Hedge V
2002
Clay
9" x 9" x 1.5"

AMANDA JAFFE
Las Cruces
New Leaves
2003
Clay
9" x 7.5" x 1.5"

AMANDA JAFFE
Las Cruces
Yellow Leaves III
2003
Clay
9" x 7.5" x 1.5"

LUIS JIMENEZ
Hondo
Eagle
2001 - 2002
Fiberglass
55" x 75" x 52.5"
Lent by Moody Gallery, Houston, TX

SUZANNE KANE
Las Cruces
Two Lines in Space / Dona Ana
2003
Clay, steel
104" x 48" x 32"

JOHN LATHROP
Hobbs
Getting Ready
2001
Clay, wood, copper, glaze, acrylic
32"x 13" diameter

BUD LATVEN
Tajique
Torsion (Torsion Series #8)
2002
Tulipwood
20" x 20" x 14"
Lent by Patina Gallery, Santa Fe, NM

ANN LOWE
Sherman
Clean, Dirty, Happy, Creepy
2001
Plexiglas, dolls, cleaning products, computer labels
16.5" x 28" x 4"

LORETTA LOWMAN
Socorro
Fish Out of Water I
2001
Digital photograph
22.5" x15"

LORETTA LOWMAN
Socorro
Fish Out of Water II
2001
Digital photograph
21" x 14"

LORETTA LOWMAN
Socorro
Fish Out of Water III
2001
Digital photograph
22.5" x 15"

BRUCE LOWNEY
El Morro
The Hermitage
2002
Oil on canvas
38" x 54"

JOYCE T. MACRORIE
Las Cruces
Before Rain - Bosque del Apache
2002
Acrylic on canvas
40" x 46"

JOYCE T. MACRORIE
Las Cruces
Early Morning Someplace Else
2002
Acrylic on canvas
30" x 40"

BEVERLY MAGENNIS
Apache Creek
Garden Lady
1995
Clay, cement
60" x 32" diameter
Lent by the Albuquerque Museum,
Albuquerque, NM,
Gift of The Fund
at the Albuquerque
Community Foundation

BEVERLY MAGENNIS
Apache Creek
Good Fortune Dolls
2001
clay, glass, wood, cotton fabric
16.5" x 51.5" x 5.5"

NOEL MÁRQUEZ
Artesia
Agave #1
1990, 2003
Lithograph
30" x 41"

TIMOTHY McANDREWS
Columbus
Dogs
2000
Oil on canvas
20" x 30"

ROSEMARY McLOUGHLIN
Mesilla
Goodbye Pleiades, Hello Coney Island
2001
Oil on canvas
36" x 24"
Lent by John and Sharon Meier,
Las Cruces, NM

ROSEMARY McLOUGHLIN
Mesilla
Ice Cream and Alex Haley
2002
Oil on canvas
18" x 24"
Lent by John and Sharon Meier,
Las Cruces, NM

FERNANDO MERCADO
San Acacia
Crossroads
2002
Oil, oil stick, pastel on linen
56" x 66"

FERNANDO MERCADO
San Acacia
Summer Light - San Acacia
2002
Oil, oil stick, pastel on linen
49" x 62"

JACKIE MITCHELL
Las Cruces
No Thank-You
2001
Oil, oil stick, pencil on canvas
7.75" x 7.75"

IVA MORRIS
Veguita
Birds of a Feather
2002
Oil on canvas
55" x 71.25"
Lent by Timothy & Kimberly
Custer, Lake Forest, CA

IVA MORRIS
Veguita
Bull's Eye
2000
Oil on linen on metal
43" x 60" x 2"
Lent by Ygal & Hon. Sheila
Sonenshine, Laguna Beach, CA

IVA MORRIS
Veguita
Our Lady of Perpetual Housework
2002
Oil on canvas
67" x 67"

BRIAN NORWOOD
Jal
Photo documentation
The Trail Ahead
2000
Steel
20 feet x 400 feet

BRIAN O'CONNOR
Veguita
93 Million Miles II
2002
Oil on canvas on panel
16" x 11"

BRIAN O'CONNOR
Veguita
The Expulsion: Mother Earth, Father Time
2002
Oil on canvas on panel
14" x 12.5"

BRIAN O'CONNOR
Veguita
Garbage Pants, The Imperialist
2003
Oil on canvas
60" x 23"

BRIAN O'CONNOR
Veguita
Perfect Circle
2000
Oil on canvas on panel/ oil on linen
73" x 48"
Collection of the Museum of Fine Arts, Santa Fe, purchased with funds donated by the Herzstein Family Acquisitions Endowment Fund, Lynn Marchand and George Goldstein, and Christopher Han

WILLIE RAY PARISH
La Union
Photo documentation
Undeterred, They Continued Driving South
La Union, NM
2000
Steel, wood
12 feet x 18 feet x 7 feet

PRISCILLA PEYNETSA
Zuni
Untitled
2003
Clay
11.25" x 11.25" diameter
Lent by Andrea Fisher Fine Pottery, Santa Fe, NM

KAREN PRITCHETT
Capitan
Lassie, My Last Dog
2002
Hand sewn quilted fabric
48" x 38"
Lent by Blue Dome Gallery, Silver City, NM

LEA RANO
Alamogordo
Embrace
2002
Clay
49.5" x 11" diameter

JOSHUA ROSE
Las Cruces
Autumn
2002
Acrylic on paper
30" x 22"

JOSHUA ROSE
Las Cruces
Summer
2002
Acrylic on paper
30" x 22"

JOSHUA ROSE
Las Cruces
Winter
2002
Acrylic on paper
30" x 22"

CARLENE ROTERS
Silver City
Serenade of the Thrashers
2002
Oil on canvas
36" x 48"
Lent by Blue Dome Gallery, Silver City, NM

CARLENE ROTERS
Silver City
Life's Tapestry with Prickly Poppies
2001
Oil on canvas
48" x 36"
Lent by Blue Dome Gallery, Silver City, NM

ELMER SCHOOLEY
Roswell
Freedom and Responsibility
1989
Oil on canvas
80" x 90"
Lent by The Munson Gallery, Santa Fe, NM

MARY SILVERWOOD
Belen
San Juan Range, No. 2
2003
Pastel on paper
20" x 28"
Lent by Joyce Robins Gallery, Santa Fe, NM

MARY SILVERWOOD
Belen
Searching for Riley, Ladrones Mountains
2003
Pastel on paper
25" x 31"
Lent by Joyce Robins Gallery, Santa Fe, NM

MARY SILVERWOOD
Belen
Yellow Bird Wash
2000
Pastel on paper
27" x 38"
Lent by Joyce Robins Gallery, Santa Fe, NM

CHIP SIMONS
Bosque Farms
Bunnies
2002
Iris print
20" x 16"

CHIP SIMONS
Bosque Farms
Bunnies
2002
Iris print
20" x 16"

CHIP SIMONS
Bosque Farms
Bunnies
2002
Iris print
20" x 16"

MATTHEW SOMMERVILLE
Gila
INSIDEOUT
2002
DVD

MATTHEW SOMMERVILLE
Gila
Lifeline
2002
DVD

NANCY SPENCER
AND ERIC RENNER
San Lorenzo
Miss America in Uncle Sam's Frying Pan
(from On Deaf Ears series)
2001
Type C pinhole photograph
20" x 16"

NANCY SPENCER
AND ERIC RENNER
San Lorenzo
Sambo and the Ghost of Jim Crow
(from On Deaf Ears series)
2002
Type C pinhole photograph
20" x 16"

NANCY SPENCER
AND ERIC RENNER
San Lorenzo
Topsy and the Ghost of Jim Crow
(from On Deaf Ears series)
2002
Type C pinhole photograph
20" x 16"

NANCY SPENCER
AND ERIC RENNER
San Lorenzo
Troubled Child I
(from On Deaf Ears series)
2001
Type C pinhole photograph
20" x 16"

RACHEL STEVENS
Las Cruces
Foam Flip Flops with Flowers
2003
Steel
7" x 16" x 16"

RACHEL STEVENS
Las Cruces
Gita
2003
Steel and flock
8" x 16" x 18.5"

RACHEL STEVENS
Las Cruces
Spanish Dancing Shoes
2003
Steel
10" x 16" x 16.5"

CARRIE SWENSON
Lovington
Chaps
2000
Pastel on paper
20" x 26"

CARRIE SWENSON
Lovington
Tools of the Trade
2000
Pastel on paper
27" x 21"

DAVID TAYLOR
Las Cruces
Pivot Irrigation/Burning House
2000
Gelatin silver print, ink jet print, steel
33" x 19.5" x 2"

JEFF TURNER
Silver City
A Day Like Any Other
2003
Steel
11.25" x 14.25" x 13"

SANDRA VICTORINO
Acoma
Untitled
2002
Clay
11" x 9.75" diameter
Lent by Earl and Suzanne Swenson,
Franklin, TN

LAURA WACHA
Bernardo
Not Responsible
2000
Acrylic on canvas
48" x 68"

H. JOE WALDRUM
Truth or Consequences
La cruz arriba de la iglesia
abandonada de Hernandez
2003
Acrylic on canvas
64" x 64"

JASON S. WILLAFORD
Silver City
Nash
2003
Encaustic on canvas and panel
34" x 42"

SUSAN WINK
Roswell
Loteria
2002
Clay
52" x 24.25"

ACKNOWLEDGMENTS

In organizing this exhibition I was given the title of "guest curator," but working in the Museum of Fine Arts from the first day onward, I was made to feel like family rather than a guest. For making all this possible I want to first give my deepest and most sincere thanks to Dr. Marsha Bol for her belief in this project and her unfailing support throughout the organization of *SoQ*. She had the vision to realize the importance of the museum extending its reach to all corners of the state. To make a show with so many artists from so many locations I welcomed assistance from many people. As curatorial assistant, Martha Landry managed the complicated task of arranging photographs of the artwork and assisted in compiling the biographies and checklist for the catalogue. Curators Joseph Traugott and Laura Addison each suggested artists whose work I included in this exhibition. Museum staff members Aline Brandauer, Mary Jebsen, Velma Rodriguez and Joan Tafoya each in her own way helped with various details in *SoQ*'s organization. Many thanks are due to David J. Mendez, catalogue designer; Antoine R. Leriche, exhibition designer; Laura Addison, curator of contemporary art and itinerant über-editor; and photographers Blair Clark of the Museum of New Mexico and Jack Diven in Las Cruces. Bonnie Anderson, assistant director and project manager, shepherded this project throughout its duration. Barbara Hagood, deputy director of the Museum of New Mexico, facilitated design and production matters with much grace and aplomb. Additional thanks for special assistance go to Theresa Garcia, Jennifer Marshall, Judy Martinez and Cheryle Mitchell. Other museum staff who offered advice toward this project are Christine Mather and Steve Yates.

Many people offered suggestions of artists and I here record my thanks to Virginia Dodier, director of the Carlsbad Museum and Art Center; Bruce de Foor from the Clovis Community College art department; Sharon Bode-Hempton, director of cultural activities for the museum system in Las Cruces; Al McDonald, New Mexico State University–Alamogordo; and Joshua Rose, head of the art department at New Mexico State University, Las Cruces, for each providing me with lists of artists whose work I might want to see. I send a special thank-you to all the artists who suggested other artists, always a great way to learn the newest and best. Others who shared ideas and offered support are Charmay Allred, Ann Bagby, Judy Chicago, Bob Ewing, Mortimer Herzstein, Judy Just, Suzanne Kane, Jackie Schmeal and Janice Spence. My sincere appreciation also goes to all who generously lent works for the exhibition. I heartily thank the Friends of Contemporary Art (FOCA) for their financial support.

Lastly I want to respectfully express my gratitude to Representative J. Paul Taylor, whose deep interest in the arts of southern New Mexico made *SoQ* possible.

Betty Gold, Guest Curator

This exhibition is dedicated to the memory of artist H. Joe Waldrum, who died December 13, 2003, after a brief illness.

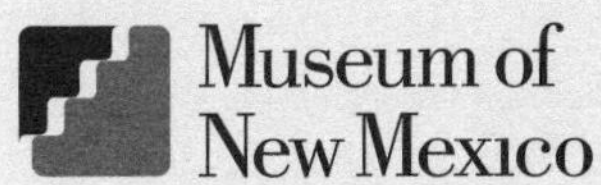

Museum of Fine Arts

SoQ: CONTEMPORARY ART IN SOUTHERN NEW MEXICO

January 23–April 25, 2004

Museum of Fine Arts, Santa Fe, New Mexico

Guest Curator
Betty Gold

Foreword
Marsha C. Bol, Ph.D.

Exhibition design
Antoine R. Leriche

Graphic and catalogue design
David J. Mendez

Photo credits:
Photos of artwork by the artist unless stated otherwise.
Photos by Blair Clark: pages 38, 39, 43, 62, 63, 65, 69, 71, 73, 75, 81,89.
Photos by Jack Diven: pages 30, 31, 32, 33, 34, 36, 37, 41, 44, 45, 46, 48, 49, 51, 52, 53, 54, 56, 58, 59, 61, 64, 66, 67, 68, 70, 76, 77, 78, 79, 84, 85, 86, 87, 88, 90, 91, 92, 93.
Photo by Tim Hearsum: page 72.
Photo by Herb Lotz: page 80.
Landscape and artist snapshots by Betty Gold.

SoQ: Contemporary Art in Southern New Mexico has been funded through the support of Representative John Paul Taylor and the State Legislature of New Mexico, and the Friends of Contemporary Art.

ISBN 0-9675106-6-x

Published by Museum of Fine Arts
P.O. Box 2087
Santa Fe, New Mexico 87504-2087
505-476-5059; FAX 505-476-5076

The Museum of Fine Arts is a Division of the Department of Cultural Affairs, State of New Mexico

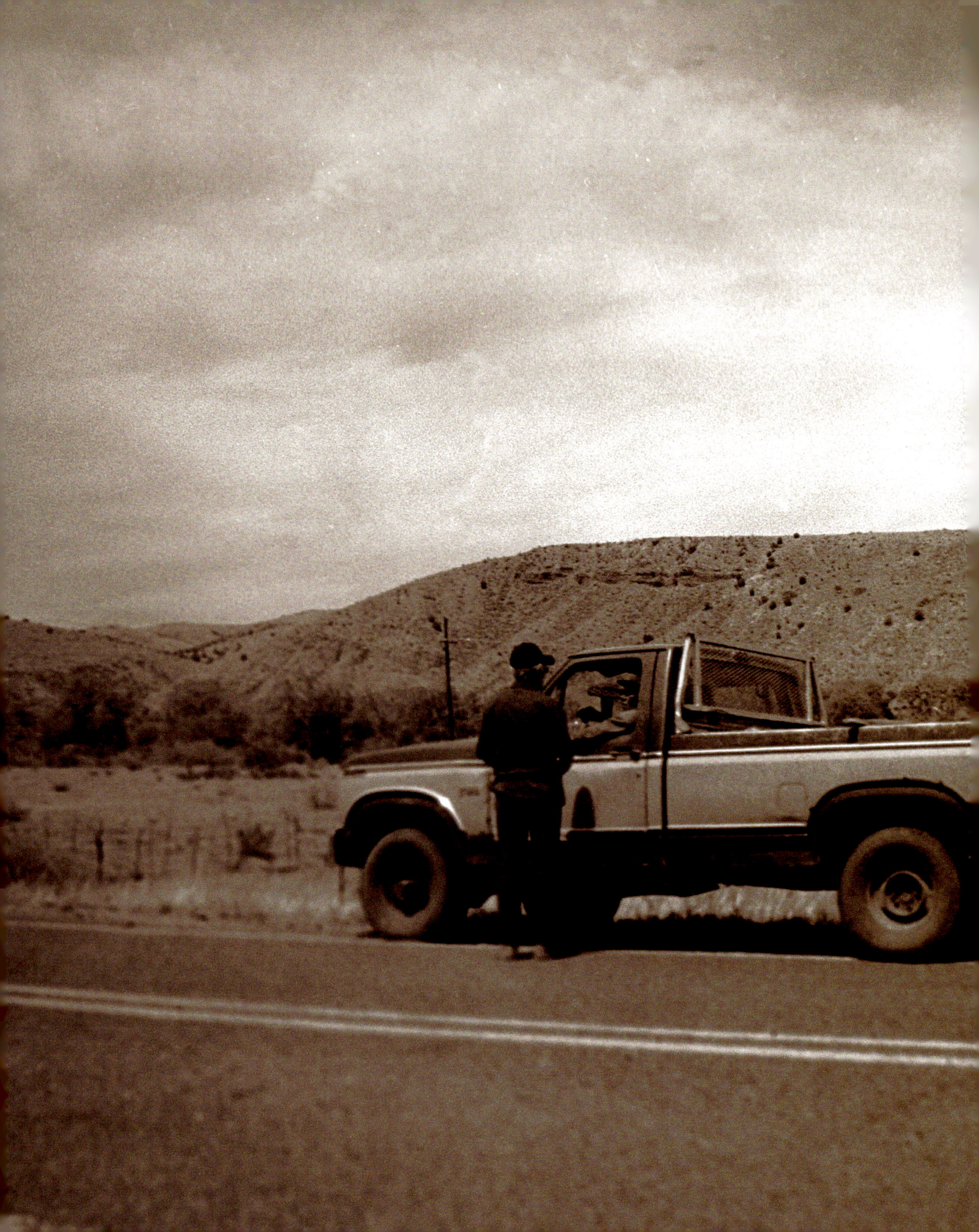

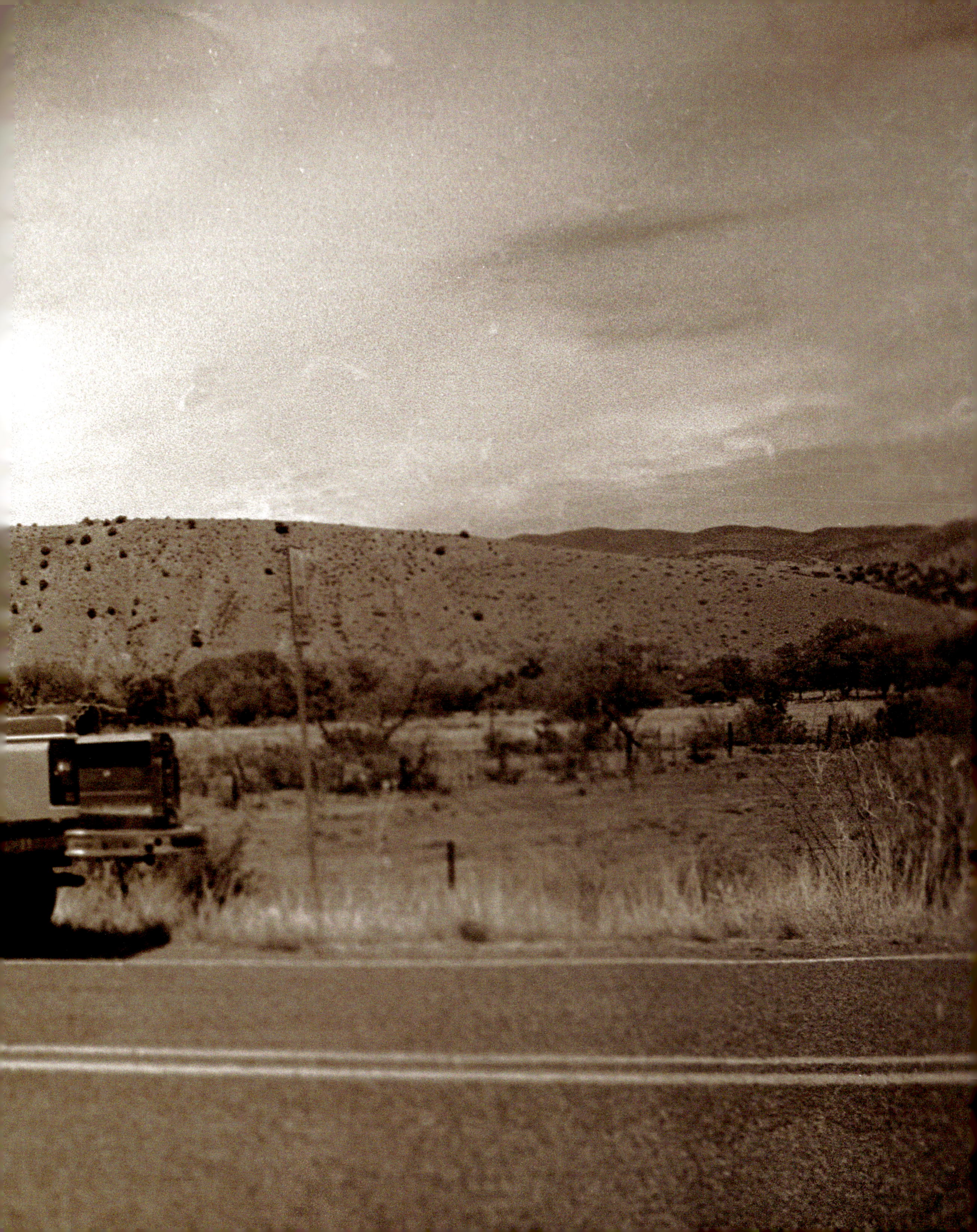

Reservation
El Malpais Nat'l Mon And Nat'l Conservation Area
CIBOLA
Los Lunas
Bosque Farms
Valencia
Belen
Sen. Willie M. Chavez State Park
Manzano
Forest
Manzano Mtns St Pk
Bosque
Veguita
Salt Lake
Tres Lagunas
Quemado
Pie Town
Alamo Band Navajo Indian Reservation
LADRON
Bernardo
Cibola
GALLINAS MTNS
LOS PINTOS MTNS
Apache-
Sitgreaves
Quemado Lake
National
Forests
Datil
Magdalena
Chamisal
Polvadera
Escondida
SOCORRO
National
PLAINS OF SAN AGUSTIN
Old Horse Springs
Aragon
Apache Creek
FRANCISCO
San Antonio
Bingham
CATRON
SAN MATEO MOUNTAINS
Forest
White
Reserve
TULAROSA
San Marcial
LAVA
BEDS
National
Mogollon
Monticello
Winston
Chloride (Ghost Town)
BLACK
Rio Grande
State
Park
JORNADA
Elephant Butte Res
SIERRA
Pleasanton
MOGOLLON BALDY
MOGOLLON MOUNTAINS
Gila Hot Springs
Gila Cliff Dwellings Nat'l Mon
Cuchillo
US Customs Inspection Station
Williamsburg
Elephant Butte
Truth Or Consequences
Buckhorn
Forest
RANGE
MIMBRES
Lake
Caballo
Caballo Res State Park
Caballo Dam
CABALLO MTNS
Percha Dam State Park
Gila
Cliff
GRANT
Pinos
Silver City
Santa Clara
Hanover
Mimbres
Kingston
Hillsboro
San Lorenzo
Arrey
Derry
Garfield
Salem
Bayard
Santa Rita (Ghost Town)
Redrock
Tyrone
Hurley
Sherman
City Of Rocks State Park
Dwyer
Lake Valley (Ghost town)
Hatch
Rincon
San Andres
National
Wildlife
Refuge
White Sands National Monument
SAN ANDRES MOUNTAINS
National
Whitewater
Fort Selden St Mon
Radium Springs
Leasburg Dam St Park
Lordsburg
Forest
CONTINENTAL
Dona Ana
Inspection Station
Akela
Separ
ORGAN MOUNTAINS